B. Mairéad Pratschke

D1471750

# Visions of Ireland

## Gael Linn's *Amharc Éireann* Film Series, 1956–1964

PETER LANG

Oxford • Bern • Berlin • Bruxelles • Frankfurt am Main • New York • Wien

Bibliographic information published by Die Deutsche Nationalbibliothek.
Die Deutsche Nationalbibliothek lists this publication in the Deutsche
Nationalbibliografie; detailed bibliographic data is available on the Internet at
http://dnb.d-nb.de.

A catalogue record for this book is available from the British Library.

Library of Congress Control Number: 2015939714

ISSN 1662-9094
ISBN 978-3-0343-1872-3 (print)
ISBN 978-3-0353-0742-9 (eBook)

Cover image: Still from *Mná Spéire* [Air Hostess Training], May 1957 © Irish
Photo Archive, <http://www.irishphotoarchive.ie>

© Peter Lang AG, International Academic Publishers, Bern 2015
Hochfeldstrasse 32, CH-3012 Bern, Switzerland
info@peterlang.com, www.peterlang.com, www.peterlang.net

This publication has been peer reviewed.

Printed in Germany

# Contents

# Acknowledgements

I would like to express my gratitude to Stephen Heathorn at McMaster University and Imre Szeman at the University of Alberta for their generous mentoring throughout my doctoral studies and their unflagging support in the years that followed.

A special note of thanks goes to Jim Rogers, who got this project started by enthusiastically publishing my first work on the series in the *New Hibernia Review*, and to Terry Byrne at The College of New Jersey, who invited me to share my research with the Irish Studies Seminar at Columbia University.

I am especially grateful to Sunniva O'Flynn, Curator at the Irish Film Archive, who went to great lengths to facilitate my research, and to Máire Harris at Gael Linn, who generously responded to my various requests for information and material.

But most of all, I am grateful to my parents, John and Máire Pratschke, who instilled in me a love of learning and language, of adventure and discovery and of personal and intellectual growth from the earliest days. Thank you, from the bottom of my heart, for your endless love and support.

86-year-old Peter Cloherty and his two sons, Marcin and Joseph, at work. 14 May 1959.
*Reproduced with permission from the Irish Photo Archive.*

# CHAPTER ONE

# Introduction

This book is about the representation of Ireland in a series of short documentary films and newsreels made in the 1950s and 1960s called *Amharc Éireann*. The title means *Views of Ireland* in Irish, and conveys exactly what the producer and sponsors intended – that Irish cinema audiences look at images of Ireland, rather than of Britain or the United States – or worse, at foreign-made representations of Ireland. The *Amharc Éireann* series was sponsored by Gael Linn, a cultural organization whose purpose was, and continues to be, the promotion and protection of the Irish language and culture through the use of modern media. The films are all in Irish, and the series constituted the first of its kind in Irish history.[1] This is Ireland for the Irish, a cultural nationalist project that finally put the native language on the screen.[2] Irish-language filmmaking began with the *Amharc Éireann* series. Indeed, it was the risk taken by Gael Linn in producing it that led to the sponsorship of the other, higher profile Irish-language productions such as George Morrison's *Mise Éire* and *Saoirse*?

The period in which the series was made (1956–64) is generally seen as a watershed in Irish history, during which Ireland began its economic,

---

1   The Gael Linn film series and related paper collection is preserved at the Irish Film Institute's Irish Film Archive in Dublin. I am very grateful to curator Sunniva O'Flynn, who initially encouraged me to work on the *Amharc Éireann* series and facilitated my research. I am also indebted to Máire Harris of Gael Linn, who gave generously of her time whenever I requested her help.

2   Content from the article, "A Look at (Irish) Ireland: Gael Linn's Amharc Éireann series, 1956–64," which appeared in the Autumn 2005 issue of *New Hibernia Review* (volume 9, number 3), is reproduced throughout this book. My heartfelt thanks extend to Jim Rogers of the NHR for his enthusiastic encouragement of my work on this topic in its earliest days.

political and social transformation into a modern member of the international community. Production began during a deep depression and the series' lifetime overlapped with the much-applauded recovery and rapid growth of the economy over the following eight years. It also coincided with the post-war revival, which saw an increased awareness of the need to protect traditional Irish culture from destruction. This began with the growth of Irish-language publishing in the 1940s and ended with the political and social movements for language rights in the late 1960s and early 1970s. Ireland's entry into the European Economic Community (EEC) in 1973 marked the end of an era for the Irish language movement. Ireland joined as the only member-state whose first and official language was *not* recognized as an official language of the EEC. This act – or lack of action – marked the culmination of decades of neglect and poor planning on the part of a state that had failed in its half-hearted and misconceived attempt to save the language from the threat of extinction. It is ironic then that only recently, in the context of European Union measures to protect minority languages, Irish has actually begun to receive the attention it needs in order to survive.[3]

The *Amharc Éireann* series records and reflects upon this key period in Irish history, beginning in 1956 with short documentary films and proceeding in 1959 to newsreel format, before concluding in 1964. Louis Marcus used this archival footage to produce the 1996 historical documentary series, *The Years of Change*, shown on Raidió Teilifís Éireann. However, as Harvey O'Brien has argued, because of the uncritical use of the *Amharc Éireann* footage, the period "is robbed of its specificity by historical distance, and has been commodified and repackaged in a sanitized form as tamed history."[4] He therefore called attention to the need to critically engage with the history represented in the *Amharc Éireann* series and to

---

3    Irish was given official and working language status in the European Union in June 2005.

4    Harvey O'Brien, 2004, *The Real Ireland: the evolution of Ireland in documentary film* (Manchester: Manchester University Press), 123.

assess the context in which it was originally filmed.[5] This book does just that – using the visual content, Irish-language commentary and historical context of these films, it critically engages with the picture of Ireland presented in the *Amharc Éireann* series. What emerges is an Irish-Ireland[6] perspective of the country, and a rather contradictory one at that: in the short documentary phase, the series presents a progressive picture of the country's development, but in the newsreel phase there is a tendency – often expressed in the commentary – to resist the implications of modernization as it appears in the visual text. This unresolved tension demonstrates that Irish nationalists were caught in the same Janus-faced predicament as many other nationalist movements in the twentieth century.[7]

## Irish cinema history

Irish film exhibition began on 20 April 1896 – only four months after the Lumière brothers' first screenings in Paris on 28 December 1895 and exactly two months after the first screenings in London. During the early years, films were shown in village halls, on exterior walls, at village fairs or in any other available indoor or outdoor location. It was not until James Joyce opened the Volta in Dublin in 1909 that Ireland had its first cinema.

5    Harvey O'Brien, "Projecting the Past: historical documentary in Ireland" *Historical Journal of Film, Radio and Television* 20, no. 3 (2000), p. 345.

6    Generic term referring to the various forms of cultural nationalism that took shape in the late nineteenth and early twentieth century, whose immediate source can be linked to Douglas Hyde's 1892 address on "The necessity of de-anglicizing Ireland," in which he argued that Ireland should follow its own cultural traditions, and D.P. Moran's 1905 essays entitled, "A Philosophy of Irish Ireland" (1893–1905).

7    See Tom Nairn, *Faces of Nationalism: Janus revisited* (London & New York: Verso, 1997); Eric J. Hobsbawm and Terence Ranger, eds, *The Invention of Tradition* (Cambridge: Cambridge University Press, 1983); David Miller, *On Nationality* (Oxford: Clarendon Press, 1995).

Its opening was the catalyst for further development and by 1916 there were 149 cinemas and halls in Ireland. Although viewing conditions were comparable to those in Britain and Europe, with cinemas showing both non-fiction newsreels and fictional narrative films by 1910, the films that were shown in Ireland were almost always foreign-produced. The country's island status and undeveloped industrial infrastructure made it very susceptible to the uneven development of the world cinema industry and by 1915 Hollywood's was already the main product in Irish cinemas.

Irish nationalists recognized the propaganda value of newsreels and resented the foreign, particularly British, domination of the newsreel market in Ireland. Foreign companies – the *Pathé Gazette*, the *Gaumont Graphic* and the *War Office Gazette* during World War One – supplied the majority of the newsreel or actuality images shown to Irish audiences. For nationalists, films like the British Army recruitment film screened in late 1913 and early 1914 in Dublin's Grafton Cinema were seen as British propaganda and provoked resistance by two of the radical nationalist constituent organizations, Inghinidhe na h-Eireann (Daughters of Ireland)[8] and Na Fianna (The Fianna).[9] Efforts were made to counter the overwhelmingly British influence on the market by showing Irish news films instead. In 1913 the Wolfe Tone commemoration ceremony was filmed and the footage shown sometimes as much as three times nightly.

Ireland's turbulent political history between 1916 and 1923 made film exhibition difficult. During the War of Independence and the Civil War that followed, cinemas were attacked and even bombed. The Grand Cinema in Sackville Street was burned down in 1916 and threats were made on others, as authorities in Dublin Castle increasingly viewed them as potential meeting places for Sinn Féin suspects. In 1917 English-born Norman

8    An Irish nationalist women's organization led by Maud Gonne from 1900 to 1914, when it merged with Cumann na mBán (The Irishwomen's Council), which in turn became an auxiliary of the Irish Volunteers in 1916.
9    A nationalist youth organization for boys, founded in 1909 by Countess Constance Markievicz.

Whitten's[10] General Film Supply began the newsreel, *Irish Events*, which quickly established itself as a regular feature of Irish cinema programmes by filming events of interest to Irish audiences. It recorded a number of events with nationalist themes, including a Redmond rally in the Phoenix Park and the first footage of Michael Collins giving a speech in Armagh. One of the more controversial items was on the return of the Sinn Féin prisoners in June 1917, but others included the opening of the Irish Convention, the Phoenix Park demonstrations, and the Twelfth of July celebrations in Belfast. *Irish Events* eventually ran into trouble with the British authorities, however, when in 1919 it created a half-hour compilation newsreel, *The Sinn Féin Review*, which included a film of de Valera taken in Dublin following his escape from prison two months earlier. Predictably, the authorities prohibited the screening of the film. Once the military struggle began, the filming of such events became too dangerous for newsreel cameramen and the company ceased production in 1920.[11]

The Irish Free State that emerged from the debris was politically, economically and culturally conservative, shunning the foreign film imports that failed to meet the national moral criteria as outlined by the newly appointed film censor, James Montgomery, under the Censorship of Films Act (1923).[12] The Irish government preferred to promote traditional cultural activities associated with rural life, such as storytelling, Irish dancing, music and singing to cinema and jazz, which were characterized as cultural invasions threatening to Irish social and moral life.[13] At the same time, the introduction of sound to cinema spelled the decline in popularity of

10  Whitten had worked with British film pioneer Cecil Hepworth in the early 1900s, before moving to Ireland in the 1910s. He also shot fictional films, including the bilingual life of St. Patrick, *Aimsir Padraig/In the Days of St. Patrick* (1920).

11  Kevin Rocket, Luke Gibbons and John Hill, *Cinema and Ireland* (London: Croom Helm, 1987), 34–8.

12  For the history of Irish film censorship, see Kevin Rockett's *Irish Film Censorship: A Cultural Journey from Silent Cinema to Internet Pornography* (Dublin: Four Courts Press, 2004).

13  Lance Pettitt, *Screening Ireland: Film and television representation* (Manchester: Manchester University Press, 2000), 35.

Continental productions, so that the majority of films seen in local cinemas became either British or American.

The introduction of British and American sound films prompted numerous objections from the Irish political establishment. Before becoming Minister of Finance after Fianna Fáil's victory in the 1932 general election, Sean MacEntee supported the redirection of film distributors' policies in the hopes of gaining an alternative supply of films, citing Russian director Pudovkin's *Storm Over Asia* (1928), one of his revolutionary triology, as the type of film that should be distributed instead. A rather less cerebral objection was voiced by the President of the Gaelic League over the American and British accents accompanying sound films, complaining that the volume of English being spoken in Irish cinemas gave the English language an unfair advantage over Irish.[14]

Overall, however, it was the content rather than the sound of the films that formed the basis for objections. The conservative nationalism of the Irish state, which only deepened during the 1930s, created a mood in the 1940s that characterized film as a "celluloid menace."[15] American cinema was perceived as an immoral influence on Catholic Ireland, bringing images of infidelity, the destruction of the traditional nuclear family, and jazz music. Instead, the powers that be called for uniquely Irish values to be the mainstay of Irish cinema and promoted the idea of a Dublin Documentary Film Unit imbued with Irish Christian and Catholic history, rather than the Marxism and materialism of John Grierson's British documentary movement.

American-made stage-Irish films like *Smiling Irish Eyes* (1929) prompted the first direct attack by an Irish group against an offending film, which was followed by other intermittent attacks and threats throughout the 1930s and 1940s. In 1934 an attack by republicans on the Savoy Cinema in Dublin and others throughout the country over a newsreel of a royal wedding led to its withdrawal, as well as the George V celebration film, *Royal Cavalcade* (1935), the following year. When World War II began,

14   Rockett *et al*, 51–2.
15   Brian McIlroy, *World Cinema 4: Ireland* (Trowbridge: Flicks Books, 1989) 31.

the Emergency Powers Order (1939) blocked the showing of films deemed prejudicial to the national interest and any film showing foreign troops could be withdrawn with as little as a complaint from a Dáil member. Even after the war, protests against the showing of British newsreels took place. Between 1949 and 1953, a series of incidents occurred involving young men identifying themselves as Sinn Féin members, who threatened some Dublin cinemas and instructed the management not to show newsreels on a variety of British topics.

Despite state censorship, between the 1920s and 1950s cinema going was a popular leisure activity. In the mid-1930s there were 190 cinemas in the Irish Free State and over eighteen million tickets sold. A 1953 study found that one third of the national population, one half in urban centres alone, went to the cinema at least once a week and spent 3.5 million pounds.[16] The government cashed in on this by exacting a flat rate import tax on each film, as well as receiving money from the processing traffic between Ireland and England. When the British Rank Organization expanded in Ireland after World War Two, it took a major share in Allied Cinemas and Irish Cinema, both of which were owned by Maurice Elliman, and subsequently controlled the Irish distribution and exhibition market. By the 1950s, the peak of cinema's popularity, exhibition was well established in Ireland, with annual admission in 1954 totaling 54,100,000.[17] The introduction of television came later to Ireland than it did Britain and North America, so the cinema continued to prosper until the early 1960s. Once Teilifís Éireann was introduced in 1962, however, cinema attendance declined in Ireland as it did elsewhere.[18]

The history of Irish filmmaking is overwhelmingly a history of non-fiction film production, mainly thanks to the utter lack of interest on the part of the Irish Free State from its foundation and continuing with the

---

16  McIlroy, 39.
17  Pettitt, 33.
18  For discussions on the origins of Irish television and its effects on Irish society, see Robert J. Savage, *Irish Television: The Political and Social Origins* (Cork University Press/Greenwood Press, 1996) and *A Loss of Innocence? Television and Irish Society, 1960–72* (Manchester University Press/Palgrave Macmillan, 2010).

Irish Republic until the 1980s in fostering a native film production industry. The first native Irish company to exhibit and distribute film was the Irish Animated Picture Company, whose projectionist, Louis de Clerq, made the first Irish documentary, *Life on the Great Southern and Western Railway* (1904). But in spite of sustained native output during the 1910s, including Walter MacNamara's *Ireland a Nation* (1914) focusing on the life of Robert Emmett, independence did not bring a continuation of film production from the nationalists that found themselves in positions of power. For a combination of economic and moral reasons, the newly independent Irish Free State was reluctant to encourage native production. The insularity of the nationalist movement's perception of culture meant that film production would have been associated with the Irish Republican Army (IRA) and radical Sinn Féin, and was thus deemed to have a negative influence on social stability. Meanwhile, the economic and logistical problems faced by the new state left little room for interest in film production – there were other much more pressing areas of development to focus on and the conservative political establishment frowned on the potentially corrosive influence of film on its Catholic population. As a result, the American film industry's position was expanded and consolidated, while European production was decimated – directly or indirectly – by the First World War.

Despite the state's antipathy towards native film production, there were some significant developments during the 1930s. While the introduction of sound films effectively destroyed what remained of European cinema for the majority of the cinema-going population, regret over its loss by the intellectuals led to the formation of the Dublin Amateur Film Society in 1930 and the Irish Film Society in 1936. These film societies were an oasis in an otherwise parched cultural landscape for the soon-to-be first generation of Irish filmmakers; the source of inspiration, education and eventually action. It was in the 1930s that Irish productions found their feet, creating films in the tradition of the American Kalem silent films of the 1910s that focused on themes of Irish political history but using Irish resources. Some of the more notable productions included Denis Johnston's *Guests of the Nation* (1935) based on the Frank O'Connor story of the IRA and two British prisoners, Tom Cooper's *The Dawn* (1937), which drew its characters and background from Irish history and was made entirely with local resources from Killarney, and Donal O'Cahill's *The Islandman (West of Kerry)* (1939) on life in the Blasket Islands.

It was also during the 1930s the Irish-American Robert Flaherty's British-produced documentary *Man of Aran* (1934) was made. The film was not well received by the Aran Islanders themselves, who found it a deceptively old-fashioned portrait of their traditional lifestyle made all the worse because it was made to look like contemporary island life. On the other hand, critics' positive reception to the film as realistic reinforced the general tendency to reject Irish economic and social reality. This retreat from reality into depoliticized documentary was symptomatic of Irish filmmakers' preference for the reproduction of an "ahistorical ethnicity and its economic offshoot, the tourist-landscape film,"[19] compared to the oppositional style being pursued by the British documentary movement's focus on working-class social problems. *Man of Aran* did, however, inspire the government to make its only documentary project of the 1930s, an Irish-language short film to accompany Flaherty's main feature, entitled *Oidhche Sheanchais (Storyteller's Night)*, featuring a well-known *seanchaí* Thomas Ó Diorain telling a sea fishing story from the hearth of a rural cottage.

The first documentary overviews of Ireland were also made by foreign companies and produced similarly unsatisfactory results for Irish audiences. In 1936 and 1943 the American series *March of Time* made editions on Ireland. However, the 1943 issue on "The Irish Question" presented negative stereotypes of rural, southern Ireland, while the North was characterized as vigorous and aggressive; and the most important contemporary issue – southern Irish neutrality during World War Two – was explained by means of the stereotype of the Irish as irrational and illogical.[20] During the war years, the paternalistic tone of the British newsreels played in Irish cinemas was infuriating but there was no homemade alternative. The only films made of the war made from the Irish perspective were a promotional film for the army commissioned by the Education Film Company of Ireland, entitled *Step Together* (1940), which featured training techniques, new technology

---

19 Rocket et al, p. 72.
20 Ibid., p. 73.

and weapons, and the Irish Army's Spearhead Film Unit's *Eire's Progress* (1941), a record of its own wartime activities.

In the 1940s state investment was generally limited to support for government promotional, educational and informational films that would not threaten the national moral standard to which the conservative political establishment aspired. Sources of funding for Irish film production were usually cultural, religious and educational institutions promoting specific political or social messages, rather than independent commercial enterprise or entrepreneurs. But The Emergency – the Irish euphemism for World War Two – was a watershed in the revitalization of Ireland's cultural life. The Irish Film Society publicized its activities and screenings in the new periodical, *The Bell* (1940–54), edited initially by Sean O'Faolain, and Lucy Glazebrook's regular "Tour of Films" column on feature films shown in Irish cinemas sparked enough interest to lead to more involved articles by other authors.

*The Bell* provided an alternative forum to the reactionary *Irish Catholic*, the Dublin paper, which in 1944 set up a Film Information Bureau aiming to encourage the proper use of the cinema. Since the publication of Pope Pius XI's 1936 encyclical, *Vigilanti Cura*, the Roman Catholic Church had been deciding whether or not to take an active part in film culture. The National Film Institute (NFI) was set up in 1943, partly thanks to John Charles MacQuaid, Archbishop of Dublin until 1947, to encourage the use of film in the Irish national and cultural interest, as well as promoting the use of film in adult education, schools, Irish language teaching, and the establishment of a National Film Library. Initially the NFI's committee was composed of a mixed body of laypeople and priests but disagreements soon turned into hostility and all four priests resigned, leaving the future of the NFI in the hands of laypeople. A number of films on religious themes were made during the 1940s, including *Pioneer Celebrations* (1943), filmed by the NFI; *Out of the Darkness* (1948), by the Holy Rosary Sisters of Killeshandra on their life and work in Nigeria called; and *The Silent Order* (1948), a portrait of the monks of Roscrea. The National Film Institute also published its own journals, *Irish Film Quarterly* (1957–59) and *Vision* (1965–68), which featured articles on the educational use of film and on the film scene at home and around the world.

Shortly after the foundation of the National Film Institute in 1943, two government films were made on Irish national themes, the *Inauguration of President O'Kelly* (1945) featuring future Taoiseach Sean Lemass, and Sean MacEntee in *A Nation Once Again* (1946), made to commemorate the 100th anniversary of Thomas Davis' death. But the idea of the government producing films did not appeal to everyone, particularly when they were made for anything more than informational purposes. Liam O'Leary wrote about the film, "one can see the easy primrose path to ballyhoo propaganda, chauvinistic and false, geared to the machinery of Party."[21] O'Leary is a giant in Irish film-production history, the man single-handedly responsible for much of the national film archive housed in the National Library of Ireland (now known as the Liam O'Leary Collection) and the first Irish Film School, created as an offshoot of the Irish Film Society, which he also co-founded. O'Leary was very critical of the state's language revival failure and argued for the establishment of an indigenous film industry and a native newsreel service. In the first book written on Irish cinema, *Invitation to the Film* (1945), O'Leary argued that film had a unique role to play in the national rebirth – that "not to use it would be almost an acknowledgement of terrible failure" – and he made the case for the use of documentary as a social tool in the tradition of Grierson's British Documentary Movement, arguing that "cinema must be used to open the eyes as well as the hearts of our people."[22]

O'Leary's commitment to social and political issues was given an outlet when in 1947 he was asked to make an election campaign film for a new socially radical political party. Dr. Noel Browne – who had already made a film on the *Newcastle Sanitorium* (1946) dealing with Ireland's battle against tuberculosis – joined forces with Sean MacBride and Noel Harnett to form Clann na Poblachta (People of the Republic or Republican Family). *Our Country* (1948), made under the banner of Irish Civic Films in December 1947, was essentially a criticism of Fianna Fáil's failure to deal with a variety

21    Quoted in Rockett *et al*, 74.
22    Roderick Flynn & Patrick Brereton, *Historical Dictionary of Irish Cinema* (New York: Scarecrow Press), 276.

of social problems. On 16 January 1948 the government had introduced the unpopular Supplementary Budget, which included increases to entertainments tax, so the cinema owners were certainly motivated to show the film. Irish scenes were interspersed with direct camera statements filmed in secret in England by MacBride, Hartnett and Browne. The result of this publicity was an increase in anti-Fianna Fáil sentiment and the party's defeat in the February 1948 general election.

Clann na Poblachta, now in office, continued with its utilization of film as a tool for communication and began to use film for government information campaigns. Dr. Noel Browne became Minister for Health in 1948 and followed the example of the Department of Local Government, for which Liam O'Leary made a number of films on social issues, including *Mr. Careless Goes to Town* (1949) on road accidents, *Safe Cycling* (1949) on the perils of cycling among Dublin traffic, *Gnó Gach Éine / Everybody's Business* (1949) on food hygiene, and *Voyage to Recovery* (1952) on tuberculosis. Finally, *The Promise of Barty O'Brien* (1950), written by Seán Ó Faoláin and funded in part by the Marshall Aid Programme's Economic Co-operation Administration, was made to publicize the long-awaited Rural Electrification Scheme.

During the same period, non-governmental native film production grew. Hibernia Films made promotional and information films such as *Next Please* (1948), the First National Film Corporation made the first attempt at an Irish newsreel (1949) since Norman Whitten's *Irish Events*, and the Irish Hospital Sweepstakes Films made *Irish Travel Club* for foreign consumption. One of the more important indigenous projects was the foundation of Comhar Cínó: Substandard Film Services by Colm Ó Laoghaire (1919–2007) and Kevin O'Kelly (1924–94), journalist and broadcaster with the Irish Press before joining Radio Éireann in 1954, who together made a silent film for the Gaelic Athletic Association on the *All-Ireland Football Final 1946: Kerry vs. Roscommon* (1946).[23] Ironically, it was an American film made the following year that sparked interest in Ireland in making

---

23    Comhar Cínó also made a sound film on the annual *Meath Pilgrimage to Lourdes* (1948).

future newsreels of football and hurling matches: Padraig O'Keefe, one of the directors of the National Film Institute and a member of the Gaelic Athletic Association, saw an American-made newsreel of the *All-Ireland Football Finals* (1947) between Kerry and Cavan, held in the New York City Polo Grounds. He was so impressed by the film that he brought it to Ireland for distribution and decided to have a short film made every year on the All-Ireland final.

The other major development in Irish film production in the late 1940s was the establishment of Peter Hunt's sound studios in Dublin. Hunt – an internationally recognized expert who did consulting work on the building of EMI sound machinery – and his wife came to Ireland from England and set up a sound recording studio in St. Stephen's Green. Abbey Film's *Who Fears to Speak of '98?* (1948) was the result of collaboration between Hunt and George Fleischman, the German pilot who had been interned in the Curragh Camp along with his film machinery during World War Two, but subsequently granted long-term parole to attend university in Dublin. Fleischman and Hunt worked on many credits in the post-war period. Liam O'Leary wrote the script for the film and Cyril Cusack (1910–93)[24] the commentary.

In 1950 the Minister for Industry and Commerce, Liam Cosgrave, reported that the Industrial Development Authority (IDA) was investigating the feasibility of establishing a national film industry in Ireland. Sean Mac Bride, as Minister for External Affairs, appointed Liam O'Leary to sit on the newly created Cultural Relations Committee, which commissioned a number of films. O'Leary made *W.B. Yeats – A Tribute* (1950); *Ireland-Rome* (1950), a record of President O'Kelly's pilgrimage to the Vatican; and *Portrait of Dublin* (1952) on eighteenth-century Dublin. Unfortunately

---

24  Born in South Africa to an Irish father and English mother, Cusack moved to Ireland at the age of 6, where she met an actor and they set up their own theatre company. Cusack made his own acting debut at the age of 7, joined the Abbey Theatre in 1932, and appeared in 65 plays in 13 years. He was widely regarded as Ireland's greatest actor. He formed his own touring company and by the 1950s had regular film roles in Hollywood. In 1963 he joined the Royal Shakespeare Company and the Old Vic the following year. He died in October 1993 at the age of 82.

for O'Leary, when Fianna Fáil returned to power in 1951, Sean MacEntee exacted his revenge by refusing to release *Portrait of Dublin*, which effectively ended O'Leary's directing career. He left Ireland for London in 1953, where he became acquisitions officer of the British National Film Archive. In that role, O'Leary negotiated a deal that allowed him to use their facilities to preserve historic Irish films, including several productions from the Kalem Company and the Film Company of Ireland.[25] The new Fianna Fáil government jumped on board and made its own External Affairs-sponsored film, *Fintona – A Study of Housing Discrimination* (1954) on alleged anti-Catholic discrimination in Co. Tyrone. This was intended to be the first in a series of documentaries but the project never came to fruition, as the Second Inter-Party Government again replaced Fianna Fáil as the party of government in 1954.

During the 1950s and early 1960s, some of the most innovative steps were taken in Irish film production. In 1953 Pronsias Ó Conluain's *Scéal na Scannán (The Story of Film)*, the first Irish-language account of the history of Irish cinema, was published. Like O'Leary, Ó Conluain (1919–2013) is an incredibly important figure in the history of Irish film. He was an RTÉ broadcaster, author, and promoter of the Irish language. His broadcasting career spanned the 1940s to the mid-1980s, specializing in Irish language and music programs. He played a major role in preserving and promoting the Irish language and heritage, and produced many RTÉ programs on the subject. He started by joining Radio Éireann in 1947 as a scriptwriter before joining the Mobile Recording Unit to travel the country with colleagues Séamus Ennis and Seán Mac Réamoinn, capturing the traditional music, dialects and local lore for the RTÉ Archives. He chronicled the lives of west-coast islanders and recorded the last Irish speakers in Co. Tyrone's Sperrin Mountains.[26] He also co-founded An Club Leabhar to encourage

---

25    O'Leary returned to Dublin in the 1960s to work with Radio Telifís Éireann as a film viewer, and held this position until his retirement in 1986. He continued to collect and store valuable material on Irish cinema, which eventually became his archive. Flynn and Brereton, 276.

26    See the O'Neill Country Historical Society tribute to Proinsias Ó Conluain at oneillcountryhistoricalsociety.com.

secondary school students to read in Irish, an initiative that is featured in one of the *Amharc Éireann* newsreels. He retired from RTE in 1983 and passed away in 2013 at the age of 93.

In 1956 the Cork Film Festival[27] was established as part of An Tóstal,[28] opening with Jack Lee's *A Town Like Alice* (1956), thus beginning a new era in Irish film culture. The same year, Louis Marcus established the periodical *Guth na Scannán (The Voice of Film)* for the festival and the Cork branch of the Irish Film Society. Marcus continued to publish it until 1961, while other more traditional reports on the cinema scene appeared by Michael Paul Gallagher in *Studies* and by Anthony Slide and Pat Billings in the *International Film Guide*.

Meanwhile, in contrast to Cork's internationalist orientation, Gael Linn focused on the domestic context by sponsoring the *Amharc Éireann (Look at Ireland)* series and the production of two compilation documentary films on the early history of the Irish state by George Morrison, *Mise Éire (I am Ireland)* (1959) and *Saoirse? (Freedom?)* (1961), both of which were shown at the Cork Film Festival. *Mise Éire* was extremely popular with the Irish public, presenting as it did a glorious view of the Irish struggle for independence but in *Saoirse?* Morrison conveyed his skepticism regarding the success of the independent Irish state. The somewhat less self-congratulatory tone of *Saoirse?* meant that it was also less well received. Meanwhile, the *Amharc Éireann* series graced Irish screens in the early 1960s because of the withdrawal of the British Rank Organization's newsreel from Irish cinemas, along with those in Britain. While in other countries, newsreels were being phased *out* while television was being phased in, in Ireland's case the phasing *in* of newsreels occurred at the same time that the government was seeking a means to set up a national television service. The series did not come to an end until two years after the introduction of television and Ó Laoghaire also went on to make more films, including

---

27    The Festival continues as one of Europe's oldest film festivals. For information, see
      <www.corkfilmfest.org>.

28    An Tóstal was the name for the series of festivals that ran all over the country from
      1953 to 1958 as a celebration of Irish life. The festival in Drumshanbo, Co. Leitrim is
      the only one that continues to this day.

*Our Neighbours' Children* (1960), a fund-raiser focusing on the challenges faced by the physically handicapped children at Baldoyle Hospital, and *The Most Gallant Gentleman* (1966), on the removal of Roger Casement's body from England and his reburial in Ireland.

## Ireland in the 1950s and 1960s

The late-1950s mark the beginning in popular consciousness of Ireland's internal and external transformation from an economically underdeveloped and politically isolated nation on Europe's western fringe into a modern member of the international community. With the publication in November 1958 of the *First Programme for Economic Expansion*, a five-year-plan for growth, Sean Lemass's Fianna Fáil government embarked on a modernization policy from 1959–63 that opened the door to further policy initiatives throughout the 1960s, brought Ireland into the welfare state system of post-war Europe, and finally into Europe itself as a member of the European Economic Community in 1973. The *First Programme*, as it was known, was based on T.K. Whitaker's paper *Economic Development*, the impact of which on the official mind has been compared to Britain's Beveridge Report, and followed the basics of Keynesian economics already well-known and implemented in other Western European countries. Its implementation marked the formal end to the protectionist economic policy of the de Valera era and the beginning of the new period of trade liberalization and economic development. The programme yielded impressive results almost immediately – the anticipated growth rate of 2% per annum was easily surpassed by the 4% average, prompting the government to follow the *First Programme* with a second, more ambitious, programme in 1964 for the period 1964–68. When it became obvious that the momentum of 1959–63 could not be sustained and the new targets could not be met, this programme was pre-empted by a third, more modest one in 1967, which was in turn quietly set aside in the increasingly difficult international economic climate of the late-1960s.

The dramatic nature of the programme's impact was accentuated by the remarkable scale of the economy's recovery from the seemingly bottomless pit of depression of the mid-1950s. More important, however, in terms of the first economic programme's impact on the Irish population and policy-makers was the *perception* of success in the public mind rather than the actual figures. After decades of isolation, shortages and rationing during and after the Emergency, and a sequence of balance of payments crises from 1948 to 1955, a sense of excitement spread through the population. The psychological effects of economic revival were lasting and felt in all areas of Irish social life. The heightened expectations and new optimism were characterized at the time as a mental virus infecting the population of Ireland, as traditional Irish values and social mores were challenged from within and without. In the cities, and especially Dublin, urbanization established the concept of the nuclear family and revised gender roles, altering traditional family dynamics. Consumerism was embraced along with the introduction of new media. All over the country emigration began to decline, albeit slowly. The Roman Catholic Church faced the implications of modernization both domestically and internationally through the work of the Second Vatican Council. Educational reform in the late 1960s updated the system inherited from the British, which had remained essentially unchanged since independence. Ireland joined the twentieth-century welfare-state system with the introduction of new government policies on health and welfare, while even the civil service and government administration initiated reform from within.

This economic revival and its social consequences coincided with an apparent upheaval in the Irish political establishment. Since independence, the legacy of the Civil War had continued in the composition of the ranks and leadership of the two main political parties. Fianna Fáil – the Republican Party and the anti-Treaty forces in the Civil War – led the country with Éamon de Valera as Taoiseach for many years, while Fine Gael, representing the former pro-Treaty forces, remained in opposition. The status quo remained for the most part uninterrupted until two Inter-Party Governments took office, each for a period of three years, first in 1948 and again in 1954. When de Valera retired as Taoiseach in 1959, Seán Lemass became leader of Fianna Fáil. Lemass's name has become synonymous with the revival, thanks to the many policy changes and new programmes his government oversaw. His tenure has been characterized as the changing of the guard from the older, Civil War-era politicians, to the new, younger generation of leaders which would guide Ireland toward the bright future of European membership and its new identity as the so-called Celtic Tiger. But the reality is that although Lemass's leadership of Fianna Fáil did coincide with a changing of the guard to a certain extent – there was a new leader of Fine Gael (James Dillon) in the same year, and of Labour (Brendan Corish) shortly thereafter – the politicians serving in Lemass's cabinet were essentially those who had served under de Valera, and the core group did not change substantially until after Lemass's retirement. In fact, Lemass himself was a member of the old guard, having fought for the anti-Treaty forces in the Civil War. Lemass's tenure was also relatively short (certainly compared to his predecessor) and many of the more dramatic changes that are commonly associated with Ireland's transformation actually came after he retired in 1966 and was succeeded by Jack Lynch.

To a great extent then, the publication of the *First Programme* in 1958 and the arrival of Seán Lemass as Taoiseach in 1959 do mark a turning-point in Ireland's history in the public mind – but the popular perception of Ireland as completely politically, socially and culturally stagnant *prior* to 1958 is false. Lemass's political philosophy and the movement towards political internationalism, Whitaker's economic programme and trade liberalization, the social impact of emigration, internal migration and urbanization, and the cultural movements which commented upon and criticized these and other aspects of Irish life had all existed, at least in embryo, for years before the dramatic events of the late-1950s. This is not to downplay the importance of the economic revival and its consequences, but simply to point out that there were other watersheds that occurred in other areas of Irish life, at other times. So, instead of seeing Ireland simply as being rapidly transformed in a few short years, it is more useful to see the period from 1958 to the late 1960s as the con-centrated results of ideas that had been fermenting for some time, as it was the dramatic coincidence of these political, economic, social and cultural forces from 1958 onwards that has lent this period such power in the popular historical memory.

Ireland, like other Western European nations, had enjoyed a postwar boom from 1945 to 1949, which disguised the country's economic problems in the short-term and fuelled the consumer spending that drove imports upwards. Meanwhile, food exports were protected by Ireland's preferential trading relationship with the UK, so the widening gap between imports and exports was never addressed. When it became apparent to the government after the 1951 balance of payments crisis that something was amiss, deflationary measures were taken in February 1952 and increased in July of that year. While succeeding in terms of decreasing the gap somewhat between imports and exports, these measures were not sufficient to stem the tide of expectation that had arisen among the Irish population, which had grown increasingly aware of the discrepancy between its standard of living and its neighbour to the east. The ball finally dropped in 1955 when food exports to the UK ended and the state of the country's finances became disastrously apparent. The immediate impact of the balance of payments crisis of 1955 was a drop in employment in industry, construction and associated trades, while the outflow from the land continued.

The tide of emigration had been flowing at a rapid rate of over 40,000 per year since 1948 but in 1956 the level of emigration was higher than at any time since the 1880s. Not only were young men and women leaving the country in droves in hopes of economic independence and of having a family, whole groups of workers were leaving secure jobs in Ireland in the quest for a future for themselves and their children that they could simply not envisage at home. And while there had been a Commission on the Gaeltacht (Irish-speaking areas) in 1926, which drew attention to the numerous problems in the Irish-speaking areas of the country, it was – incredibly – only in 1956 that these regions were officially defined by the government as the Gaeltacht areas.

There were, however, some positive steps taken before T.K. Whitaker became Secretary of Finance and Seán Lemass became Taoiseach. While the Second Coalition Government of 1954–57 can definitely be faulted for failing sufficiently to address the problems at hand, three important measures were taken, also in that landmark year of 1956, to address some of the problems in industrial manufacturing, export production and redistributive investment. The Coalition Government started to use industrial grants to attract foreign activity and introduced an export tax relief scheme, which exempted income tax and corporation tax profits earned from new or increased exports. Both schemes contributed notably to the economic revival from 1959 onwards, by focusing industrialists' energies on export markets and attracting foreign industrialists to Ireland in great numbers than ever. They also brought concrete results in the years prior to the revival as it is generally understood: Although the figures for the Irish economic revival are typically quoted as a lump from 1959 to 1973, exports actually rose as a result of these schemes from 12 million pounds in 1956 to 32.5 million in 1960, while the number of new factories established annually by external interests trebled between 1957 and 1960. Thus, although it is true that it was the crisis year of 1958 that finally prompted the government to act and implement the *First Economic Programme*, measures taken before that date – in 1956 and 1957 – had a beneficial effect on the outlook for the national economy before 1959.

The coincidence of these events with the beginning of the *Amharc Éireann* series was not accidental. Ó Laoghaire was well aware of their potential consequences, and focused on these – and on some of the problems yet to be rectified – in his single-item documentary films. Production of the early series of short documentary films began in June 1956 and continued until April 1959. Thus it was into the depths of nation-wide depression and demoralization that Colm Ó Laoghaire launched a new image of Ireland, destined for an audience not yet particularly optimistic regarding Ireland's future economic growth. The vision he presented is one of a country that is down but not out, depressed but not without hope for the future. For while in many concrete senses 1956–58 signified the depths of Ireland's economic crisis and material and psychological depression, in *Amharc Éireann*'s "Eyes of Ireland" short documentary series there is more than a glimmer of hope for the future. The cultural organization behind this projected glimmer was Gael Linn.

## The language revival movement and Gael Linn

The strength of the Irish language had been steadily declining since before the Great Famine of 1845–49, which saw 1.5 million people emigrate and another million die of starvation. The impact of the famine was felt most strongly in the poorer Irish-speaking communities in the west of the country and the resulting shift in the demographic balance between Irish and English gave rise to practical concerns about the long-term survival of Irish among sections of the educated classes. The Gaelic League was formed in 1893 by Douglas Hyde and Eoin MacNeill to promote the Irish language. It was closely affiliated with two other cultural movements – the Gaelic Athletic Association and the Anglo-Irish literary revival spearheaded by Lady Gregory and W.B. Yeats. As the movement for political independence grew in the early years of the twentieth century, the Gaelic League split – reflecting the split in the Volunteer movement – with MacNeill joining the Irish Volunteers in their fight for national independence. After the formation of the Irish Free State in 1922, the leading members of the Gaelic League became leaders of the new conservative state. A Department of the National Language was established, with the then president of the Gaelic League as its Minister, and the language revival was instituted as national policy. Unfortunately, it was precisely this institutionalization that effectively destroyed the impetus for revival and the use of Irish continued to decline dramatically into the twentieth century.

The Irish Constitution defined Irish as "the national language" but still recognized English as an official language. The state's strategy consisted of the maintenance of Irish in areas where it was still the community language – elsewhere the objective was revival – as well as the use of Irish in the public service and the standardization and modernization of the language itself. By the twentieth century, however, the areas in which Irish was the community language had shrunk to a fragmented group of districts on the western and south-western periphery of the country. These Gaeltacht areas were subsistence economies characterized by out-migration, depopulation and deprivation, so the state policy in the Gaeltacht took on the character of a regional development programme, beginning in 1926 with the Gaeltacht Commission. The policy focused on the critical role of agriculture and defined the areas as being either fully Irish-speaking (80% or more) or partly Irish-speaking (25% to 79%), on the basis of a census undertaken in 1925. Maintaining Irish was tied to the issue of stabilizing the population and the economy through land reorganization, fishing and rural industries from about 1930 to 1950.

In 1956 the government finally acknowledged that the Gaeltacht communities were on the verge of extinction and established Roinn na Gaeltachta (the Department of the Gaeltacht), which redefined the area boundaries for the first time since 1926. The new Gaeltacht corresponded closely to the area previously defined as the core area of fully Irish-speaking persons, but by now it only contained 85,700 people, down from 168,279 in 1926. A new revival programme was launched by the Department to provide employment opportunities and essential amenities, and to nurture a more positive self-image and sense of pride in the Gaeltacht population. In 1958 Roinn na Gaeltachta established Gaeltarra Éireann, a statutory board, as its instrument for industrial development in the Gaeltacht. Its purpose was, however, only to assist in the continued operation of the few traditional industries, many of which were outdated and incapable of modernization. For the first seven years of its operation, Gaeltarra Éireann simply operated and renovated its inherited industries.

In 1963 the report of the Commission on the Restoration of the Irish Language (1958–63) made a number of recommendations for development in the fields of forestry, fishing and tourism, and recommended small-scale industry as well as the establishment of at least one large-scale enterprise in each of the three larger Gaeltacht districts. It was not until 1965 that its powers were augmented to include the development of new industries and enter into development schemes with nongovernmental organizations and firms, by which time the Gaeltacht population had declined by a further 12,000.

In spite of such efforts on behalf of development in the Gaeltacht areas, the state's approach to the revival from 1948 to 1971 was one of stagnation, detachment and retreat from responsibility for the language policy. The government accepted many of the recommendations made by the Commission on the Restoration of Irish in 1963, but argued in its own White Paper published in 1965 that the public had a part to play in fostering positive attitudes towards Irish. This emphasis on public attitudes reflected government views that the major obstacle was the absence of sustained public support for the language, rather than state action.

During this very same period, however, a movement was underway to promote the revival of the Irish language. In the 1940s, after twenty years of failure in government hands, language revivalists took up the task of renewal of the movement, rejecting the association of Irish with the poor and backward west and looking to the urban centres as sources of renewal. This new activism led to the establishment of a number of urban-based language organizations and new publications. In 1943, the periodical *Inniú* (*Today*) and the journal *Comhar* (*Co-operation*) were founded. The same year, key members of An Comhchaidreamh (The Association), an organization of Irish-speaking university students formed in the 1930s, created Comhdhail Naisiúnta na Gaeilge (CNG) (the Irish National Congress), as an umbrella body for all Irish language organizations – and from *that* organization came Gael Linn in 1953.

## The *Amharc Éireann* series

Gael Linn began as a fund-raising project initiated by a small group of university students and graduates that, in effect, wanted to shame the government into paying more attention to the language.[29] The name Gael Linn is a play on words, meaning both "Irish pool," referring to the football pools or private members' lottery which was created to raise the funds, and "Irish with us," or "Our Irish," referring to Gael Linn's purposes of promoting of Irish language and culture. After independence, the institutionalization of the Irish language and traditional culture by the conservative state –

---

29 See <www.gael-linn.com> for information on the organization and its history.

especially its heavy-handed and compulsion-oriented policy towards language revival – had dampened people's concern for the survival of Irish. In March 1953, Dónall Ó Móráin, who came to be regarded as the founder of Gael Linn, recommended that an organization be formed under the patronage of Comhdháil Náisiúnta na Gaeilge (Irish National Congress) to raise the funds for Irish film production. This use of modern media to promote the Irish language cause was in itself was a significant departure from earlier attempts at language revitalization, which was motivated by the fact that – as Riobard MacGóráin, another future Gael Linn member – put it: "The magic spell of the screen made faraway hills beautiful and made our people doubt the worth of their own bitter barley. It was at the top of Gael Linn's aims to possess this field for Irish – and, indeed, for Ireland."[30]

Ó Móráin initially approached Ó Laoghaire to discuss the prospects for a series of monthly short Irish-language documentary films. Ó Móráin knew Ó Laoghaire from university as a long-time member of the Irish Film Society and as a nephew of Joseph Mary Plunkett, a hero of the 1916 Rising and member of a well-known nationalist family interested in the language.[31] Ó Laoghaire had recently discussed the need to produce films on 35mm for distribution in Irish cinemas with Vincent Corcoran, who had just acquired an Arriflex 35mm camera. Ó Móráin's original idea had been to produce a weekly newsreel that would cover such political topics as party meetings and Dáil debates. Ó Laoghaire argued against this; he felt the resources were not available to generate enough material for a weekly series and the subject matter would be too boring for a cinema audience.

---

30   Riobárd MacGóráin, "Scannáin, Amhráin agus Dramaí," in unknown collection: 67–76 (my translation).

31   Horace Plunkett was the founder of Irish co-operative movement and Count George Noble Plunkett, Colm's grandfather, was a member of the first Dáil in 1919. More recently, James Plunkett is the author of the novel *Strumpet City* on the 1913 Dublin lock-out, and his cousin Eilís Dillon, also a novelist, is most famous for her work, *Across the Bitter Sea*, on Irish emigration to America. Colm Ó Laoghaire was thus part of a fairly long and illustrious line of national political and literary figures. I am grateful to his wife for facilitating our meeting as part of the early research for this book. Colm passed away in December 2007.

He was concerned that Irish had come to be regarded as tiresome, given the association of the Irish language with compulsion. He was, for the same reason, determined to dissociate Irish approaches to making documentaries from those of John Grierson's British Documentary Movement, which he saw as entirely too rational and too British in tone and content for Irish Catholic sensibilities.[32] Instead, they decided to produce a monthly series, each focusing on just one subject. These were conceived as "magazine-style" documentary films. The producers stressed the similarity to magazines by referring to each film as an *éagrán*, the Irish word for "edition" or "issue." Ó Laoghaire was given editorial freedom to choose the subjects covered. To keep production costs down, each issue was kept to four minutes.

The first *Amharc Éireann* film was released in June 1956. The series ran from June 1956 to July 1964, beginning as monthly, single-item short documentary films from 1956 to 1959, and then as a weekly, multi-item newsreel from 1959 to 1964. The whole series was known to the general public as *Amharc Éireann*, but internally – in Ó Laoghaire's correspondence and on the copies of the scripts – the monthly documentary films were referred to as the "Eyes of Ireland" series, and the later newsreels were called "Gaelic News." Both series were shot on 35mm film. Several Irish distributors were contacted, but all wanted to charge a fee; only Rank Film Distributors in Britain was prepared to distribute the films free of charge, as a public-relations demonstration of its recognition of Ireland as a separate country with an indigenous culture. The monthly issues were attached to the end of the Universal Newsreel screened in all Rank-owned cinemas in the Republic of Ireland. Eight to ten prints were made of each film, which first went to four or five city-centre cinemas in Dublin and then to the rest of the country. As the films were not topical, the delay in distribution to rural cinemas was not a concern. Gael Linn handled all of the publicity for the series, which included the production of a poster for each issue. In

---

32    Colm Ó Laoghaire, "Gael Linn 'Vest Pocket' Documentaries" in *Irish Film Quarterly* March 1957, vol. 1, no. 1.

total, thirty-eight magazine-style single item short documentary films in the "Eyes of Ireland" were shot.[33]

By 1959, television had come to Britain and, in its wake, the Rank Organziation withdrew its newsreels from Irish cinemas. To fill the gap in the viewing program, Ó Móráin envisaged the "Gaelic News" series of weekly Irish newsreels. The transition from monthly to weekly films was relatively smooth because the production procedures were already in place. The main changes were due to the demands of a faster turnover with a great amount of material to cover, which necessitated that Gael Linn hire a director and cameraman, Jim Mulkerns, and an assistant, Val Ennis, on a permanent basis. Usually four items were covered per week, in one-minute clips that formed a four-minute issue. Sometimes an issue would focus on a single special event and compilation issues were made at the end of the year, but the 4-minute maximum length was firm. Two hundred and seventy issues in total were released (including a non-numbered trial issue). Editorial control remained with Ó Laoghaire, though Gael Linn did suggest items to be covered – particularly the events in which they were involved. But Gael Linn's involvement remained chiefly at the level of publicity, in the translation into Irish of the commentary scripts, and in the provision of commentators and distribution. The newsreels series ended in July 1964, owing to the influence of the newly established national television service, Telefís Éireann, and the decline in cinema audiences.

The nature of newsreel production makes it difficult to outline specifically the responsibilities of each member of the crew for individual items and issues. Ó Laoghaire produced, edited, researched and scripted the newsreel series from its inception in 1959 to mid-1961, with the exception of two films, which were shot and directed by George Morrison,[34] after which he assumed the role of executive producer. From that point on, Jim Mulkerns assumed the responsibilities for week-to-week production. Jim Mulkerns

---

33   Two of these were never made into films; one on hurling skills, and another on shamrock picking deemed too out of date and stage-Irish.

34   "Réadlann Rathfearnáin" (Rathfarnam Observatory) #24: May 1958 and "Gáirdíní na Lús" (Botanic Gardens) #25: June 1958. The *Amharc Éireann* series was numbered in sequence, which will appear after each title throughout these footnotes.

was the director and cameraman and Vincent Corcoran photographed thirty-three of the thirty-eight issues. Mulkerns[35] and Corcoran went on to become respected filmmakers in their own right. Val Ennis worked as assistant cameraperson on the series and was responsible for indoor lighting. Nick O'Neill was initially taken on as a trainee, and worked as production assistant. Robin Bestick-Williams, Morrison's preferred cameraman, also shot three issues.[36] The film scripts were first drafted in English by Ó Laoghaire, but supervised and then translated into Irish by Gael Linn employees, all of whom were to become major figures in Irish literary and cultural history. Máirtín Ó Cadhain – best known for his novel *Cré na Cille* (1948) – worked the first six issues, and Mícheál Ó Gríofa for the rest of the series. The commentary was read by Pádraig Ó Raghaillaigh, a noted Irish-language broadcaster with Radio Éireann. He was occasionally replaced by Breandán Ó hEithir, also a prominent print and broadcast journalist and novelist, and less frequently by Donnacha Ó Míochán. The pace of speech and the dialects of Irish represented varied from film to film, because Gael Linn consciously sought to present a mixture of voices.

Laboratories in London processed the film and generated the titles, which were all in Irish for the short documentary films of the "Eyes of Ireland" series. This practice changed with the "Gaelic News" films, for which the titles are in English. With no processing facilities in Ireland the production crew was on an extremely tight and demanding schedule. All four items had to be shot by Sunday evening, when the film was canned and packed and sent to Denham Laboratories in London on the last flight. The following Monday, the lab processed the film and produced rush prints, which were returned to Dublin on Tuesday morning and brought to

35  Mulkerns made the Irish-language documentary film, *An tOileánach a d'Fhill (The Return of the Islander)* in 1969, which earned him a certificate of merit at the Cork Film Festival in 1970 and an Oscar nomination in 1975. Like Ó Laoghaire, he had strong family ties to the 1916 Rising and the artistic and literary life of Dublin. His father was a veteran of the 1916 Rising interned in Frongoch, and his uncle, Frank O'Neill, was the manager of the Gaiety Theatre in Dublin in the mid-1920s.

36  "Caiseal na Rí" (Rock of Cashel) #26: July 1948; "Snámh Sábhála" (Safety Swimming) #28: September 1958; "Madraí ar Saoire" (Dogs on Holiday) #30: November 1958.

Peter Hunt's sound studios, where the film was cut and Hunt did the recording and dubbing at with the assistance of Gene Martin. All of the films were shot mute, except for the music festivals, which Peter Hunt recorded live. At around 6pm on Tuesday a Gael Linn staff member would type up the narration, the sound staff would chose the music for the items, and at 7pm the voice over was recorded by projecting the film in Peter Hunt's recording room and recording the commentary live. Gerald Victory, one of Ireland's most prominent composers and later director of music for RTÉ, composed eight pieces of music for the series. Once the soundtrack was complete, the films were returned to London. On Wednesday and Thursday the finished prints were produced and returned to Dublin on Friday morning for screening in cinemas that same day.

Gael Linn proceeded to bring the *Amharc Éireann* series to a country that in 1956 did not have a particularly positive opinion of itself or its native language. The period during which it was made overlapped with both the depths of depression of the 1950s and the heights of the Lemass years of the 1960s. The series was a cultural nationalist project, which began before Whitaker's economic miracle, as a call to the people of Ireland to look at their own country and to take pride in it and the language. Ó Laoghaire attempted to change the prevailing attitude to Irish by producing films that also aimed to inspire a confidence in Ireland – in its capacity to produce valuable goods, to promote its own industrial development, to compete internationally, to sustain its population, and to generally reassure the Irish of their collective self-worth at a time when depression had taken its toll on the national psyche. It is to these films that we now turn.

# PART I

# "The Eyes of Ireland" short documentary films[1]

Garret FitzGerald, former Taoiseach, wrote that the 1950s were the first decade of normalcy in Ireland since independence.[2] The sequence of crises since then – the Civil War in 1922–23, the Depression, the Economic War from 1932–38, closely followed by the Second World War from 1939–45 – meant that the state's protectionist economic policies were never tested in normal circumstances. As such the 1950s presented the first real test of the independent state's economic policies – and it failed that test rather badly. 1956 was a landmark year in two negative senses. First, in 1956 the report of the Commission on Emigration completed in 1954 was published for general readership, and the numbers were horrifyingly clear: The level of emigration was higher than at any time since the 1880s, when people were being driven forcibly from the land. Second, a Commission on the Restoration of the Irish Language was launched. Located in the isolated and rural western seabord districts of the country, these areas were underdeveloped, even by standards of 1950s Ireland, and the prospects for employment were even worse than elsewhere in the country. Thus by 1956, confidence in Ireland – especially confidence in Irish-speaking Ireland – had reached a new low. It was into these depths of nation-wide depression and demoralization that Colm Ó Laoghaire and Gael Linn launched a new image of Ireland.

---

1  This section on the short documentary films contains content previously published as part of an essay entitled, "The *Amharc Éireann* Early Documentary Series: Milled Peat, Music and Mná Spéire," in *Ireland in Focus: Film, Photography and Popular Culture*, edited by Eoin Flannery and Michael Griffin (Syracuse University Press, 2009), pp. 17–34.

2  Garret FitzGerald *Planning in Ireland: a P.E.P. Study* (Dublin: Institute of Public Administration & London: Political and Economic Planning, 1968): 8.

In 1956, Irish was associated in the public mind with compulsory schooling rather than popular entertainment. The primary purpose of the *Amharc Éireann* series was to put Irish on the screen, to present hearing it in the cinema as a normal occurrence, which it clearly was not in the mid-1950s. While the series did not purport to "teach" Irish in the off-putting sense that the state's compulsory educational system did, its mere existence was sufficient to spark interest in, and call attention to, the language at a time when the population did not hold Irish in very high esteem. In the "Eyes of Ireland" short documentary films, the country is presented as a source of pride – the land itself is a source of wealth and resources, the people are innovative and hard-working and there is no reason why anyone should be forced to leave a country so full of potential. Ó Laoghaire's vision – of an Ireland that was rural as well as modern, industrious, motivated, innovative and successful – undermined the long-held association of the language with rural backwardness and poverty, while the validity of the Irish language as a means of communication outside the Irish-speaking Gaeltacht was reinforced by its association with a popular form of modern media. So while in many concrete senses 1956–58 signified the depths of Ireland's economic crisis and material and psychological depression, in *Amharc Éireann*'s "Eyes of Ireland" series there is also hope for the future.

Ó Laoghaire was keenly aware of the need to counteract audience prejudice against films in Irish by providing subject matter beyond the realm of the expected in terms of Irish-language material. The Irish cinema audience, accustomed as it was to British newsreels and Hollywood-produced feature films, was discerning enough to demand a certain level of professionalism. It was vital that the topics not be perceived as boring and Ó Laoghaire had a clear idea of the type of documentaries he wanted to avoid. He was interested in the development of an identifiably Irish documentary style and was at pains to dissociate the content and style of his films from John Grierson and his followers in the British Documentary Movement. The Irish moral-philosophical basis for documentary-making was fundamentally different, as Ó Laoghaire saw it, based on Catholic Christianity rather than Liberal Humanism, and he hoped that Irish documentaries would emulate the Continental rather than the British style.[3]

The opening title of the *Amharc Éireann* series is emblazoned on the screen in large block white capital letters, with the sub-title "produced by Gael Linn." The issue title follows, against a background silhouette of a cameraman holding his camera, cleverly constructed to also look like a shamrock. Each issue ends with another silhouette, this one a map of Ireland, with the word "end" superimposed upon it. These images instantly communicate the overriding purpose of the films – the presentation of Ireland to the national cinema-going public. The presentation style is obviously modeled on the British newsreels that traditionally preceded the main features in Irish cinemas but in this case the large bold lettering announces the content to the audience: "Views of Ireland" – for a change!

---

3    Colm Ó Laoghaire, "Gael Linn 'Vest Pocket' Documentaries," *Irish Film Quarterly* 1, no. 1 (March 1957): 9–11.

Lobster fishing boats from Carna, Galway arrive in Ringsend, Dublin.
Donal Ó Morain of Gael Linn (3rd from left) meets with the fishermen. 24 June 1959.
*Reproduced with permission from the Irish Photo Archive.*

# CHAPTER TWO

# Industrial and rural development

The Coalition Government took a number of steps in 1956 in order to encourage industrial development in Ireland and many of these short documentary films focus on the specific areas in which these steps were to prove extremely beneficial in the long term. The foresight Ó Laoghaire displayed in choosing the topics for a number of these films is quite striking, as he drew attention to some of the innovative and exploratory work being conducted while highlighting areas still in need of attention. Films on the Shannon airport, Bord na Mona's milled peat operation, copper mining in the Avoca valley, a technical school for fishermen in Howth, and on the Waterford Glass factory[1] draw attention to the new and innovative ways of conducting traditional industries – some welcome and some not – and indicate the potential importance of these industries for Ireland's future economic success. In the mining and peat development areas specifically, the films send a message regarding Ireland's future development that was uncanny given the events that transpired in the 1960s and 1970s, while one on the dying art of barrel-making serves as a postscript to the otherwise bright future anticipated by Irish industry.

A common thread throughout this group of films is the uniquely Irish nature of the subject-matter. Sea fishing, copper mining, turf cutting, and glass making were all Irish indigenous industries, based on the landscape, seascape and natural resources embedded in the earth itself. Unfortunately, until the 1950s none of these potential sources of wealth were sufficiently

---

1    "Aerphort na Sionainne" (Shannon Airport) #2: July 1956; "Bua na Móna" (Milled Peat Production) #13: June 1957; "Mianaigh Thrá Dhá Abhainn" (Mining in Avoca) #3: August 1956; "Iascairí ar Scoil" (Howth Fishing School) #1: June 1956; "Gloine Phortláirge" (Waterford Glass) #20: January 1958.

utilized in their traditional form to make a significant contribution to the Irish economy. As small-scale or short-term enterprises, their significance in terms of economic contribution on a national scale was limited to the symbolic. The purpose of these "Eyes of Ireland" films was, then, to show the public how these industries could, with the necessary resources, contribute to the national economy. Foreign technical expertise combined with domestic state-sponsored assistance was to be the catalyst for development, complemented on the local level by individual educational initiatives.

The very first film made for the series, "Fishermen at School,"[2] illustrates the characteristics necessary to create a productive Irish society on an individual level, by focusing on one fisherman in a rural village. The first view of the harbour sets the scene into which the fishing boat "Howth Head" comes. Fishermen unload crates of fish onto the dock and Jim Deeling is introduced by the narrator. We follow Jim as he goes home for tea, only to emerge shortly afterwards to make his way through town. The narrator wonders aloud where he is off to next. "Where to now? To the pub?" But to the viewer's surprise, Jim finally makes his way to entrance of the Technical School, the sign for which is displayed prominently, where he joins the other "fishermen at school" from which the film gets its title.

Jim Deeling is an example of the pro-active and self-motivated fisherman, who not only works hard at sea during the day, but is committed to increasing his skills during his free time rather than wasting it at the pub or elsewhere. At the school, the small group of fishermen stands around watching as the instructor teaches them navigation skills. Next, they proceed to a class on charting the course, where the fishermen again watch and listen closely to the instructor. The focus in the technical school is on theoretical knowledge that can be applied as a complement to their practical working lives. The film ends by returning to the opening scene outdoors, where the theory of the classroom meets the practical world of the fishing boats. For those in any doubt, the feature ends with a clear enunciation of the message. "Early in the morning they sail to the seas again with new knowledge about fishing that they learned at school." The closing scene is an exact reversal of

2    "Iascairí ar Scoil" (Howth Fishing School) #1: June 1956.

the opening one, as the boats leave the docks and proceed out beyond the harbour on their way to the open seas. The difference this time, however, is that the fishermen carry with them the valuable navigation and charting skills, which can now be applied to their trade.

One of the obstacles to development in the Irish fisheries was the perception of the job of fisherman as low-status. Perceptions of poor working conditions and low pay added to the social stigma already attached to fishing. It was not considered a job in its own right and was generally done only as a part-time activity done by farmers to supplement their income from the land. Education was needed not only for the fishermen at school but also for the public in order to erase fishing's social stigma. Professionalization of the industry and the resulting change in public perception of its status was part of the modernization process, and this school is ahead of its time as an example of the sort of schemes that were introduced on a more comprehensive level in the 1970s.

"Mining in Avoca"[3] deals with the re-opening of an old nineteenth-century copper mine in Avoca, Co. Wicklow. Here, innovation is coupled with tradition, as natural domestic wealth is combined with international expertise, allowing for the continued exploitation of a resource previously assumed to be exhausted. Mining in Avoca had taken place over many centuries, focusing on different minerals at different times. It declined after a sixty-year peak in 1890 due to technological limitations and falling world metal prices, but popular memory held that exhausted resources had been the cause of the industry's decline.

The film opens with a view of the road sign to Avoca, followed by a view of the valley where the mine is located. "In Avoca in Co. Wicklow you see in this beautiful glen here, the old mine that has been closed for one hundred years." The scenery is lovely and it is an unlikely looking location for an industrial enterprise. "Today brand new work is beginning as a copper-mine is being opened by a Canadian group." This apparently rural area is being revitalized through the input of international resources. We follow the work of the miners after entering the tunnel, where the men are

---

3    "Mianaigh Thrá Dhá Abhainn" (Mining in Avoca) #3: August 1956.

shown drilling the rock in a very watery cavern. They place explosives in the rock and then the tunnel is seen from the outside again, with smoke coming out of the entranceway. The commentator explains that this activity is the result of foreign investment. "A special mechanical dumper came from Canada to take out the rock." The tyres alone cost eight hundred pounds but the dumper can carry up to thirty-one tons of rock, as the camera zooms on the words "31 ton capacity" on its side.

There is no mention of the role of the Irish state in this enterprise but without the co-operation of the Canadians this crucial element in the mining operation would be missing. The dumper enters the mine to remove the rock, while the miners look on. "When the tunnel and the structures are ready, they will get copper from the mine" and this revamped industry will supply more jobs for Irish miners. There are sixty miners working here already and that there will be two hundred when the project is complete. The camera pans back out from the mine into the valley with which the film began, providing a sense of perspective on the immediate and more long-term significance of the mining industry for the surrounding area. In spite of present good fortunes, the landscape inspires humility, if not outright cynicism. "Men are working here again as they did long ago; but the glens and the hills were here before them and will continue to be after them!" This sense of the land as the provider of resources, detached from the fate of the people, appears as a typically Irish philosophical attitude. Although they have found a way to make it provide for them, this will only last as long as ingenuity does and there are no guarantees for long-term success.

The shortage of sulphur during the Second World War led to renewed interest in mining of pyrites for sulphuric acid at Avoca from 1942 to 1947, which revealed an extensive copper deposit at the site. The Irish government had already made some moves to facilitate increased mining activity by foreign companies. The Minerals Development Act of 1940 alleviated the complications of land ownership which led to haggling over mineral rights and dissuaded companies from initiating exploration, by allowing the State to issue licenses without regard to land ownership and to sometimes acquire mineral rights. Demand for metals rose during the early 1950s but Ireland was still technologically ill equipped to engage in mining alone.

The 1956 Finance Act was the first major effort on the part of the state to stimulate mining activity. It included tax concessions exempting new mining enterprises from income tax and corporations profits tax for four years, and from half of the profits tax for a further four. The new tax holiday scheme immediately attracted a Canadian company to the project. St. Patrick's Copper Mines Ltd., a subsidiary of the Canadian Mogul organization, began production on the Avoca mine two years later in 1958, continuing until 1964 and encouraging the subsequent influx of other Canadian firms. That first exploration in Avoca from 1958–64 recorded in the "Eyes of Ireland" film was thus a foreshadowing of the good things to come in Ireland's near economic and industrial future.

The impact of mining on the community in the late-1950s is noted in the film, in terms of the employment it would generate. This impact was felt on the local and regional level, in the form of a sense of newfound pride, achievement and optimism among residents of mining towns, and reduced emigration. It was thanks to the descendants of earlier Irish emigrants to Canada that this community was able to prevent the cycle from repeating itself. Mining at Avoca was thus an example of a successful measure used to stave off the cycle of unemployment, poverty, emigration and demoralization that had wreaked havoc on Irish society since the Famine.

"Winning (Harvesting) of the Peat"[4] is a film on Bord na Móna (the Peat Board)'s milled peat-making industry and is essentially a display of the power of machinery to transform an underutilized part of the Irish landscape into a usable source of power for the whole country. The film opens with a shot of a signpost on a country road reading Lullymore. "Bord na Móna works on many bogs and Lullymore is one such. In olden times the turf was cut with a turf spade but now Bord na Móna has new machines and methods. One of these is called Milled Peat." A group of little boys watches as a large machine cuts a ditch to drain water. "At first, the ditches are cut 50 feet apart. This dries the bog." Other machines are being driven along the bog, which cut an inch off the top of it to form powdered peat, "crushed peat". Tractors then drag large rakes across the bog surface to aid the drying.

4    "Bua na Móna" (Milled Peat Production) #13: June 1957.

More machines are then shown gathering the powder peat and loading it into trucks, piling it up high. The turf is carried on special railway tracks and taken to the briquette factory, where the briquettes are made. Shots follow of large piles of them as we are told, "two other briquette factories are being built at the moment." Most of the turf is taken to the electricity board's turf-powered generating station; a shot of the large chimneys of the power station is followed by another of large cylinders spinning around as the turf is unloaded from the containers. With a shot of the electrical wires the commentator informs us, "Turf is cheaper than coal for making electricity. In the end, peat wins/the peat is harvested/won. It provides heat, light and power to the people of Ireland!" The point here is the translation of the phrase "tá bua ag an móin," which has multiple meanings in Irish – it can mean "peat wins" as in "peat saves the day," "the advantage of peat", or "the peat is won", as in "the peat is harvested". The multiple meanings are apt – peat *is* won and its advantages save the day – and the Irish win because it is an indigenous form of energy in apparently abundant supply.

The film is a testament to the power of technology; the message is that the country can be self-sustaining with the aid of modern technology and machinery. The images are reminiscent of Soviet films depicting the USSR's massive industrial progress during the period of Stalin's five-year plans. Shot after shot shows machines moving over the land, back and forth, tracing and retracing the steps involved in creating the miracle of electricity. Peat, or turf, harvesting is an activity that has connected the Irish to the land for centuries, going back to the days of Celtic tribesmen who burned it to warm their homes. Ireland's 3 million acres of bogland, composed of 95% water and covering nearly one seventh of the country's surface, is divided into two types – 10,000-year-old raised bogs and the 2,500-year-old blanket bogs, of which only the deeper raised bogs are suitable for development on a large scale. However, as in the case of mining, until recently the technological expertise and financial resources were not available to embark on any sort of a large-scale enterprise. As the film shows, this began to change in the 1950s and, by the 1960s turf production was transformed into a fully mechanized industry.

As in the case of mining, while the history of large-scale peat production can be traced to the pre-Emergency years – in this case the 1930s – the mechanical innovation displayed in this film was very recent and a product of the 1950s. After Fianna Fáil came to power in 1932 the government formed the Turf Development Board (1934) and visited the Continent to learn about other peat production methods the following year. It recommended adoption of the German system of machine peat production but continued to monitor the Soviet system of milled peat production. It is the latter that is featured in the "Eyes of Ireland" film. In 1936 two bogs were acquired, drained and put into production but activities halted with the onset of World War Two. In 1946 the Turf Development Board was reorganized and replaced by the autonomous statutory corporation, Bórd na Móna (Peat Development Board), along with its plans for national programme for peat production. In 1950 Bord na Móna's Second Peat Development Programme represented a major shift in policy, now directed toward the Soviet style of milled peat operation rather than the traditional sod peat. As in "Mining in Avoca", it is thanks to foreign technology and machinery – in this case from the Continent[5] rather than from Canada – that the Irish are able to make the most of their indigenous resources. The peat industry also contributed to national social and economic development by providing employment in rural areas and buttressing the nation's balance of payments.

"Shannon Airport"[6] offers a glimpse into the successful enterprise that is Shannon Airport in Co. Clare, on the west coast of Ireland, in 1956. Built in what was once a quiet rural area, the airport is presented as an example of successful Irish innovation, which has put the country on the map in the area of international travel. Airport facilities featured in the film include various airline administration desks, the Duty Free Shop, weather forecast office, control tower, restaurant and kitchens. The film opens with a shot of a number of airplanes on the runway at Shannon airport and the words: "A few years ago Rineanna was just a quiet place in Co. Clare." We are instantly alerted to the transformation that has taken place. "Today it's the crossroads of the world!" Passengers are seen disembarking and entering

5    Turfcutters were ordered from Germany in 1936.
6    "Aerphort na Sionainne" (Shannon Airport) #2: July 1956.

the airport, where they find themselves in what is described as the spacious and comfortable lounge area. "Every service is here for them," as one family is greeted by a friendly air hostess, while others wait at the various service facilities. The montage of signs shows an airport equipped with a post office, a Bank of Ireland and a number of offices associated with major airlines.

The airport is presented as a showroom for Irish goods, where the international visitors are a captive audience. The camera pans over the shops displaying Irish linen, lace and Waterford Glass with the subtle reminder: "The shops are lovely and they encourage people to buy Irish goods." Entering the duty-free shop, we learn that not only is Shannon the major stop-over point for international flights, it is also an innovator in the industry. "This is the first duty-free airport in the world," where travelers can buy "whiskey" and other luxuries, including watches and perfumes. Shannon airport and its surrounding location, far from being the rural backwater it once was, is now a successful hub of international travel and a path-breaker in the industry worldwide.

In the restaurant, the camera pans over a large group of chefs, who are all busy preparing the enormous quantities of food for the airport restaurant and in-flight trays for airline passengers. The commentator boasts, "The restaurant is famous – outside of Ireland." Next, we visit the airport manager in his office, the control tower and the area tower, where men are checking the weather with balloons and charts. "They give information to the airplanes on the sort of weather above the Atlantic." The film ends with the view of a plane taking off into the night sky and the words, "At night the planes go overseas." The planes are North America-bound, as were so many of the Irish during this period. Now, however, the area from which so many continued to leave due to lack of economic prospects is being hailed as an international success. Shannon airport and Rineanna represent all that can be accomplished in Ireland on a micro-scale. If this unlikely candidate for modernization could be successful, so can the entire country.

The building of Shannon airport in Rineanna, Co. Clare was tied up with both Irish-British relations and aviation history. In the final draft of the Anglo-Irish Treaty of 6 December 1921, Ireland retained the right to negotiate with any nation for the right of its airplanes to land or take off from Irish soil. This right later became an Irish bargaining tool; once the news broke in 1935 that the Germans were building a landplane for the North American route, the British sought an arrangement to secure the path. Sean Lemass, then Minister for Industry and Commerce, convinced the British in May 1935 to pay for the equipment for a joint company that had an Irish image. The British needed a stopover point in Ireland for transatlantic flights and the combined Anglo-Irish survey team chose Rineanna, on the northwest bank of the Shannon River, as the permanent base.

The "Shannon stopover" was mentioned for the first time at the Imperial Economic Conference of 1932 in Ottawa and the first commercial flight arrived in June 1939. World War Two brought civil aviation to a standstill but after the United States entered the war, American flights returned to Ireland in 1942 on the understanding that they would land at a predetermined airport. After the war this stopover policy was formalized in an agreement signed on February 3, 1945 that required all US flights to land at Shannon but by the early 1950s jet aircraft technology removed the need for the stopover. The response of the Government was to designate the airport as a duty-free zone – the world's first airport duty-free facility for passengers – and in 1957 the Minister for Industry and Commerce prepared Aer Lingus, the national airline, to open a transatlantic route of its own, which it did in 1958. Although the stopover clause was officially dropped, Shannon remained Ireland's international airport as American planes were forbidden from landing in Dublin. Shannon was designated as Ireland's only gateway for transatlantic services – all flights to and from Ireland had to terminate or initiate at Shannon, a policy that lasted up to the 1990s.

The Shannon Free Airport Development Corporation,[7] established in the large area surrounding the airport designated and promoted as a duty-free industrial estate, was created to save the airport and ensure its continued future. The new industrial complex later became a symbol of Ireland's success in the early 1960s. By 1962 the new town, which by then employed 2,500, was running out of workers for the booming construction industry, as many of the companies established there expanded – even

---

7   SFADCo is covered in the news films section on industry in the early 1960s.

doubled – their factory space. The airport therefore represents one of the earliest large scale state initiatives for the industrialization and moderniza-tion of Irish economic and commercial life in the post-war period, bringing with it significant regional development benefits.

While some films focus on the benefits of innovation and new tech-nology, others stress the traditional craftsmanship that goes into making distinctly Irish products. "Funeral of the Barrel?"[8] is a lament for the passing of such skill-based industries, in this case the old wooden barrels hand-made by coopers that were being replaced in the late-1950s by metal barrels. While the industrial progress such as that taking place at Avoca and on the bogs was recognized for its value on the regional and national economic level, these smaller craft-based industries were cherished for their contribution to the maintenance of Irish traditional Irish identity and culture.

"Waterford Glass"[9] traces the steps involved in making this distinctly Irish product. The factory was first established in Waterford town in 1783 by two Quaker brothers, George and William Penrose. That company failed less than a hundred years later and it was not until 1947 that it was revived. After World War Two a number of Dublin-based business families, led by the McGraths, decided to recreate the Waterford crystal industry. They established the small factory, recruited master glass makers from Bohemia and established a German-style meister system of master crafts-men and an apprenticeship system. The designs developed were based on the original Penrose designs. Waterford Glass also developed marketing, sales and distribution in the United States, which became its main outlet for the product. The resurrected version was a successful, native, craft-based industry that also produced for export.[10]

8    "Tórramh an Bhairille" (Coopering in Guinness) #38: April 1959.
9    "Gloine Phortláirge" (Waterford Glass) #20: January 1958.
10   There is no mention of the fact that the original company was an Anglo-Irish enterprise. This is typical of the series' use of any and all examples of "Irish" success throughout the ages and recurs in the news film section in the context of a call for the protection of Dublin's Georgian architectural heritage at a time when rather less culturally sophisticated nationalist politicians were making statements about being glad to be rid of this visual reminder of Ireland's colonial history.

The film opens with shot of a large glass chandelier, followed by an assortment of glass decanters and glasses. "Long ago Waterford Glass was world famous. The craft died about one hundred years ago but now Waterford glass is being manufactured again." The interior of a shed reveals two men mixing sand with a shovel and taking lumps of molten glass from the foundry. Some craftsmen are blowing, coding and shipping glass, while others roll it to make the base of crystal goblets. In case we are unaware of the long apprenticeship and high level of skill involved in such work, the narrator reminds viewers that, "maybe this looks like simple enough work but this man spent seven years learning the skills."

As an old man works on a glass jug with the foreman standing by, the commentator reveals the international influence in Waterford Glass: "When the factory started in 1947, these two came with other craftsmen from the Continent." The spirit is co-operative rather than competitive, as "over five hundred Irish people work here." International expertise is welcome and recognized as the necessary vehicle with which to revitally the industry that in turn creates jobs for the Irish. The return is evident in the export value of the glass. "The glassware is sold all over the world; to the United States, to Australia, to the European countries. It is sold in the East and recently an inquiry came about it from Russia!" The remaining scenes are of various people working on the glass at each of its stages of manufacture. Some women are seen working at tables, where they are decorating the glasses used at home or in pubs; others paint "Irish Coffee" on glasses. A man works on a large vase, another works on a sherry glass, while a third designs a portrait of a woman on a large vase. As hot tea is poured into crystal glasses for a line of men sipping on a bench, "At lunchtime who would be bothered with a cup!" Women wrap and pack the finished glassware and others place it on the display shelves, and the film ends with a close-up of the display and the closing salute, "The reputation of Waterford Glass is growing again, and this shows us that we have the cream of craftsmanship here in Ireland." The not-so-subtle message is a reminder of the quality of Irish craftsmanship. The Continental teachers are merely the catalyst in this revival, in the same way that the Canadian firm in Avoca and the Soviets/Germans for Bord na Móna provide the necessary technological expertise and machinery.

"Funeral of the Barrel?"[11] is about the traditional craft of barrel-making, which was becoming obsolete due to the introduction of metal barrels. It illustrates the skills employed by the coopers, and the traditional tools still used by them to repair the used porter barrels. The film is a lament for the old craftsmanship, which was dying in Ireland and everywhere thanks to the introduction of new materials and methods. It opens with a shot of the outside of pub, where three wrecked barrels are standing looking rather forlorn. "It's likely that people take much more of an interest in the drink than in the poor barrels!" A pyramid of barrels stands in a yard beside a shop; there were almost half a million barrels such as these in use in Ireland and over three hundred men employed to work on them years ago. The large cooper's workshop is smoky with industry. "In the biggest company in Ireland there are 160 men working as coopers repairing the barrels." The foreman inspects a barrel and points out the damage to it, as the commentator reminds us, "The barrel is an ancient vessel, in use for thousands of years. The trade is all hand work that is 'as old as the hills'." "This is no automated, modern industry, but one which has remained unchanged over the centuries. Little change has come to the cooper's tools over hundreds of years." When a board is broken, it is the cooper's job to repair the barrel by replacing it.

The barrels themselves are made only from oak, which comes from Texas, the Baltic area and Persia. As a man is pictured hitting a timber stave and shaving it into shape the commentator proclaims: "These coopers are ultra-trained craftsmen. They don't use rulers or measurements." Once all of the staves are shaped to put one barrel together they are moved into position so they can be easily bent. "Then, they are squeezed and twisted together into the shape of the barrel with a special apparatus and the hoops are put on them. New barrels are not made now but only broken ones repaired." The camera captures the blazing barrel, the inside of which is burnt to get rid of the moisture. By now the barrel is correctly shaped and all that is left to do is place the head onto it. The hoops are driven down over the staves

11   "Tórramh an Bhairille" (Coopering in Guinness) #38: April 1959.

and the men hammer them tightly into place. Any gaps in the wood are closed and the barrel is ready to fill again.

A tall pyramid of barrels stands in the yard but these are not the same wooden ones as shown being repaired and made in the film – none of the barrels here are new. By way of explanation: "The day of the barrel is past in America and England; and in Ireland itself, this company isn't making any new ones from now on. The metal keg is available. It's really the 'funeral of the barrel'!" So although some traditional craft industries are being saved through transformation, others that do not bear the unique Irish stamp fit for tourist or export approval are subject to the rigours of international competition. While glass can be marketed as made in the old style and therefore more "authentic," as well as distinctly Irish, there is no comparable justification for the old wooden barrel. New technology and materials have simply taken over the market and the craft, which remained unchanged for centuries, will soon be forgotten.[12]

Ó Laoghaire attempted to raise awareness of the losses that accompanied modernization and development. The old craft industries were losing their place and were only deemed salvageable when they could be suitably marketed in the new economy. This film displays his awareness of the value of such "relics" at a time when they were not yet valued as such. While these traditions were, by and large, dying out, Ó Laoghaire was communicating the message to the Irish public that, even in the context of modernization, there were aspects of Irish traditional crafts and culture worth saving simply for their own sake.

The period during which these documentaries were being made and shown to Irish audiences coincided with a national economic crisis of severe proportions. At a time when the population of Ireland had lost faith in its own ability to succeed, Ó Laoghaire demonstrated not only that it could succeed, but that it had been quietly doing so for some time. Most of the progress and innovation reflected in these films dated back to steps taken in the 1930s and 1940s, which was then built upon in the 1950s. Thus the

---

12   This would also change in the early 1960s, as seen in a news film featuring miniature barrels made for the souvenir industry.

independent state that appeared to be utterly failing its population in the mid- to late-1950s was partially redeemed, and could actually be applauded for some of its more innovative measures. Its openness to international influence is also noteworthy, as this is commonly assumed to be a characteristic that Ireland only acquired from 1959 onwards, once given the nod from the more internationally minded Lemass.

Sadly, however, it is still the case that while the government could be praised for some of its more farsighted measures, there were other areas in which its policies were simply inadequate. The flight from the land that was driving emigration rates in the 1950s to record levels was taking place overwhelmingly from the western, Irish-speaking areas. While some areas of national development were receiving government attention before the late-1950s, the rural and Gaeltacht areas were not among them. In fact, it was those areas most in need of assistance that suffered the most dramatic losses due to emigration because, in spite of the impressive degree of innovation and enterprise being exhibited in the area of Irish industrial development, the same level of interest was not generally taken by the government in rural enterprise.

Several films in the *Amharc Éireann* series illustrate the uneven pace of development in rural Ireland, in particular those that focus on the state of the herring fishery in Dunmore East, the workings of a Donegal tweed factory in Kilcar, and on the bringing of electricity to Connemara, in the rocky west of Ireland.[13] Donegal Tweed operates successfully in a rural setting thanks to government assistance, while the fishery in Dunmore East suffers from lack of the same. Meanwhile, the film on the rural electrification scheme's arrival in the west is a look at the largest-scale development programme in post-war Ireland, fascinating in its depiction of the arrival of modernity in a most tangible form into traditional rural life. These films are intended to drive home the uneven pace and nature of rural development in Ireland, and to indicate that the modernization process took place

---

13    "Dún Mór na Scadán" (Dunmore Herring Catch) #21: February 1958; "Bréidín Thír Chonaill" (Donegal Tweeds) #5: October 1956; "Leictriú Chonamara" (Rural Electrification in Connemara) #15: August 1957.

more as a consequence of progress in other areas than from any activity specifically directed towards rural areas.

"Dunmore of the Herring"[14] shows a rural industry before its period of transition into a modern state-subsidized industry. It deals with the seasonal fishing industry in Dunmore East, where international rather than domestic fishermen are depicted as benefiting from Ireland's wealth of natural resources. The Irish government is conspicuous in its absence as the more technologically advanced international competitors from England, Scotland and elsewhere are presented as cheating the Irish of their share of the herring. The film opens with a view of the village of Dunmore East, where boats are docked in the small bay and seagulls fly overhead. "For the majority of the year Dunmore East on the coast of Waterford is a quiet village." Scenes depicting the uneventful nature of everyday life in the village follow; old men walking in the street, a roof being thatched and a man passing by with a dog. "Sometimes, in the summer, there is entertainment and dancing, as the visitors who come like the people." The atmosphere is one of quiet hospitality, where visitors are welcome.

"But when Spring comes the village is busy as the herring boats arrive." The scene switches to the harbour, where nets are being mended and unraveled as a fishing boat prepares to leave. The harbour is crammed tightly with boats and supplies are stacked on the quay. Unfortunately, all of this activity does not translate into increased productivity or wealth for Ireland. "The herring provide wealth and work but it is the big foreign boats that benefit, unfortunately! – those are the boats that take the most of it – the English boats, Scottish, French, and just one from the Continent!" As evidence, shots follow of close-ups of boat names: Agnes Palmer, Raingoose, Joanna Mary, Runmondv Katwukazee, Janny, Tonny – all clearly foreign names. Surprisingly however, the impotence of the Irish is not strictly due to any wrongdoing on the part of the foreigners, but simply to the Irish lack of proper fishing vessels. "The Irish boats don't take much of the herring because they are not as big and there aren't enough of them." Clearly,

14    "Dún Mór na Scadán" (Dunmore Herring Catch) #21: February 1958.

such limitations on the Irish fishing industry were deserving of government attention.

The boats in the film catch 1,000 to 2,000 pounds worth of herring per day, which are packed into wooden boxes on the quay. The names written on the boxes stacked into piles indicate their destination: "Irish Fishing Board", "John Reid & Sons, Howth", "W. Hines London", "N. Kerrick Waterford", "D.S.C. Dunmore East", "W.F. Furlong Dunmore East". All of the boxes shown except one are for the domestic market, while the herring destined for the Continent and Britain are packed into wooden barrels with salt. To add insult to injury, some of the foreign fishing crews bring their own packers rather than employing locals to do it. Scottish boats are shown with women at work, followed by a man hammering lids onto barrels. "The Scottish boats bring their own packing women with them. They sell this herring in England and all over Europe." Scenes from the loading and unloading process follow and crates are loaded onto the back of a lorry but all of the activity is channeling wealth out of, rather into, Ireland. The implication is clear – the Irish could just as easily be profiting by selling their fish on the Continent, while providing employment for Irish men and women rather than for foreigners.

As the film ends a lorry drives away from the quay and the commentator tells us: "The visitors that come to Dunmore each season prove that we are losing millions of pounds from the Irish coasts annually, and that the generosity and harvest of the seas is leaving in streams!" The film is an indictment of the Irish government for its lack of action on the issue. The contrast between the opening scenes of the quiet village with the hustle and bustle associated with the coming of herring season highlights the irrationality of the situation in Dunmore East. Rather than celebrating the increased level of activity in the small harbour – and what the viewer initially presumes will be increased wealth for the fishermen who live there – the visitors, normally welcomed as tourists, are depicted as intruders and thieves, while the Irish are shown as impotent thanks to their lack of resources. The situation is humiliating and unnecessary – there is no good reason why the Irish should not be able to avail of the produce in their own area while others can. This period is well before the days of moratoria, when the only limitations on Irish fishing capacity are those imposed by their own shortage of decently sized vessels and their technological backwardness. By not providing the Irish fishermen with the necessary crafts, the government is implicitly charged with cheating the nation of its own wealth.

Beginning in 1950, the Irish fishery underwent an enormous expansion that increased the volume of the catch sixteen times. It had never been stable or acquired an industrialized structure, due to the lack of investment and research that went into other areas.[15] The low level of technology in the 1950s was comparable to that of biblical times, consisting of obsolete equipment and small boats suitable only for inshore fishing. Expansion occurred in two stages, the first of which increased the herring catch from 3,400 tons in 1950 to 47,800 tons in 1972. The agency responsible for the eventual transformation was Bord Iascaigh Mhara, or BIM (the Irish Sea Fisheries Board), founded in 1952 under the Sea Fisheries Act from the earlier Sea Fisheries Association, a state-sponsored co-operative organization established in 1931. Modernization was promoted through grants and low-interest loans and in its first decade of operation, from 1952 to 1962, BIM's activities included boat building and vessel operation. However, it is obvious from this film that those benefits were yet to be felt in Dunmore East.

Changes in the form of international competition were just being detected in the late-1950s, as witnessed by the complaint over the inadequacies of the Irish fleet compared to its foreign counterparts. The issue of international fleets encroaching on Irish territory was not a new one in the 1950s, nor was the perception that this was an injustice. Irish resources have drawn foreign fishermen to the island for a thousand years. However, the level of animosity communicated in the film on Dunmore East is indicative of the increased pressure on resources as early as the late-1950s, and those to come in the near future, as foreign activity – complete with greater technological capacity and range – in the waters off Ireland intensified beginning in 1957.

15   Desmond A. Gillmor, "The Irish Sea Fisheries: Development and Curtailment of a Renewable Resource Industry," *American Journal of Economics and Sociology* 46, no. 2 (April 1987): 165–6.

Some of the problems highlighted in the film on Dunmore East were eventually addressed. The state adopted a *Programme of Sea Fisheries Development* in 1962, at the same time that investment was increased and concentrated at a limited number of ports. Modernization meant centralization of activity to larger and better equipped ports, where half of state expenditure was focused on five main fishery centres, two of which had been identified years earlier and featured as subjects of "Eyes of Ireland" documentaries: Howth, the home of the technical school featured in "Fishermen at School", and Dunmore East, which was eventually transformed into one of Ireland's major sea fishing centres.

"Donegal Tweed"[16] focuses on Gaeltarra Éireann's tweed factory in Kilcar, Co. Donegal, in the northwest of Ireland, tracing the manufacturing process from the wool's arrival at the factory to the final stage of display in a Dublin shop. Home spun and woven tweed lasted in Donegal until into the nineteenth century but in the early twentieth century a number of important developments took place, which were the precursors to the operations of Gaeltarra Éireann, the state-sponsored body created in 1958 to help revitalize the underdeveloped Gaeltacht areas of the country. The factory featured in this film is one example of that state-sponsored attempt to revitalize the rural economy in an Irish-speaking area.

The film opens with a shot of the advertising brochure that reads "handwoven tweeds" followed by one of the road sign for Kilcar. "There's talk everywhere about Donegal Tweed. It's made in here in Kilcar, a small town in Donegal, in the Gaeltarra Éireann factory." The view is of the village of Kilcar in the distance, with the mountains rising on either side. It is followed by another, closer view of the small town with a large white factory to the fore. The factory building displays the Gaeltarra Éireann sign on the front, "Gaeltarra Éireann Kilcar and Dublin," recognizing and advertising the state's role in this initiative. The film follows the tweed-making process through its various steps, from loading the wool into the machine to be washed and dried, then dyed and blended, before it is blown through pipes to be dried again. Although there is a production-line process

16    "Bréidín Thír Chonaill" (Donegal Tweeds) #5: October 1956.

involved, the factory is a small-scale operation. The work overwhelmingly low-tech; at every stage there is one person working with one machine and nothing is automated. The tour begins with a view of the tweed factory, where a man unloads the wool, as others throw the dried wool into a vat of dye. The dyed wool is then packed into a machine which mixes strands of different colours together before it is dried thoroughly and mixed by a fan-machine. The wool is wound into yarn and sent to the weaver, who is seated at a hand-loom. The alternative to the small factory operation is the cottage-industry scenario. "Some of the weavers work in the factory. When they work at home the loom is in the house or in a small hut beside it." The camera follows a man leaving his house to enter a smaller version of the cottage adjacent to it, the outhouse, where he weaves on a loom. A signpost reads Glencolumbcille and commentator notes: "There is a weaving site in Ard Ratha and a new one at Glencolumbcille." The exterior of the weavers' building is shown, then the interior where there are some thirty weavers working. Once the tweed is woven, it goes back to the factory in Kilcar, where the women put the finishing touches on it before it is washed again and smoothed. The completed cloth is then sent to Dublin to be sold.

The new site at Glencolumbcille turned out to be extremely important. The state-sponsored initative at Kilcar in fact preceded the better-known co-operative experiment set up by Father McDyer in Glencolumbcille, just down the road from Kilcar, in 1962. Along with Shannon airport, Glencolumbcille was considered to be Ireland's rural development success story of the decade. It was not to last, however, as even after proving its potential for success, the state failed to provide it with the funds it needed to expand and continue into the late-1960s. Such evidence appears to support the accusation[17] that the *First Programme* – intended as Lemass put it to "lift all boats" – failed to take account of the isolated rural communities like Glencolumbcille in need of special assistance. However, the

17 Vincent Tucker, "Images of Development and Underdevelopment in Glencolumbcille, County Donegal, 1830–1970," *Rural Change in Ireland* Belfast: The Queen's University of Belfast; The Institute of Irish Studies, 1999: 84–115.

Donegal tweed venture set up by Gaeltarra Éireann featured in this "Eyes of Ireland" film was at least one example of the way in which Irish traditional crafts and cottage industries were promoted and made successful in the pre-Lemass state.

The final film is about the arrival of electricity to the isolated rural area of Connemara, in the west of Ireland.[18] The fact that this film was even being made in the late-1950s speaks volumes about the underdevelopment of the rural west compared to the urban centres, where by this time electricity was commonplace. Although the commentator does not mention the government at all, the film – by simply highlighting the inadequate facilities in the part of Connemara – illustrates the government's reluctance to act to improve the quality of life in isolated Gaeltacht areas like this one. The Electricity Supply Board (ESB), a semi-state body, was established by the government in 1927 and developed a hydro power station at Ardnacrusha on the River Shannon. The Rural Electrification Scheme began in 1946 but priority areas were determined by the ESB according to financial return rather than quality of life issues. The rural areas which would deliver the best return on the ESB's investment were given priority, thus the easily accessible areas received service first, while more isolated places, like Connemara or parts of Donegal, were relegated to the bottom of the list. Of course, isolated rural areas needed electricity as much if not more than other areas in order to stimulate new industry and bring technology to outmoded agricultural practices, but these factors were apparently not taken into account by either the government or the ESB.

The film is related to "Peat Wins/The Winning of the Peat,"[19] by virtue of the importance of the ESB to both ventures. The giant ESB power station featured in that film feeds the electrical wires shown being hung up here, finally connecting the people of Connemara to the rest of the country. The bogs were the source of fuel for the same people of the west, but they had to cut them in the old-fashioned manner before the advent of the ESB's peat powered generating stations. Now the same people will

18   "Leictriú Chonamara" (Rural Electrification in Connemara) #15: August 1957.
19   "Bua na Móna" (Milled Peat Production) #13: June 1957.

receive electricity powered from the station, thanks to the machinery which eliminates the need for them to engage in the manual labour as they used to. The land is thus still the source of energy, but technology has interfered to make life easier.

In fairness to the ESB, the task of rural electrification was enormous and there were significant challenges involved in bringing electricity to these areas – the land itself was often rock or bog, which posed problems in erecting the tall wooden poles, and access was often an issue, as in the case of Donegal where poles had to be brought in by small boats along the northwest coastline, rather than via the one available road that did not pass through Northern Ireland.[20] Also, the hesitancy borne of superstition or simple stubbornness on the part of some rural dwellers – generally male – was a minor factor. These were, however, challenges that arose as the scheme progressed; the fact remains that the ESB's schedule of priorities was initially determined according to potential financial gain rather than any other social factors, and that presumably the government could have intervened in the scheduling if it saw fit. Also, in bringing electricity to the country, ESB developed networks throughout Ireland and became one of the country's major employers.

"Electrification of Connemara"[21] opens with a panoramic view of the Connemara landscape, followed by a closer view of the characteristic fences made of rock that divide the shallow fields in the west of Ireland. The commentator immediately draws our attention to the significance of the location with the words: "Connemara! The biggest Irish-speaking area in Ireland. It's a hard life for the Gaels who came here during the Cromwellian plantations." This is the land of the true Irish, those who speak the language as natives and eek out a difficult existence on the harsh land to which their ancestors were pushed back centuries ago. There is no sense that times might have changed for these Gaels in the context of the twentieth-century independent Irish state. The sacrifice the Gaelic martyrs

20    Michael J. Shiel, *The Quiet Revolution: The Electrification of Rural Ireland, 1946–76* (Dublin: The O'Brien Press, 1984): 96–104.
21    "Leictriú Chonamara" (Rural Electrification in Connemara) #15: August 1957.

endured in the 1600s at the hands of the English colonists continues by
virtue of the poor quality of the land. A lorry approaches on the narrow
road, laden with long poles. "But at long last, new help and opportunity is
coming to them – electricity!" This modern technology is what will finally
deliver the people of Connemara from their fate, by ushering in the new
age of light into the dark west.

The shot then switches the view of the landscape from the perspective of the ESB men on the truck. They pass various people on the way
to their destination. During its journey the natives are subject to the
stranger's gaze and respond in a variety of ways. First, we pass a woman
walking alone down the road in the opposite direction, dressed in the
traditional dark clothes of the Irish countrywoman, driving cattle ahead
of her. She looks over her shoulder at us as the lorry passes, glaring somewhat sullenly into the camera. "They have been looking forward to it for a
long time, but now, the people of Connemara will have light and power."
Second, we pass a group of young men and boys working in a typically
small field with primitive farming implements. They pause as the lorry
passes them and stare openly and curiously at it. Next, we pass the front
gate of a house where some children are gathered, before finally passing a
cottage from which the occupants wave, welcoming the group. This cottage does not fit the picture of a cottage in the west of Ireland. Although
it is small and whitewashed, instead of the traditional thatched roof and
small painted front door, it has a modern slate roof and good windows.
The progression of greetings the lorry passengers receive from onlookers
of decreasing age, from the first lonely woman's cold and unwelcoming
glare to the warm wave from the occupants of the modern cottage at
the end of the journey, appears to be a metaphor for the opening up of
Connemara itself to the outside world, as the lorry brings modernity and
technology to the land of the Gaels. The commentator rhymes off Irish
names: "Ag Flathartaigh, Seoigh, Máilligh, Breathnaigh agus Raghallaigh;
ag Clann Dhonncha, Clann 'ac Conghaola, as Catháin agus Cadhain."
These are the names of the old families of Connemara, where as in other
long-settled Irish landscapes, the family name was synonymous with

certain locations.²² These families have been here, waiting for redemption, since the days of Cromwell.

A man is pictured drilling a hole into the ground but it is not an easy task to erect an electrical pole in an area mostly composed of rock. When a small hole is ready he places the explosives inside and we then watch the explosion of a landmine from a distance. The commentator warns: "Every mountain glen throughout Ireland will be shaking." The poles are then hauled upright by a group of people, which the commentator tells us prompts the reminiscing of the elderly about other less-optimistic times. "The straightening of the poles reminds the old people of the straightening of the masts." We have now progressed from Cromwell to the Great Famine, when the masts on the old "coffin ships" took thousands away to the New World in search of a better future. Although the coffin ships are now a thing of the past, emigration is not, especially from poverty-striken Gaeltacht areas like Connemara, where the prospects for success are dim. "Electrification brings work with it too, but sadly, it is in England and America that most of the Connemara Irish-speakers are working." Electricity has come too late for the many of those who have already left for Britain and the United States. But hopefully these new "masts" – planted into the rock rather than drifting westward on the seas – will help to stem the tide of emigration by bringing hitherto unknown opportunities to the west.

The next scene of men and boys holding the electrical cables up over their shoulders as they unfurl from the drums, walking across the fields to the houses, appears to gather everyone in the community together symbolically with the wire. All of the work is communal – done by the group for those that live there. The sense is conveyed of a very tight-knit community that shares in its fortunes, good or bad. Indeed, the rural electrification drive involved the entire community in its work, and included the ESB men from away who employed locals and became themselves temporary members of the community for the duration of their stay. Some said that rural areas

22   David Lowenthal, "European and English Landscapes as National Symbols" *Geography and National Identity* (Oxford: Blackwell, 1994): 17.

– and particularly the women – had not seen such excitement since the war, thanks to the influx of "new blood" into stagnant and isolated areas.[23]

The film then changes topic rather abruptly to demonstrate the various uses of electricity in the home and the community. The first scene is of a cookery demonstration, using a small electrical cooker, to an eager group of women who all turn around curiously to face the camera. The ESB regularly staged demonstrations like this one to illustrate the benefits of electricity in the home. Farmwives had much to gain from electricity in terms of easing the drudgery of daily household work like washing and cleaning; women were often the modernizing force in the rural household, persuading reluctant farmers to sign on for electrical service.[24] After the cookery demonstration they head back outside to the glasshouses, where the food to be cooked by the women will grow. We are told that: "There is no factory using the power here yet, but the electricity will help the glasshouses with heat and water." Although the people of Connemara do not expect to have a factory in their area any time soon, the power will at least help with their most basic needs. Unfortunately, the government's priorities in terms of men/women and farm/cottage mirrored the case of the rural/urban divide in that women's needs were apparently not considered a priority – hot running water and electricity often came later to the rural cottage than to the farm itself.

The closing scene presents the rural housewife as the real beneficiary. "But more than anyone else in the house, this new opportunity brings happiness and comfort to the woman of the house." As the woman holds up an old paraffin lamp, the commentator reminds viewers, "When the paraffin oil came she was afraid." Once the electrician screws in the fuse the woman presses the switch – the kitchen lights up and the watching children shield their faces from the light. The commentator compares the past with the present: "But tonight the Connemara woman is not afraid, but welcomes

23    Shiel, 129.
24    The ESB worked in conjunction with other rural groups like the Irish Countrywomen's Association (ICA), which is discussed in more detail in the section on women and work.

the new light." The woman does not shy away from the light but instead smiles broadly at the camera, looking slightly embarrassed but unable to conceal her pleasure. The benefit to the rural woman is clearly the message here. The film began with a woman in black glaring with hostility at the intruders coming with new technology to "the land of the Gaels" but the closing scene is of the rural woman transformed – happy, smiling, appreciative and glad to have the benefit of new technology to assist her at home.

These films all deal with the common theme of rural underdevelopment and the government's plans – or lack thereof – to assist the situation. The fishing industry in Dunmore East is portrayed as suffering from unfair international competition due to the lack of state assistance, while the Donegal Tweed factory is a more positive example of the rural industry that manages to succeed with state aid. The film on the electrification of Connemara presents the west and all of its historic baggage as it enters the modern world – or, more correctly, as modern technology enters *it*. Each of the three locations holds assets for the country in terms of potential material and spiritual wealth: The fisheries need only to be modernized in order to be competitive on an international level; Donegal Tweed can be sold in urban centres and around the world; Connemara can now join the twentieth century and leave behind the negative aspects of its identity.

Ó Laoghaire clearly points to the value of traditional industry and identity in these films, calling on viewers to pay attention to the history of neglect by the Irish state and the English colonizers that preceded it. In doing so, he points to efforts that can be seen as latter-day versions of the self-help movements of the late nineteenth- and early twentieth-century cultural revival.[25] Just as the Irish Agricultural Organization Society and Sinn Féin aimed to encourage local modes of development and economic self-sufficiency, Ó Laoghaire's focus in these films is a reminder of Horace Plunkett's aim in founding the co-operative movement and Arthur Griffith's in founding Sinn Féin.

---

25   See P.J. Mathews, *Revival: The Abbey Theatre, Sinn Féin, The Gaelic League and the Co-operative Movement* (Notre Dame, Indiana: University of Notre Dame Press in association with Field Day, 2003).

Kate Kearney's Cottage, Killarney. 5 May 1958.
*Reproduced with permission from the Irish Photo Archive.*

CHAPTER THREE

# Landscape, heritage tourism and women's work

In a number of the "Eyes of Ireland" documentary films, the landscape itself is presented as the locus of national identity and the repository of national culture. Specific locations, events, monuments and artifacts are presented as lessons in national history, while also serving to promote the heritage tourism industry. In this sense, these "Eyes of Ireland" films intersect with the government's Bord Fáilte (Tourist Board) promotional films but while the latter were targeting international audiences, Ó Laoghaire's films were meant to promote Ireland, Irish history and Irishness to its own population.

Some of these films record the journey taken by a group of tourists to a particular location and their experience along the way. Each deals with a specific historical site, national monument, geographical feature or cultural event, and serves as a means to stimulate contemporary national consciousness. Three films are on popular tourist destinations; a new pleasure boat tour of the River Shannon, a visit to the Killarney area long favoured by international tourists, and a guided architectural tour of the Rock of Cashel in Co. Tipperary.[1] Tourists are the vehicle to record the real subject of the film, the location itself. In Killarney and on the Shannon they retrace old routes using old-fashioned means of transportation, in an effort to experience the "authentic" journey. Collectively, these films explore the growth of heritage tourism in Ireland, while investigating the symbolic value of the landscape as the locus of national history and identity.

[1]	"Saoire ar Sionainn" (Shannon Cruises) #16: September 1957; "Cuairt ar Chill Áirne" (Visit to Killarney) #33: February 1959; "Caiseal an Rí" (Rock of Cashel) #26: July 1958.

"Holiday on the Shannon"[2] follows the new river boat tour along the
River Shannon from Athlone to Killaloe, past a number of islands and
monasteries of national historical interest. The film opens with a view of an
old Córas Iompair Éireann (CIE – the national transportation body) bus
traveling down a country road, followed by an interior shot of the group
of seniors sitting on the bus. "Years ago there were CIE tourist buses for
holiday-makers. They started in the big cities and made visits to beautiful
places all over the country. Now they have another delightful kind of tour
and the visitors are coming to enjoy this new holiday." Long and short
pleasure boat tours take place every day of the season, and this particular
tour follows the group on a long tour. "From the historical town of Athlone,
the pleasure boats sail – the St. Breandán and the St. Ciarán – for the big
water of the Shannon." The River Shannon, which cuts Ireland in two –
separating east from west – was the country's water highway before the
days of railways and roads and played a key role in national history. The
Vikings used it to penetrate the interior of the country when they invaded
in the ninth century, plundering the monasteries along the way, as did the
lesser-known Irish raiders who followed in their footsteps. Athlone is an
important crossing point on the river that has long been recognized for
its strategic military significance, and was frequently the site of battles for
control of the river crossing. Most famously, the Jacobites retreated west
and held the line of the Shannon against the Williamite forces during the
winter of 1690/91.

In the film, the tourists travel from Lough Ree through Carrick-on-
Shannon and south to Killaloe. Some pleasure boating took place on
Lough Ree as early as the 1730s. In 1897 a daily passenger service began
between Athlone and Killaloe, but lasted for only six years before being
reduced to a summer operation. Their journey takes them past a number of
small islands once home to Irish monks. "Long ago there were monks and
monasteries on them; call to prayer and holy music." The monastic settle-
ments on the islands of Lough Ree survived both the Vikings and the Irish
raiders. St. Diarmuid chose the Inchcleraun as his sixth-century monastic

2    "Saoire ar Sionainn" (Shannon Cruises) #16: September 1957.

site because of its connection in legend to the sister of Queen Maeve, who was supposedly killed there. The camera tracks past the ruins on the banks. "Going south, we see the famous old monastery Clonmacnois that St. Ciarán founded in the sixth century." Clonmacnois sits on an esker ridge overlooking a large area of bog through which the Shannon flows. It was its location, at the crossroads of Ireland that contributed to the site's development as a major centre of religion, learning, craftsmanship and political influence. The journey, however, is not supposed to be all work and no play. At the risk of getting too serious, the commentator exclaims: "But a drink is closer to hand than a story! The healthy river air makes them thirsty and hungry!" The people sit at the table in the cabin, drinking and talking, listening to the accordion player. "Wherever there is drink there is music, and wherever there is music there is dancing!" The group dances and the commentator notes somewhat gleefully: "Ha! If St. Ciarán could see them now!" There is obviously no prayer time on the Shannon now. "From the start the passengers see one hundred miles of the river and two lakes before they reach journey's end!" Once the boat arrives in Killaloe, it sails through Loch Derg, the biggest lake on the Shannon.

The film combines some of the highlights of Irish history with modern tourism – a big dose of recreation and scenery with a little bit of history thrown in for good measure. The River Shannon, once the symbolic national divide, now joins old and new Ireland, while the piety and solemnity of the old monasteries is juxtaposed with the lighthearted party on board the boat. The focus here is not on understanding the real significance of the monasteries but rather to note their presence and add authenticity to the atmosphere, making for a more satisfying tourist experience. The focus is also on the mode of transportation and the experience of being on the River Shannon itself. In this sense, the journey is a re-enactment of the historic route taken by the Vikings and many others through the country and through the ages; a means of reliving history in the present.

The two boats featured in the film, the St. Ciarán and the St. Breandán, played an important part in keeping the Shannon open to navigation at a time when it was threatened by shortsighted policymakers. In so doing, they opened the way for future tourist and recreational development along the river. After World War Two, commercial traffic had virtually ceased on the river and the local authorities planned to replace the opening bridges with fixed structures. In response, Colonel Harry Rice, a resident of Athlone, launched a campaign to save the river. In January 1954 the inaugural meeting of the Inland Waterways Association of Ireland (IWAI) was held and attended by over 200 people opposed to the obstruction of the Shannon Navigation. In August 1954 the Tánaiste (Deputy Prime Minister) William Norton and the chairman of CIE were taken on a trip on the river and were sufficiently convinced of its tourism potential that the CIE was charged by the government to develop boating on the Shannon. The CIE's passenger service began on 26 June 1955, which assured a clearance of 8ft at all bridges, so opposition to fixing the Bridge of Athlone was withdrawn. The CIE bought the two boats and installed new engines, maple decks, canopies for dancing, coloured lights and a public address systems. It ran day tours from Dublin, giving many people their first trip on the river. As a result of this venture, the water highway of the Shannon stood out once more as it did before the days of railways and cars, and the river itself was opened up for boating business. This promotion of Irish heritage tourism in its early stages of development reflects Ó Laoghaire's keen awareness of the aspects of national heritage, culture and history in need of conservation.

In a similar vein, "A Visit to Killarney"[3] follows the tour taken by a group of tourists to this picturesque area. It presents a film-postcard of this famously scenic part of Ireland, long popular with tourists for its rugged beauty. The tour is popular because of the scenery and the location's evocation of the national past. The focus is on the lyrical beauty of the area, which is highlighted by allusions to well-known poems and operas that decorate the commentary. Like the film on the Shannon, the modes of transportation used in the tour are important, as they serve to authenticate the tourist experience by enabling them to travel through the area in the once customary fashion. History appears in the film but only as a sound bite serving as decoration, adding interest to the locale by calling attention to the rich and turbulent history of the area but not in a manner in-depth enough to stimulate serious thought or to risk boring the cinema audience.

3    "Cuairt ar Chill Áirne" (Visit to Killarney) #33: February 1959.

History in this context is merely a prop with which to sell the tourist destination – arguably one of the main characteristics of heritage tourism.[4]

The film begins with a view of the Great Southern Hotel in Killarney. The commentary begins: "Killarney in the summer! Visitors from every place on earth." Tourists are milling around outside, climbing into jaunting carts and leaving the hotel. They pass a sign for Kate Kearney's cottage, where the cars are left behind and the tourists proceed on horseback into the Gap of Dunloe. The group heads up in single file along a narrow track beside the water, crossing a small bridge and enjoying a view of the mountains. "The views are amazing. This is the wildest area of Killarney; small lakes, streams and solemn mountains on every side; and at last, out in front, the Gap of Dunloe itself!" The wildness of Killarney has drawn tourists to the area since the eighteenth-century's Romantic sensibility. However, the characterization of Killarney as wild was as much a result of the area's turbulent history and lawlessness as the landscape itself, which was then marked by the Whiteboy disturbances, which occurred as a direct result of English colonization of the country.[5]

In the film, the group stops at midday for lunch. They sit at a table outside where they eat salads put on by the hotel and talk. "Hunger makes the food taste good but the healthy mountain air is better." The view of the lake sets up the next segment of their trip across Lough Lene in a rowing boat. The men row the boat while the women enjoy the scenery. The camera fixes on the oarlock, followed by a close-up of the oars cutting into the water as one of the women is pictured looking out at the view, her hand trailing lightly through the water. The voice-over quotes lines from the well-known poem "Fáinne Geal an Lae": "Early in the morning I went out on the banks of Lough Lene; Who did I find by my side but the fairheaded girl coming through the dawn!" Once they reach Ross Castle, the visitors will return to their hotel by land.

---

4   See Barbara O'Connor and Michael Cronin, eds, *Tourism in Ireland: a critical analysis* (Cork: Cork University Press, 1993).

5   See Luke Gibbons, "Topographies of Terror: Killarney and the Politics of the Sublime," in *South Atlantic Quarterly* 95, no. 1 (1996)

The history of this castle, their final destination, encapsulates centuries of Irish political history. It was built by the O'Donoghue Mór family, descendants of the kings of Munster who established themselves in the area around the eleventh century, during the sixteenth century building revival and supplanted by the Browne family in the aftermath of the Elizabethan conquest. The military outpost was seen as impregnable and was the last stronghold to fall to Cromwell's forces during the siege of 1652. The Browne home beside the castle was converted into a barracks during the Williamite wars and a military presence was maintained there until 1815. Ross Castle was the site of displacement and upheaval at the hands of foreigners, and it was this upheaval which gave the area its descriptive character in the eighteenth century and continued to draw visitors in the 1950s. But although the choice of location and buildings are inherently political, none of this is directly communicated in the film. Rather, Killarney is presented simply as a pleasant and scenic day-trip and the tourists are not troubled with the layers of meaning enveloping the area. "It's worth getting one last look from the top of the Castle at the beautiful mountains and Killarney Lake!" The final shots are of the Killarney scenery as the sun sets over the lake, naturally framed by the mountains.

The film represents the Killarney area as a moving-postcard, with camera-worthy views, lyrical music and poetry to add to the romance of the scenes. All of the stock pictures of Killarney are presented – horses and jaunting carts, views of the Gap of Dunloe, Lough Lene and the surrounding mountains, The Twelve Pins. The tourists' itinerary is also a set piece – tours on horseback up the Gap, with Kate Kearney's cottage, the eternal starting point, perched at the entrance way. The visitors are passive receptors of these images of rural Ireland, set to music and choreographed from start to finish including all of the appropriate sights, and yet active participants in the experience. Killarney is seen on foot, on horseback, and from a rowing boat –not from a giant tour-bus. It is by reliving the experience of ordinary people who traveled on horseback through the Gap of Dunloe and rowed their boats across Lough Lene that the tourists' experience is made "authentic." The absence of gimmicks, or new technology, or other such innovations, is precisely what draws the tourists to the area to sample a piece of "timeless" Ireland.[6] The tourists thus enjoy all of the loveliness of Ireland without engaging with any of the hardship or political struggle that actually gave the locations their tourist value.

The third film in this section, "Rock of Cashel,"[7] is named for the famous national monument and popular tourist destination, a large outcrop on which is located a large monastic and ecclesiastical ruin, one of the more spectacular archaeological sites from Christian Ireland. The oldest feature is a round tower, while other elements of the complex are estimated to date from the tenth century and later. The film follows the tourists on a visual tour of the area, showing various features of the site including exteriors, the courtyard, the chapel and its tombs, architectural reliefs, and Christian sculptures. Thus "Rock of Cashel" is a visual summary – part lesson on those who built the various structures, part architectural lesson on the various features of those structures. Again, the landscape is the monument to Irish history, an exterior museum parallel to those in which the smaller relics are housed.

The film opens with a view out over the landscape to a distant rock and the words: "In the plain beside Castle Thiobrad Árann, an historical rock hangs its head in the air, firmly and boldly – the Rock of Cashel." Various views of the Rock are followed by closer shots of the buildings on the rock accompanied by the commentary: "Here kings and Munster bishops reigned for hundreds of years. On the rock they built fortresses, churches and a round tower that are one thousand years old." The shot closes in on a view of the buildings, focusing on the round tower and then on the old stone cross of St. Patrick, who apparently baptized a Munster king here. Cashel was the seat of the provincial chieftain or king, Brian Boru. Brian, king of Munster, seized the High Kingship or overlordship of Celtic Ireland during the tenth century. He was slain at the Battle of Clontarf in Dublin, a battle between his own armies and forces led by the Vikings or Norsemen

---

6   "Timeless" is one of the stock characterizations of Ireland in promotional tourist information; see Barbara O'Connor "Myths and Mirrors: Tourist Images and National Identity," Chp. 4 in Barbara O'Connor and Michael Cronin, eds, *Tourism in Ireland: a critical analysis* (Cork: Cork University Press, 1993): 75.

7   "Caiseal an Rí" (Rock of Cashel) #26: July 1958.

in which the Vikings were defeated, in 1014. In popular history Brian Boru is seen as the last effective High King of Ireland. His descendents are the Uí Bhriain (Ó Brians). In the story Brian's own action in contesting and seizing the overlordship from the traditional holders of the title, the Uí Neill (or Ó Neills) of Ulster undermined the very kingship and its stability.

The area is a popular destination, completely open to visitors. "There are few days that visitors are not seen," as a couple is shown sitting on a ledge. Then, on a model version of the area, a hand points out Chapel Cormac, built in the twelfth century. Subsequent to its role as a centre of secular/tribal power of Celtic society, Cashel developed as an important ecclesiastical centre in Christian Ireland. In this role it was constituted in the early twelfth century as an archdiocese. Cashel today remains one of the four archdioceses of the Catholic Church in Ireland. It was also a diocesan centre in the (Anglican) Church of Ireland structure of administration, but lost this status as a Church of Ireland archdiocese in 1839. The view switches to the roof of the chapel, followed by the front. "This is the most wonderful old chapel in Ireland, with decorations, ornaments and engraved stones." Inside the archway is the mausoleum. "They say that the descendants of the kings were put in this tomb." The scene changes back to the same shot of the couple, linking life and death, present and past.

Next, the camera pans over the biggest ruin on the site, a thirteenth century church. It tilts down to the church interior to show the row of windows, then up to see the arches from the church interior. "The roof of the Church fell years ago but still, there is solemnity and nobility there in the high walls; the slender windows; the polished columns and in the decorated polished arches. Bishops and noblemen from Munster visited here, both Gaels and Normans." The ruins on the Rock include structures from both the pre-Norman (Norse) and Norman phases. The town of Cashel dates from the Norman conquest; towns were unknown to Celtic society, the urban form in Ireland being a creation of the Vikings or Norse. This site, which has seen waves of visitors over hundreds of years, bears witness to the history of Ireland – its architectural structures provide a tangible link to this past. As the camera pans over the figures of animals carved into the rock, the commentator notes: "And aren't they odd, the ornaments they made long ago? Clever craftspeople did this work. They did not last but the Rock of Kings stands proudly on their behalf!" The film closes with a view from the window to the church below, then of the tower framed in the arch – a reminder that the Rock of Cashel itself provides a window through which to look at the Irish past and ponder the course of Irish history.

The next two films present entirely opposing ways of experiencing Irish culture in its contrasting manifestations of high and low, archaic and contemporary, dead and living. The first is of a visit to the National Museum in Dublin, to view some of the relics of the Early Christian era; the second is a record of a day at one of the national music festivals, the Fleadh Cheoil, where traditional Irish culture is shown to be alive and well, being passed on to the next generation rather than stagnating in the shadow of imported international culture. The contrast between the passive museum experience to the much more participatory living landscape of the Fleadh is striking. Although the object of the museum piece is to enlighten the cinema audience about some of Ireland's national treasures, the music festival is infinitely more enjoyable to watch – and presumably in which to participate.

"Irish Metalwork"[8] is simply a record of a visit to the National Museum, during which the camera follows visitors viewing various relics from Ireland's Early Christian era (eighth and ninth centuries), the high period of Celtic metalwork. The film opens with a sign reading Department of Education, Ard-Músaem na hÉireann, National Museum of Ireland, followed by a couple of shots of the exterior of the National Museum. People are seen entering the door of the Museum. "Thousands of people visit the National Museum in Dublin, a place where there are tools, goods, weapons and clothes – historical relics that people have used since the beginning of life." In the central hall relics from the era after St. Patrick are displayed. "It is the metalwork that is most interesting." After a sign which reads Ré na Críostaíochta (Early Christian Period) we see some of the relics, including boxes for storing gospels and a view of some intricate metalwork pictures. The museum official directs the young boys to an exhibit of the cover of St. Patrick's Bell, which dates from later, and the St. Patrick's Bell itself.

8   "Obair Miotal na hÉireann" (Irish Metalwork) #19: December 1957.

The children look at the cover, which is jeweled and engraved. Some of the metalwork is not religious, such as a metal buckle from the eighth century. We see the Tara Brooch and the Cross of Cong, made for the High King of Ireland as a reliquary for a piece of the True Cross. A man and a woman look at the display, intercut with views of the detailed work on the cross. The children at the display case inspect the Ardagh Chalice and the film closes with a close-up of its ornamentation. The film obviously refers to Ireland's Celtic origins, but also again ties the Irish landscape to the notion of wealth – this time in terms of historical artifacts drawn from the earth. The same mineral wealth that is being drawn attention to in the film on "Mining in Avoca"[9] – in that case the copper-mine – is the root of the great Celtic metalwork in gold and bronze as well. Once again, although this time less directly, the landscape is the repository of national wealth.

In a completely different vein, "Music Festival"[10] is about one of the famous national music festivals put on by the Association of Irish Musicians[11] all over the country. It was during this time period that traditional music was beginning to be actively preserved in sound recordings saved in archives as a record of a way of life that was disappearing. This festival is the live, communal experience of Irish traditional music, in which the whole community participated and others from all over the country attended. The atmosphere is lively and informal, and traditional music is shown as an art form not restricted to a disappearing generation, but being passed down to the children, along with the traditional Irish dancing that accompanied so much of it.

The topic is introduced in the opening shot of a sign reading "The Association of Irish Musicians has music festivals every summer." The location for this one is Dungarven, Co. Cork. The huge crowd watches as the procession of marchers and drummers approaches. Everywhere there are crowds, watching the procession, watching musicians, dancing in the streets,

---

9    "Mianaigh Thrá Dhá Abhainn" (Mining in Avoca) #3: August 1956.
10   "Fleadh Cheoil" (Music Festival) # 14: July 1957.
11   The Association goes by its Irish name, Comhaltas Ceoltóirí Éireann, or simply Comhaltas.

some drinking, all obviously having a great time. An old man is standing in the background watching as a fiddler plays for two judges. "Irish traditional music is played and there are competitions on Saturday and Monday in which the best musicians in Ireland participate." The pipers are playing in the courtroom and the commentator notes, "it's funny to be judging the pipers in the court-house." The liveliness of the pipers' music is highlighted by their location in what is normally quiet and solemn building. Obviously the normal rules do not apply in Dungarven on this occasion.

Next we see three young accordionists playing for another two judges: "The old style of music is not disappearing with the old people: The young people prove that it is alive and dynamic." This is the key message – the crowds and the youthfulness of so many of them is, quite literally, living proof that the old ways will not die with this last generation of "old Irish". While many other ways of life have died out, the music is still played and still valued – and, most importantly, still fun. Next are the flutist and the concertina player, followed by the harpists in the garden. "One hears every kind of instrument at the Festival and the music spreads all over the town, even inside the convent." There is no elitism to this event or this music – all participate and all enjoy it, each in their own way. The mood is simultaneously lively, relaxed and spontaneous. A man is pictured Irish dancing in front of the line of nuns. "The music surprises and delights the visitors, and dancing breaks out naturally everywhere."

Out in the street, the band plays as the commentator quotes from the blind poet's "I am Raftery:" "The drummers delightfully carefree, playing music to empty pockets." Meanwhile, inside the pub a group of fiddlers and accordionists are gathered, playing for another enthusiastic crowd with empty pockets that is instead clapping along and stamping its feet. At this point whatever normal musical score usually accompanies the documentary films is cast off in favour of the music being played in the pub. As the commentator explains that all the old Irish traditional favorites are heard: "Inside the pub, 'the full jug', the 'pulse of the music' and 'the filling woman' are being played from night until day!" We hear these well-known songs with the noise of the crowd and get a real sense of the liveliness of the atmosphere there – as well as of the quality of the music itself.

If Ó Laoghaire set out to prove that Irish traditional music was not dead he certainly succeeded here. The entire film is crammed with crowds, young and old people dancing, clapping, marching, listening, playing, drinking, smiling and enjoying the festival. "Music Festival" provides a fly-on-the-wall style glimpse into living Irish culture. This film is highly entertaining, depicting Irish culture as vibrant and energetic. While the museum visit, on the other hand, creates an atmosphere of respect and solemnity, it is hardly engaging. This contrast between the two approaches to celebrating Irish heritage is important because the nostalgic looking backward at Ireland's glorious past tended to glorify the earlier days, largely because of the impressive artifacts and relics. In the comparison, contemporary Irish culture lost prestige because it was considered to have declined beyond the point of redemption – hence the need to elevate the past to such a degree. This film, however, shows a version of Irish culture that is popular and alive – and leaving its own sort of relic in the musical tradition to be passed down to the next generation. In the mid- to late-1950s, this side of Irish culture needed a boost in prestige in the public imagination, and the film accomplishes this by depicting the festival not only as a part of Irish tradition of which the population could be proud, but also as something truly enjoyable – and consequently, lasting.

"Souvenirs,"[12] in keeping with the title, serves as a visual postscript to the theme of heritage tourism, warning viewers of the potential dangers inherent in this path of development. By presenting a craft-based alternative to the mass-produced norm, it implicitly confronts some of the issues involved in the growth of the Irish heritage tourism industry, the representation of "Irishness", the notion of authenticity and the commodification of national symbols. The film features various types of "traditional" souvenirs made from natural fibres, including Killarney landscapes made from pieces of tweed, dolls dressed in traditional rural Irish style, wooden figurines of Irish saints, warriors and monks, as well as pseudo-Celtic jewelry. Made by Irish women in their homes, these souvenirs are meant to replace some

12    "Féiríní Cuimhne" (Irish Souvenirs) #29: October 1958.

of the mass-produced plastic replicas of thatched cottages and leprechaun figurines made overseas.

The film opens with a shot of a typical souvenir display on a wall, including porcelain shamrocks, little thatched cottages, leprechauns and shillelaghs. The commentator tells us that although visitors from every country like to have souvenirs, "In Ireland there was nothing for them to get but leprechauns, heel straps or thatched cottages and the like." The representation of Ireland for foreign visitors was restricted to the mass produced souvenirs perpetuating the cliché image of the Emerald Isle, populated by little men and charming people living in picturesque little white-washed cottages. Things were changing, however: "Lots of people in this country are making nice, artistic souvenirs." The emergence of this cottage craft industry is presented as a response and a resistance not only to poor quality and tacky souvenirs, but more importantly, as the work of the very Irish "folk" that the mass-produced versions (mis-) represent.

In the film, two women are pictured sitting at a kitchen table in their home, making dolls. "These dolls are dressed in the old way that was seen in places until recently." Rather than presenting the Irish as a race of little mythical men, these women are presenting the Irish as they were in the very recent past, in long skirts and shawls. Next we see a woman making jewelry from pewter, decorating them by hand with recognizably Celtic ornamentation copied from paper models. The designs are the familiar spiral patterns so familiar nowadays thanks to Celtic crafts and jewelry designs, not to mention tattoos of Celtic (or pseudo-Celtic) origins modeled on the decorative lettering in the Book of Kells and engravings on megalithic tombs around the country. At this stage, however, the commodification of Ireland's Celtic heritage is still a new development. It represents the beginnings of the marketing of ethnicity and of traditional culture as part of the growing heritage tourism industry. "Indeed, other people and small factories are making goods of this type." This particular souvenir industry, however, is reformulating the stereotypical representations of Ireland: By creating dolls by hand and in authentic Irish clothing, the women are creating representations of themselves, their mothers, their grandmothers – and in doing so, they are reclaiming their rights to contribute to an industry that always threatens to be overtaken by the mass-producers of kitsch.

The third example of handcrafted souvenirs is of a woman who creates familiar landscape scenes of rural Ireland from tweed remnants. She cuts out the shapes of lakes, trees and hills to create scenes of places like Killarney's Lough Lene and other popular tourist destinations. The use of tweed to create the scenes is significant and refers back to the film on the making of Donegal Tweed – another notable effort at creating a viable rural industry using local resources in a cottage industry and small factory context. This woman is comfortable working at home with her cat on her lap. She is shown adding minute details – clouds, trees and leaves – with pieces of leftover tweed so that nothing is wasted. "She makes a pattern from a diagram and from this she cuts the pieces of cloth in the appropriate colour." Again, there is no attempt to create something truly original – the pictures are formulaic, tested and true diagrams of familiar and saleable scenes. But the use of tweed provides a natural quality and a connection to the landscape with which the viewer will engage. The tweed is the product of the rural Irish workers who made the fabric from Irish sheep's wool, drawn from landscapes like those represented in these scenes. Due to the individual care and attention that goes into making them, and the natural fabric from which they are created, the pictures are then presented as being more "authentic" than the generic, printed and mass-produced scenes generally sold to tourists.

Next is the potter's wheel and the making of crockery, complete with Irish designs: "The ornaments tidy them up and the jugs sell well." Many of the souvenirs are made from wood. A man is pictured working at a wheel, making miniature wooden figurines of saints, warriors and monks – references to Ireland's Gaelic, Celtic, Christian and monastic traditions that recall the major eras in Ireland's national and pre-colonial history.

This film attempts to reconcile the tension between Ireland's "authentic" past and its rather more commercial present by banging the "authentic Irish" drum that redeems the souvenir industry from attack. There is a tension here between the demands of modernization and the opening up of Ireland and its resources, while at the same time attempting to remain true to the "real" Ireland and its traditions. The dolls, dressed as traditional country women with long skirts and shawls represent Irish women as they appeared in the recent past. The pewter jewelry is decorated by hand with recognizably Celtic ornamentation copied from paper models. The individually constructed tweed landscapes of Killarney are more "authentic" than the generic, printed and mass-produced scenes sold to tourists, as are the wooden figurines of saints, warriors and monks that recall Ireland's precolonial Gaelic, Celtic and Christian heritage. The use of natural fibres – of Irish cloth, tweed, clay, wood – and of familiar Irish designs, historical figures and scenery, all tie the souvenirs to the land from which they came and the people who made them and resolves this tension through the use of Irish materials to sell the country's symbolic representations.

The final section on the "Eyes of Ireland" short documentary films is in one sense a new topic – on women and work – and is yet a reiteration of the previous topics. The films featured in the following discussion touch on all of the key themes already highlighted – the costs and benefits of industry and progress, the role of rural industries and communities versus the state in national development, and the growth of tourism and popular perception of the Irish landscape in the context of national depression. However, the tendency for Irish women to be rendered invisible as a result of church and state policy was such that their appearance in their own right in a number of these short documentary films is noteworthy. The nature of that depiction, however, is another matter. This group of films features the training of Aer Lingus air hostesses, modeling courses in Dublin, the Irish Countrywomen's Association's (ICA) summer courses and a hospitality training course attended by a Gaeltacht woman.[13] Each of the films presents a very different sort of work opportunity for women and corresponds to the type of woman that is portrayed as taking them. Aer Lingus air hostesses and the Dublin soon-to-be models constitute a new class of urban glamour-girls that stand in stark contrast to the wholesome rural women that attend the ICA's summer course and the hospitality industry's training courses attended by Gaeltacht women.

---

13   "Mná Spéire" (Air Hostess Training) #12: May 1957; "Oiliúint Bainicín" (Mannequin Schools) #7: December 1956; "Bantracht na Tuaithe" (Irish Countywomen's Association) # 4: September 1956; "Cúrsaí Óstán" (Hotel Training Courses) #9: February 1957.

Ó Laoghaire never overtly casts judgment on whether it is the urban or the rural "girls" – as women are unfailingly described in the commentary – that constitute the "real" Irish but it is quite plain where his sympathies lie. While the films do not display the sort of naïveté that de Valera did fifteen years earlier in his 1943 St. Patrick's Day speech, in which he referred to Ireland as the "land of comely maidens,"[14] Ó Laoghaire is clearly skeptical of the new breed of woman that is appearing in urban centres – and particularly Dublin – in the late-1950s. Rural women are represented as a practical and hardworking group that have enjoyed few of the opportunities their counterparts in the city have at their disposal. It is particularly for the Gaeltacht women that Ó Laoghaire feels sympathy, as their plight is that of the internal migrant compelled to leave home simply for lack of other options, rather than out of any overwhelming desire to join the ranks of city girls.

"Women of the Sky"[15] is about the training course for the new Aer Lingus air hostesses. The job was a novelty as well as simply as a new avenue of employment for women. These flight attendants were minor celebrities in Ireland in the 1950s, considered very elegant and cosmopolitan by their peers. Ó Laoghaire was apparently not as easily impressed. The title of the film in Irish, "Mná Spéire," literally translated as "Women of the Sky," is significant as an Irish double entendre: "Mná spéire" actually refers to the women who represented Ireland in national mythology, like Cathleen Ní Houlihan. By using this phrase to refer to the group of air hostess trainees, these women were being presented – presumably tongue in cheek – as the stuff of modern urban legends, chosen to represent Ireland in flesh and blood on the international stage.

The film opens with a front view of the Dublin airport building and the words: "Aer Lingus trains the air hostesses at Dublin Airport." Women enter and crowd around a notice board as the narrator tells us that "there

---

14   De Valera's famous "dream" broadcast of St. Patrick's Day 1943 is quoted in J.J. Lee
     *Ireland 1912–85: Politics and Society* (Cambridge: Cambridge University Press, 1989):
     334.
15   "Mná Spéire" (Air Hostess Training) #12: May 1957.

are over 75 of them and each year around 25 new girls are trained." We are told that the six-week course is broad and difficult – this group obviously represents the lucky few. As evidence, the women are next seen sitting in the classroom, dressed in their Aer Lingus uniforms, where they are listening to a lecture on the duties, responsibilities and privileges that go along with their new lives. "Out here, they will go on journeys to Paris, Amsterdam, Düsseldorf and other cities." There is a sense of these women embarking on more than a career, but also the elevated social status that went along with it.

Lest the "girls" not be taken seriously, the commentator informs us that the uniform is there to command respect and authority: "Just like the army, the air hostesses wear their hats properly and dress neatly." The role is not simply a job, but means representing the nation at its best at home and abroad. The women are shown being taught to wear their hats correctly, tilted to the side, and to walk like runway models. Despite the hopes for the authority-inspiring uniforms, even the commentator cannot help himself from commenting approvingly: "It's no surprise that they look so charming, as they walk elegantly and modestly." The film follows the women through the various stages of their training course, which consists of demanding tasks including holding a tea tray single-handedly whilst the plane is in mid-flight. Unsurprisingly, the air hostesses are not expected to learn any of the technical details associated with flying or maintaining an aircraft, but they must understand the basics of how the aircraft operates in case of emergency. They stand around the engine as the male instructor points out various aspects of its operation. They then move to the control tower, where they are shown the equipment used for talking the airplanes down. Somewhat ironically, the commentator tells us, "The air hostesses have a lot of responsibility" before proceeding to list the various tasks they actually perform: checking equipment, providing passenger reading material and doing the paperwork. We are told that the meals are prepared ahead of time by the cooks at the airport and "the food is kept warm in an electrical warmer which is brought into the airplane." The novelty of this technology is apparent, as the chef displays the warming oven to the camera before carefully plugging it in.

Finally on board the plane, the women practice serving the meal trays to each other, as the commentator once again reminds us of the extreme difficulty of the task at hand. "Steady feet and hands are needed to carry the trays one-handed 10,000 feet in the air and without spilling the tea." It is only when the women are pictured writing their exam that commentator finally makes it explicit what the job of an air hostess is perceived to entail: "There is no question on how to pick up a rich passenger!" The women pose together for their group photograph, and the film closes with the obligatory words of blessing: "Now they are real air hostesses and the planes of Ireland are calling on them. God bless them!"

The idea of a woman working for the money, or even for its own sake is never addressed in the film. This was the limited frame of reference that defined life for Irish women in the 1950s and this film does not attempt to extend that by taking it seriously. Women were allowed to work until they married, after which point they were either expected or required to retire, depending on their profession. Although it would be simplistic to argue that the representation of women is narrowly anti-urban/career woman, and while the film superficially applauds the new air hostesses and wishes them well in their new career, the tone is almost sarcastic and the commentary indicates slight disapproval of all that their new career signifies about Ireland and the path that it is taking. Yet on the other hand, the simple fact of the film's existence in the collection is indicative of the increased representation of women as workers in their own right in the late-1950s.

It is worthwhile to briefly compare this film with the other made about Aer Lingus' pilot training programme, "The Call of the Sky."[16] The topic of this film is the training course held at Dublin airport for Aer Lingus pilots. The difference in approach between this and "Women of the Sky" is clear. The film opens with a shot of Dublin airport, then a sign for the Aer Lingus Technical Divison, where the pilots are trained. Commercial flights are a growing industry in Ireland. "Aer Lingus has one hundred pilots and over fifty new ones are taken on each year, some from the Irish Flight Corps." The captain leaves his desk, puts on his jacket and goes to meet the new

---

16    "Glaoch na Spéire" (The Call of the Sky) #11: April 1957.

pupils. Then a close-up of the training manual, *Pilot Training Programme*, and a hand writing the pupil's name. These pilots are all experienced thanks to their army service, but they are here to gain experience flying passenger planes. This class on the DC3 airplane lasts four weeks, during which time they learn about the machinery involved. They then spend three weeks practicing in a flight simulator, where they do fifteen hours of flying. The shots alternate between men in the radio room, to a pupil in class, the instructor at the desk, to various shots of the instruments and the pilots. The focus is on what the men are learning, the atmosphere is serious and the message is that the pilots take this job seriously.

After completion of the basic course, some of the more experienced pilots do another course on the Viscount, Aer Lingus' biggest and newest plane. Pupils in this course spend six weeks in the classroom and one additional week learning about radio instruments. They practice again in a flight simulator, under the guidance of an instructor. We see two pilots sitting in the cockpit of the plane as its comes in for landing with the comment: "The pilots practice everyday responsibilities that come with every potential difficulty." We sit in the cockpit with the student-pilot as the instructor cuts the engine and finally, "the pilot lands safely!" The film ends with a view of the Viscount on the runway. The pilot welcomes his new co-pilot. "Now he has passed every test and the captain welcomes him to his first journey as co-pilot on the Viscount!"

The difference in approach between this and the other film on Aer Lingus' flight attendants is startling. There is no discussion at all in this film of the appearance of the men or the angle at which they must wear their hats. While the women parade around looking charming, the men sit at their desks, working with instruments, and are taken seriously as pupils. Their tests are important, compared to the women's exam, about which the only comment is on the absence of a question on how to pick up a rich man. The job with Aer Lingus was considered a sexy career, and good Catholic women were not supposed to be sexy. "Women of the Sky" attempts to dissipate the tension inherent in discussing this new and potentially problematic employment opportunity for women in Ireland by using humour and by refusing to take the job seriously at all. The easiest way to deal with the conflict presented by the idea of this new class of young, independent and attractive women was simply to ignore its social implications.

The other film dealing with the work of urban women is "Mannequin Training,"[17] in which young women train to be models. The training consists of lessons in movement, poise, clothes care, make-up and hair styling, which they take at the Betty Whelan Mannequin School, the Nora Griffin Mannequin Agency and the Charles Ward-Mills Salon of Fashion. The film opens with a view of the sign for the "Betty Whelan Mannequin Agency" and the words, "There's a special beauty connected to the newest occupation of the girls of Ireland." We are told that anyone can attend one of these schools: "If you really would like to be a model, you can attend one of the schools that have been opened up by mannequin agencies in Dublin." A young woman is greeted and interviewed by the receptionist, while at another agency, the "Norma Griffin Model Agency", the women are measured, taught to sit up straight and cross their legs properly. The women are selected "on their measurements, general appearance and personality" and the three-month modeling courses consist of lectures and various demonstrations by experts. Pupils begin with Physical Culture or Deportment "which teaches them to walk properly and acquire poise, self-confidence and a sense of balance". The women are also instructed in hair-dressing and on how to properly apply cosmetics – all important tools of the trade. The final part of the course is in modeling technique – "the wearing of clothes, the method of presenting them at dress shows, and posing for fashion photographs."

Although the air hostesses and the would-be models follow much the same training – learning to dress properly, walk elegantly and present themselves well to their audience – there is no mockery of the modeling course or the "technical" training the women undergo. Of course, the comment on their appearance is also more suitable in this context: "When the result is a pretty girl like this, you know the work has been worth while!" This type of work for women appears to be much more acceptable, in which the peddling of their "wares" simply fits the job description. Modeling work

17    "Oiliúint Bainicín" (Mannequin Schools) #7: December 1956.

fit within the boundaries of women's work and identity in Ireland in the late-1950s – while unusual and glamorous work, it posed no threat to men's identities to cast women in a traditional role as a pretty clotheshorse. The air hostesses, while also glamorous and applauded for their appearance, wore uniforms which were supposed to impart an air of authority upon them, however superficial – and this presumption to occupy a role of authority left them open to criticism.

The third film in this section, "Country Women"[18] is concerned with rural women, specifically those belonging to the Irish Countrywomen's Association (ICA). The ICA was founded in 1910 as the United Irishwomen (UI) to improve the lives of rural women, and was closely affiliated with the Irish co-operative movement initiated by Horace Plunkett, another famous relative of Ó Laoghaire's. The name reflected its non-sectarian character rather than any political aspirations – the UI (later ICA) was and continues to be an avowedly non-political movement, was closely linked to other organizations such as Muintir na Tíre (People of the Land) and was a prominent actor in the campaign for rural electrification in the 1950s. The ICA has been accused of being anti-feminist but its official historian maintains that, in fact, the ICA was quietly revolutionary in the slow but steady progress it made in the most important, if mundane, aspects of daily life for rural women, reflected in their anti-ideological motto, "deeds not words."[19]

The representation of these rural women is diametrically opposed to that of the two previous films on urban girls. The ICA women are practical and hard-working, they take their jobs as rural housewives seriously and are attending the ICA's summer course to improve their skills in this area. The topics covered in the courses offer an insight into the extent of responsibilities and the daily routine of rural women in Ireland in the late-1950s. The ICA courses, however, offer more than mere instruction; the courses are also presented as a reason for rural women to gather together

18    "Bantracht na Tuaithe" (Irish Countywomen's Association) # 4: September 1956.
19    Aileen Heverin, *The Irish Countrywomen's Association: A History, 1910–2000* (Dublin: The Irish Countrywomen's Association and Wolfhound Press, 2000): 182.

in a community, to share experiences and knowledge, and simply enjoy a week's break from the monotony and isolation of rural existence.

The film opens with a shot of An Grianán (the Solarium), the big house owned by the ICA in Termonfeckin, Co. Louth, where the courses are run. An Grianán was a new acquisition for the ICA in the late-1950s, having just been bought in 1954 with funds donated by the American Kellogg foundation. This house – symbolic of their very slowly increasing stature – was the gift of an American rather than thanks to any input from the Irish government. The ICA campaigned for years for recognition to the Irish government but to no avail, so the location of this film is significant for what this says about the (lack of) recognition of rural women. There was a small cottage adjoining the farmyard, which was refurbished to be used as a model modernized farmhouse kitchen and used as a training unit for young rural housewives. The ESB provided the electrical equipment and awarded fifty-four scholarships annually from 1954 for six-week courses for nine girls at a time from the vocational school courses held around the country.

A woman drives up the driveway to the house and is greeted by the matron, Iním Nic Ghabhann. The two women enter the house and the girl is handed a brochure entitled *Programme of Courses*. The commentator informs us: "The courses are held from May to December and cover every subject." The ICA's activities covered an incredibly wide range and the film investigates some of those options. One group is learning dressmaking while the camera crew visits. All the women are busy sewing, working individually on machines or in groups. "The women have a chance to make their own dresses and to hear what their friends think of them." The ICA encouraged women in the early years of its existence to use homemade domestic fabrics, rather than the lesser quality new fabrics imported from Britain, and promoted the wearing of traditional Irish costumes, which were better suited to the climate and the daily work of rural Irish women. Other women in the film are learning basket-weaving in a rushwork class. "Handicraft classes are always popular", the commentator assures us as the women watch the instructor demonstrating the technique. Rushwork was used to make all sorts of practical objects for use around the cottage, as well as for decoration. During their tea break the women socialize with each other and the instructors in the large drawing room. This apparently inconsequential detail is actually quite significant. Rural women had little time to socialize with neighbours, and when they did so it was in their own kitchens, unlike the men who could go to the local pub. The picture of female sociability presented here is thus quite unusual and was certainly one of the many draws the ICA courses had for rural women.

In the dairy are three women learning how to make cheese. They churn the milk and put the curd through cheesecloth and hold the cream cheese out to the camera to see. Proceeding outside, three women are standing around a cow. "Dairy students again learning how to pick out a good cow." The instructor points out the various positive attributes of the animal, as the women watch. We then enter a cottage that has been set up as a model kitchen. This was the permanent result of one of the many portable exhibits the ICA set up in earlier days and during this period at places like the Royal Dublin Society (RDS) Spring Show and various Department of Agriculture exhibits to promote and publicize the benefits of rural electrification and running water in the home. Women's needs were lowest on the government's totem pole, so running water and modern kitchens took second place to the needs of the man outside on the farm. The promotion of remodeling and the use of electricity and water in the home through exhibits like the ICA's model kitchen did a great deal to increase awareness of the needs of rural women – and the potential benefits they brought in terms of cutting down on the drudgery of daily work in rural Ireland.

The work of the rural woman is obviously highly valued and not to be mocked in the way that the aspirations of the young urban air hostesses were. We are reminded of the manifold responsibilities of the rural housewife, who is responsible not only for the cooking and cleaning, rearing of children, fetching the water from the well (if they were lucky enough to have one), but also for feeding the chickens, milking the cows and tending to the crops when her husband was away, as was often the case for wives whose husbands were seasonal migrants to England. These women are crucial to the rural economy – they choose the cattle, milk them, make the butter and cheese, feed the family, rear the children, make the clothes and keep the home. It was the loss of rural women to emigration that such an effort to increase awareness of their value to Irish society aimed to prevent, for it was from the drudgery of rural life that the bulk of young female Irish emigrants were fleeing. The increased capacity for comparison with Britain in the 1940s and 1950s, as it replaced the United States as the destination for many young Irish emigrants, fuelled much of the discontent with life in the country. Thus if conditions could be improved, hopefully the tide of female emigration could be stemmed.

The film closes with a shot of the women enjoying the quiet beauty of the location. Two are seated under a tree, reading, while another two walk by. "An Grianán is in a lovely quiet place and whether it is learning or hobbies that are going on, the Irish Countrywomen are there." Again the sense is that the house is more than a centre for learning, but a place for women to retreat to and be among a community of rural women who share the same lifestyle and values as themselves. This contact with other like-minded women could do as much or more for a demoralized population as any government programme. In fact, the progress that the ICA made in the decades before it was finally officially recognized by the government laid the foundations for much of the modernizing work in the Irish countryside. As such, the ICA was a path-breaker and a bringer of progress in small and unthreatening steps to the dark and backward homesteads that, while romanticized by de Valera, were actually one of the main reasons for female emigration from the country.

The final film, "Hotel Courses,"[20] follows a Gaeltacht girl as she attends a training course in Bundoran. The film opens with a view of the Donegal landscape, where two people are standing by the side of the otherwise empty narrow country road. Ní Bhreasláin and her male companion are waiting for a car to collect her and bring her to Bundoran, where she is going to do a hotel course. She holds a newspaper advertisement in her hand, which reads "Vacancies County Donegal Vocational Education Committee Training Course for the Hotel Staff in the Great Northern Hotel, Bundoran, October 1956 to April 1957". A Volkswagon Beetle pulls up, Áine gets into the car, and the man waves goodbye. It is a striking opening scene, in which the emptiness of the countryside and the loneliness

20    "Cúrsaí Óstán" (Hotel Training Courses) #9: February 1957.

of the two figures standing by the side of the road is suddenly shattered by the arrival of the car, the symbol of wealth and modernity. The car stops at the front of the hotel. "It [the course] takes place for six months in winter and spring, when the hotel is closed." The hotel is obviously only intended for seasonal tourists – Donegal, on Ireland's rugged northwest coast, does not lend itself to winter visitors.

The view switches to the interior of a room with lots of women in aprons and maids' costumes, performing assorted cleaning tasks. The women watch a bed-making demonstration, then fold and iron the hotel sheets for practice. In the kitchen, some women are chopping vegetables while standing at the cooker under the supervision of the cookery teacher. "Various girls prepare the meals each day under the guidance of the head-teacher. Áine likes this work." We never hear Áine's voice – it is the commentator that assures us of this. It could not be far removed from the work that Áine would be expected to do at home – cleaning and cooking – but in this context it is transformed, from unpaid drudgery to paid and thus proper, even enjoyable, work. The women learn how to serve food at the banquet tables and at lunchtime they serve each other in the lunchroom. After lunch, it is time for theory class. The teacher points to the blackboard, on which are drawings of sherry, wine and champagne glasses. Unfortunately, all of the words on the board are in English. At tea time, Áine and another woman carry out the trays from the kitchen-hatch: "It's tea time and poor Áine and another friend from the Gaeltacht are still working!" This is the only point in the film where Áine's special status as a Gaeltacht girl is highlighted. It is unclear whether or not it is just the two Gaeltacht girls who are still working, casting Áine in an Irish-language Cinderella role, or whether the commentator is simply pointing out that the course itself is hard work for everyone. It is apparent, however, that the Gaeltacht girls end up together for the same reason that emigrants do in any country with a foreign language – for comfort and ease of communication in a strange situation. The comment thus highlights Áine's identity as an internal migrant to the English-speaking country of modern tourism. After tea it is time to relax and the sixty girls are shown doing set-dancing in the large room. This is still Donegal and there is no rock and roll in this dance hall. At the end of the course, Áine says goodbye to the instructors as she leaves the hotel. Upon leaving, the commentator notes: "She is trained now and already has a job waiting for her." And so the film ends with Áine walking in the front door of the Central Hotel to take up her new position.

It is a sign of the times that the woman must leave her home in order to find work, and that she must go to an English-speaking area. She is an internal migrant, who will when she returns home inevitably compare the situation in her home to that in the more prosperous areas of the country. The growth of the service industry and tourism specifically was a mixed blessing, in that it offered such opportunities close to the Gaeltacht areas and it is thus thanks to its growth that women like this one did not leave the country entirely in search of work. The growth of the tourism industry, and with it the increase in jobs for women, will be one means of "saving" areas like this one from complete economic decline in the years to come, while the fears of the threat it posed to the survival of the Irish language will be justified. The fact that Áine can obtain a job so quickly after finishing the course is an indication of the growth in the tourism and hospitality sector in some parts of Ireland. The real message, however, is that the only way to get a good job for which one requires formal training is to leave the Gaeltacht and join the ranks of English-speaking members of the growing service sector. It appears from its name that the Central Hotel is in an English-speaking part of Ireland, though the location of the hotel is not specified. Job opportunities for Gaeltacht girls were few and far between – this is the reason for the huge emigration problem in those areas in the 1950s. The opening shot of the beautiful but empty Donegal landscape speaks volumes about the lack of opportunities for advancement in that area. Modern society appears to exist only beyond those areas, which are deemed useful only insofar as they attract tourists. For the Gaeltacht people, migration to the cities or abroad seems to be the only option.

Women's work in Ireland in the mid- to late-1950s usually meant unpaid work in the home or on the farm. Single women could work but once married they were expected to retire and those who did not were actively discriminated against in state policy. These "Eyes of Ireland" short documentary films present a view of some of the urban, rural and Gaeltacht women's work opportunities, which in turn serves as commentary on the values that Ireland was embracing or letting go of during this period. The urban-based models and air hostesses are depicted as glamour-girls on the surface but lacking the qualities that the rural women possess. Although admired, they are denied the respect that comes with "real" work such as that undertaken by members of the Irish Countrywomen's Association and it is implied that their values are somehow less than those promoted by the state and church. The ICA's rural women, on the other hand, are the embodiment of Horace Plunkett's ideal – hardworking equals in a co-operative rural Irish society, while the Gaeltacht women are the other side of the rural coin, forced to leave the land that sustains the language in order to find work.

Huge crowds lined the route of the funerals of the Irish soldiers killed in the Niemba ambush while on UN duty in the Congo. 19 November 1960.
*Reproduced with permission from the Irish Photo Archive.*

# PART 2

# The "Gaelic News" reels

Once television came to Britain, the Rank Organization withdrew its newsreels from Irish cinemas, bringing the "Eyes of Ireland" short documentary phase of the *Amharc Éireann* series to a close. In 1959 Seán Lemass became Taoiseach (1959–66), ending over twenty years with Eamon de Valera as the head of the country (1932–59), with only the brief exceptions of two inter-party governments (1948–51 and 1954–57). The next phase of the *Amharc Éireann* series coincided with the tenure of Seán Lemass as Taoiseach, the implementation of the *First Economic Programme* and the period of rapid modernization that Ireland underwent in preparation for its entry into the European Economic Community in 1973. The early 1960s are widely remembered as the start of a new era of openness, progressiveness and prosperity. In contrast to the depression and emigration of the mid-1950s, this was a period of rapid growth and economic revival that saw former emigrants return to take advantage of new employment opportunities in Ireland. The Gaelic News films tell some of that story using a newsreel format that, while now outdated elsewhere in Western Europe and North America, was oddly appropriate for Ireland as a relatively late starter in the European wave of post-war development. This phase is completely different in tone, style and content from the documentary films that preceded it. Technically a newsreel, the Gaelic News series was anything but objective news reportage. Although superficially it simply records the dramatic transformation the country underwent in the economic development, international affairs and social and cultural life of the country, the underlying message throughout is the importance of maintaining Ireland's traditional identity in the face of such changes.

1916 Commemoration at Arbour Hill, Dublin. 10 May 1961.
*Reproduced with permission from the Irish Photo Archive.*

# CHAPTER FOUR

# National commemoration and symbolic locations[1]

In contrast to other films that draw attention celebrate the economic and social changes underway in Ireland in the early 1960s, in terms of its political identity the country is represented in the *Amharc Éireann* news films of 1959–64 as an inward- and backward-looking martial society, still very much defined by Ireland's revolutionary past. The fiftieth anniversary of the 1916 Rising was due to take place in 1966 and many of the activities recorded reflect the sense of preparation and build-up in anticipation of this event. The series includes a great many films that focus on national commemoration ceremonies, celebrating Irish republican heroes, patriots and martyrs. Films of national commemorations focus almost exclusively on the remembrance of heroes, patriots and martyrs to the Irish revolution (1911–22) and on militant republicanism, beginning with Theobald Wolfe Tone and the 1798 United Irishmen rebellion. Commemorations of the Easter Rising feature the heroes of the revolutionary period, including the Irish Volunteers, the Irish Citizen Army, Cumann na mBán (The Women's Society) and the Old IRA. The War of Independence of 1919–21 is represented by University College Dublin students' annual commemoration of republican legend Kevin Barry and other films honouring those killed by the British authorities in Mountjoy Prison.

The Civil War of 1922–23 that followed was impossible to ignore but more difficult to deal with diplomatically, as the legacy of this division persisted in the identities of the two main political parties; Fianna Fáil – the anti-Treaty Republicans, and Fine Gael – the pro-Treaty Free

---

1    This chapter is derived from an article published in *National Identities* in December 2009, available online: <http://wwww.tandfonline.com/ 10.1080/14608940701737383>.

Staters. Fianna Fáil was the party in power for the entire period during which these news films were made (1959–64), with Seán Lemass – a Civil War veteran himself – as Taoiseach. The figure of Lemass personified both Ireland's revolutionary past and its stately present. While important Fine Gael figures like General Mulcahy do figure occasionally in the films as attendees, de Valera, like Lemass, is omnipresent as the former revolutionary and now head of state. The other permanent fixture in all of the films of national commemorations is the priest, the bishop or the cardinal. The faith and fatherland version of Irish history was still dominant during the early 1960s, reflecting de Valera's social conservatism as expressed in the 1937 Constitution. These films were made before the crisis of Roman Catholicism in Ireland in the later 1960s and the rise of the more secular republicanism,[2] so if the effects of the Second Vatican Council were making themselves felt in Ireland before the end of the *Amharc Éireann* series in 1964, it is certainly not reflected here, as the close relationship between the Roman Catholic Church and the state is very visible.

Republican themes are repeated in the images contained within, and commentary accompanying, the *Amharc Éireann* news films that feature various national commemorations. The use of certain images and the description of the events in the Irish-language commentary clearly demonstrate the contradiction inherent in the series between the attempt to reproduce a traditional republican nationalist narrative of Irish history, albeit in a new form, during a period otherwise defined by increasingly open and internationally oriented approach to politics and the economy, as well as significant changes in practically all other aspects of Irish social and cultural life.

A number of symbolic locations are featured as sites of national commemoration, including birthplaces, battle sites, graveyards and jails, where patriots were held, killed or buried. The sites are celebrated in the films as having commemorative power and as pilgrimage destinations whose importance continues to resonate with the Irish people. They include Bodenstown – Wolfe Tone's birthplace; Vinegar Hill – the site of the 1798

---

2    See Patrick Maume, "Young Ireland, Arthur Griffith, and Republican ideology: the question of continuity", *Éire-Ireland* 34, no. 2 (1999): 155–74.

United Irishmen rebellion; Howth Harbour – the landing place in 1914 for the *Asgard* laden with guns destined for the Irish Volunteers; Dublin Castle – the centre of British power in Ireland; Arbour Hill and Glasnevin cemeteries – the resting places of numerous patriots; as well as Mountjoy Prison and Kilmainham Gaol. The films build a Republican narrative of Irish political history by serving as reminders to the national audience of the continuing importance of these historic events, symbolic locations and pivotal republican figures to the formation of the independent Irish state, by emphasizing its colonial past and its violent birth.

Unlike the original film series, which includes a vast number of news films on a wide array of topics in no particular order other than the date on which they appeared in the cinemas, the symbolic locations are presented here in sequential order according to the period to which they refer in Irish history, thus tracing the chronological development of the Irish republican tradition from the moment of its inception in the United Irishmen rebellion of 17987 to its culmination during the War of Independence of 1919–21, and its aftermath in the Civil War of 1922–23. The sequential organization of historical events and figures then clearly illustrates the manner in which the republican narrative was built throughout the lifetime of the series. We begin with the films that treat birth and early days of Irish republicanism in 1798, before proceeding to Kilmainham Gaol – a key site that encapsulates an important period of time in Irish revolutionary history. The end of Kilmainham's lifetime coincides with the early twentieth century. Many films focus on the revolutionary period of 1913–23 by addressing the role of the Irish Volunteers in 1913–14, the 1916 Easter Rising and the 1919–21 War of Independence. But the outcome of the War of Independence also brought a division between hitherto united Irish republicans in the Civil War of 1922–23, which saw the anti-Treaty Irregulars oppose the pro-Treaty Free State forces in battle. The decidedly republican slant to the films is reflected in the invisibility of key pro-Treaty Free State figures like Michael Collins and Arthur Griffith in the few films that deal with the Civil War. This mode of analysis thus combines place and time as the criteria for organization, by using time – a specific historical moment – and place – associated with a particular figure or event, in order to trace the trajectory of the Irish republican historical narrative in these films.

## Remembering republicanism

In the two centuries since the 1798 rising, the nature of the commemorations of the United Irishmen rebellion have functioned as a gauge of contemporary Irish political opinion, as people have attempted to establish a connection backwards in time to those events. Commemoration of the 1798 United Irishmen rebellion went through a series of phases, from denial of any association with it in the immediate aftermath of the rebellion and the early nineteenth century, to renewed interest with the occasion of the 1898 centenary year, to outright celebration of 1798 in the mid-twentieth century.[3] The commemorations that took place during the early 1960s that appear in the *Amharc Éireann* series reflect the strongly republican nationalist atmosphere in the Republic of Ireland that defined the lead-up to the commemoration of the fiftieth anniversary of the Easter Rising in 1966.

"Ballinglen, Co. Wicklow: Taoiseach unveils plaque to '98 men,"[4] features the commemoration of the 1798 Battle of Vinegar Hill. This battle was a victory for the United Irishmen and the same place to which they were forced to fall back after the defeat of their forces in other parts of the country. The Ballinglen memorial is to two young men, Phillip and Patrick Lacey, who died upon returning from battle. The film opens with a shot of the parade approaching in Ballinglen, complete with drummers and pipers and following an O'Byrne flag. The audience is composed of Old IRA men,[5] young women and people of all ages looking on. Lemass stands in front of the plaque to the Lacey brothers and opens the curtain, as a priest stands by his side ready to bless it. The plaque commemorating the two young men put to death after the Battle of Vinegar Hill reads:

---

3    Peter Collins "The contest of memory: the continuing impact of 1798 commemoration", *Éire-Ireland* 34, no. 2 (1999): 28–50.

4    "Ballinglen, Co. Wicklow: Taoiseach unveils plaque to '98 men" #56: 1 July 1960.

5    The Old IRA is synonymous with the Irish Volunteers formed in 1913, who went on to fight in the War of Independence in 1919–21. During the war their name was changed from the Irish Volunteers to the Irish Republican Army to reflect their goal of achieving an Irish Republic.

"This plaque was erected by all sections of the community in memory of the brothers Phillip and Patrick Lacey, aged 22 and 20 years, who were shot at this bridge when returning from the Battle of Vinegar Hill on the 21st of June 1798 by yeomen cavalry." It is an example of the monuments commemorating local heroes that were being erected all over the country from the 1940s onwards, alongside the national versions in the capital city. The commentator assures the film's audience that the memory of the rising is still fresh in Wicklow and Wexford, where the battle took place. Of course, the function of events such as this one – and films that publicize it – is to make sure that the memory of 1798 is kept alive. In the same way that the Orange Day parades in the North remind the Orangemen of the defeat of James II at the Battle of the Boyne, this commemoration and the viewing of it on film allows both local and national participation in the commemoration of Ireland's republican heritage.

By focusing on the two young men who were killed, rather than on the battle as a whole, the events of Vinegar Hill are also personalized. This is also extended to the coverage of the attendees, which includes key figures in Irish republican history. Seán MacBride is visible in the audience, not only drawing attention to his republican nationalist lineage but also to the canon of cultural and national heroes of which his family is a part. MacBride was the son of Major John MacBride, who was executed in 1916 in the aftermath of the Easter Rising. His mother was Maude Gonne MacBride, W.B. Yeats' muse, which thus expands the republican narrative beyond the narrowly politically revolutionary to include the legacy and memory of the Anglo-Irish Literal Revival. Seán MacBride himself belonged to Clann na Poblachta (Republican Family), the left-leaning political party that formed the short-lived inter-party government with Costello's Fine Gael in 1948 and brought the Irish Republic into being in 1949. In so doing, he added himself to Ireland's canon of republican heroes, and managed to steal Fianna Fáil's thunder as the self-proclaimed "Republican Party" in the process.

The key figure in the 1798 rebellion was Theobald Wolfe Tone himself, the co-founder of the United Irishmen, the father of Irish republicanism and the first of a long canon of national heroes. Two films record the annual commemoration of his life at death at his birthplace in Bodenstown. In the first of the two, "Bodenstown: Wolfe Tone remembered,"[6] army and state officials are gathered to lay a wreath on Tone's grave. The Defense Minister, Gerald Bartley, inspects a guard of honour of graduates of the military college and members of the 6th regiment (serving under Lieutenant Corcoran), before laying the wreath on the grave as the flag is raised. In the second film, "Bodenstown: Wolfe Tone commemoration,"[7] General Sean McKeown is present with Bartley. McKeown was a very high profile military figure, who had recently led the UN forces in the Congo Crisis. His presence is a reminder of Ireland's recent role in post-colonial struggles in Africa and illustrates the perceived intersection of Ireland's republican nationalist heritage with its internationalist role as mentor to other newly independent states.

In each of the two films the commentator informs viewers that two hundred years after Tone's birth, his grave – the symbol of Irish republicanism – is the most visited and most commemorated in the country. He reminds them that Patrick Pearse, one of the leaders of the 1916 Rising, spoke here, and every year the generations that followed him assemble to remember the basic principles of republicanism that Tone taught. Just as the Ballinglen commemoration linked the local to the national, the Wolfe Tone grave site links republican generations in time and forms a link in the chain that extends back from them directly to Pearse, to the leaders of the 1916 Rising, and to Tone and the United Irishmen. The commentator also issues a challenge to the current generation, as he notes in closing that, in spite of commemorations like these, Tone's main objective has yet to be fulfilled. This final comment refers, of course, to partition. The division of Ireland into the twenty-six counties of the current Republic and the six counties of Northern Ireland occurred as a result of the "betrayal" of republican values in the signing of the Anglo-Irish Treaty in December 1921, which led directly to the Civil War in 1922–23. Although an Irish Republic now exists, a reference to which we have just seen in the figure of MacBride in the film on Ballinglen, it is incomplete and not as Tone

6    "Bodenstown: Wolfe Tone remembered" #212: 22 June 1962.
7    "Bodenstown: Wolfe Tone commemoration" #264: 21 June 1964.

envisioned it, in which Irishmen of all stripes – Catholic, Protestant and Presbyterian – live together in peace in a free, united Ireland. The implication is that it is up to the contemporary audience to complete the task that Tone began, by ending the partition of Ireland. So, rather than preaching peace, this comment is a reminder of old animosities and of the need to fulfill a centuries-old goal.

The comment is striking for two reasons. First, it amounts to a contradiction of Lemass' views on partition from 1955 onwards. Lemass' Northern policy was a departure from the recent past of de Valera's non-policy and an attempt to find common ground on economic issues as a means to address partition. From the beginning of his term as Taoiseach in 1959, Lemass made it clear he wanted to develop a dialogue with the North, and invited Lord Brookeborough, Northern Ireland's political representative, to visit Dublin. These overtures were the preamble to the meetings that Lemass would hold with Brookeborough's successor, Terence O'Neill, in 1965.[8] The comment is also noteworthy due to the resurgence of the IRA's physical force tradition with a border campaign from 1956–62, which illustrated very clearly that all republicans did not necessarily agree on Lemass' tactics. The commentator's call to arms appears to condone the illegal IRA's approach to achieving Irish unity and fulfilling Irish nationalist aspirations according to ideological criteria – rather than the more pragmatic and realistic approach to reconciliation adopted by Lemass, a former Irregular himself. The viewpoint expressed by the commentator certainly points to the discontent still existent as a result of the continuing partition of the country and is thus a troubling example of the attempt in the films – and specifically in the Irish-language commentary – to resurrect the republican tradition in its militant form.

8    Robert Savage, *Seán Lemass* (Dublin: Dundalgan Press, 1999), pp. 28–9.

Back behind bars

The defeat of the United Irishmen's 1798 rebellion precipitated the end of
Grattan's Parliament and the passing of the Act of Union in 1801, which
created the United Kingdom of Britain and Ireland that lasted until the
formation of the Irish Free State in 1922. A number of films in the *Amharc
Éireann* series feature a building that functions as a monument to the
nationalist movement and is an ongoing reminder of Ireland's revolutionary
past. Kilmainham Gaol was opened in 1796 – five years prior to the Union
with Great Britain, and closed in 1924 – two years after the establishment
of the Irish Free State, so its lifetime coincided very closely with that of
Ireland under the union. Characterized as a "political seismograph, recording most of the significant tremors in the often turbulent relations between
the two countries,"[9] few places encapsulate the shaping of modern Irish
nationalism like Kilmainham Gaol. It housed all martyrs of importance to
Irish nationalist history, including Robert Emmet, various Young Irelanders
and Fenians, Charles Stuart Parnell and, most famously, the leaders of the
1916 Rising. One of those leaders was Joseph Mary Plunkett, the uncle of
Colm Ó Laoghaire, producer of the *Amharc Éireann* series. He married
his fiancée, Grace Gifford, in the jail chapel just hours before his execution. Unfortunately for posterity, four Republican prisoners were also shot
here by the Free State Army in November 1922, not far from where the
1916 martyrs were executed. The resulting juxtaposition of the two places
of execution – for the 1916 martyrs, who symbolized the idealistic and
unified group of poet-patriots who gave their lives in a "blood sacrifice"
for the sake of Irish independence, and the Civil War victims, who were a
painful reminder of the split in the republican nationalist movement into
pro-Treaty and anti-Treaty forces – within the one building was more than
the Free State government could reconcile as the victor in the Civil War,
and it was decided in 1924 to close the jail down.

9    Padraig MacCuaig, *A History of Kilmainham Gaol, 1796–1924* (Dublin: The Stationery
     Office, 1995): 1.

Kilmainham Gaol was the subject of much attention throughout the 1960s, when Lemass' "Republican Party," Fianna Fáil, was in power. The Kilmainham Gaol Restoration Society, formed in May 1960, was composed primarily of former veterans of the revolutionary period, whose goal was the restoration of the jail so that it could play a role in the fiftieth anniversary of the Rising in 1966. Its conversion into a site for national commemoration and tourism was part of the trend during this period toward the conservation and rebuilding of buildings symbolically important to Ireland's national heritage, including the old Abbey Theatre and Liberty Hall.[10] The Society's description of Kilmainham Gaol as "The Bastille of Ireland"[11] illustrates its recognition of the extent of its historic importance as a site of national memory to Irish republicanism and the films on the restoration of Kilmainham Gaol also publicize the Society's restoration work, by drawing attention to the jail's legacy and contemporary relevance.

In one such film, in which "De Valera revisits Kilmainham jail,"[12] the former Taoiseach and now President, Eamon de Valera, is shown revisiting his old cell at the beginning of this reconstruction process. A large crowd is gathered to see de Valera arrive, the last prisoner before the jail closed in 1924. He shakes hands with Old IRA comrades in a shot taken through the gates of the jail as if picturing them again behind bars. Inside the courtyard there are gravestones and crosses belonging to some of the famous Irish martyrs who were imprisoned here. Cameramen are all over the place, taking pictures of the site, as the commentator reminds viewers that this is an historic place and such access is a novelty. A tour follows of the interior of the jail, with shots of the crowd downstairs alternating with shots of the cells, juxtaposing Kilmainham's present and past. In the interior courtyard, de Valera talks to the former governor of the prison. Showing the two men now talking together in the midst of the crowd highlights the fact that the days of British occupation, when they were on opposite

---

10  The rebuilding of the Abbey and of Liberty Hall are also recorded in the *Amharc Éireann* series.

11  Kilmainham Jail Restoration Society, *Kilmainham: The Bastille of Ireland* (Dublin: The Kilmainham Jail Restoration Society, 1961).

12  "Mr. de Valera revisits Kilmainham Gaol" #144: 9 March 1962.

sides of the door, are now over and they can safely reminisce about their shared memories of an earlier time.

The darkness of the jail is emphasized in a shot of a dark corridor with bright light coming from the full-length window at the rear, against which stands the tall silhouette of a man, calling to mind the prison-guard who patrolled these corridors. De Valera reaches his former cell where, viewers are reminded, he spent long hours under lock and key. He enters the cell, crouching down from his tall height to get through the low entrance, then stands and looks around. His expression is awkward, as if trying to absorb the memories and emotions the place evokes in him, while dealing with the camera pointed directly in his face. The shot then pans along the long corridors from below, focusing on the wires and railings that close in the cells. If only these walls could talk, says the commentator. But rather than focusing only on the past, the film closes by returning to the present, where the crowd is gathered downstairs. Their work is the fund-raising project to restore the jail, so that it may become a place for visitors and education. This is the future of Kilmainham, and de Valera's experience is the past. The era of British imperialism is over and with it the era of Kilmainham can also pass into history.

Kilmainham Gaol is revisited five years later, towards the end of the *Amharc Éireann* series. In "Kilmainham prison: restoration work continues,"[13] the work of converting the prison into a museum is still going on in 1964 in preparation for the 1966 celebrations. The commentator is more specific about the relevance of the site in this film, reminding viewers that Henry Joy McCracken (another leader of the 1798 United Irishmen rising), Robert Emmett, Charles Stewart Parnell, James Connolly, Patrick Pearse and others from 1916 were all here, as well as the fact that Joseph Mary Plunkett was married here before his death. The so-called apostolic succession of Irish nationalism is thus celebrated in the film, immortalizing it in the monument of Kilmainham Gaol. Together the films draw attention to the symbolic importance of Kilmainham Gaol for the nationalist tradition. De Valera is presented as the living embodiment of all of the

---

13    "Kilmainham prison: restoration work continues" #268: 19 July 1964.

past revolutionaries who were housed here, while the jail itself is a monument to Ireland's revolutionary history. But de Valera himself represents the republican strand of nationalism and although he subsequently turned statesman, it is to his earlier identity as a republican revolutionary that the film turns, by placing him clearly within the canon of nationalist heroes housed in the jail itself.

## Restaging the revolution

The revolutionary period that is encapsulated in Kilmainham Gaol and personified in the person of Eamon de Valera came to a head in the period from 1913 to 1922. The *Amharc Éireann* films showcase the role of the Irish Volunteers, who played a crucial part in the 1916 Rising. The Irish Volunteers were formed in November 1913 in response to the formation of the Ulster Volunteers and the increased threat of violence from the north in opposition to the Home Rule Bill. In "Memorial plaque to 1913 volunteers,"[14] the occasion is the unveiling of a plaque outside the Rotunda in Dublin, where the Irish Volunteers were founded, and the historical significance of the Volunteers is clearly stated by de Valera himself. Dublin's landscape of monuments to its heroes provides the backdrop to the film. The opening shot is of O'Connell Street, where crowds are gathered and a platform and benches are set up for the occasion. President de Valera arrives in a black car and is greeted by army personnel. The shot then switches to Lemass, who is sitting in the benches with the other veterans and dignitaries, including Defense Minister Gerald Bartley, General Sean McKeown and former president Sean T. O'Kelly. The aging de Valera, dressed in his top hat, is subtly guided along by the army personnel, and proceeds to inspect the troops. He then ascends the platform and gives his speech. In his oration, de Valera reminds the crowd that the founding of the Irish Volunteers started

14   "Memorial plaque to 1913 Volunteers" #235: 30 November 1963.

the fight for freedom, brought out the heroes of 1916, and that they have freedom "in this part of the country" as a result – the implication being, of course, is that the Irish in the North are not free. Afterwards he opens the curtain in front of the plaque to the 1913 volunteers on the wall of the Gate Theatre beside the Rotunda, which reads: "Here in the Rotunda the Irish Republican Army was founded on November 25th 1913". There is no need for any additional commentary, as de Valera's speech echoes the sentiment expressed elsewhere by the commentator regarding the evils of partition.

The role of the Irish Volunteers is more fully celebrated in the film, "Howth Harbour: the Asgard comes home."[15] This single-issue newsreel is actually a two-part film; part historical compilation film using stills from George Morrison's famous historical compilation film on the 1916 Rising, *Mise Éire* (1959), and part re-enactment of the gun-running expedition to Howth in 1914. The film begins with the caption: "Sunday, July 26th, 1914" followed by a number of stills from the original landing of the Asgard in Howth Harbour. The commentator sets the scene: "it was in Howth Harbour, forty-seven years ago, that the Asgard's first voyage took place, carrying guns and ammunition from Germany. The crew on board consisted of two Donegal fishermen – Richard O'Dugan and Padraig O'Nolan, as well as Erskine Childers, his wife Máire and her friend, Máire Spring Rice." They brought the boat safely to Howth "under the keen eyes of the English," where the Irish Volunteers were waiting to meet them on the pier.

Part two takes place in the present, in July 1961, as the Irish Volunteers are seen marching again in a re-enactment of the Asgard's arrival. The commentator stresses how much has changed since those early days – today the Old IRA men are greeted by the Irish Navy, which now uses the Asgard as a training vessel. Again, a symbol of the national resistance has been converted into an educational tool for the present, just as Kilmainham Gaol will become a museum. But the past and present are one again in the person of de Valera, one of the original Volunteers who brought the guns ashore in 1914 and now here as head of state. The Asgard also has guns and ammunition on board, just as it did then, and the Old IRA men are

15    "Howth Harbour: the Asgard comes home" #113: 4 August 1961.

lined up on the pier to unload the cargo. What follows is a moving scene of these former soldiers, now old men, as they stand in their uniforms with their medals, and lean over to grasp the boxes that are passed to them, the pride and emotion visible on their faces. The women of Cumann na mBán march along the pier, unlikely looking revolutionaries now as stout old ladies carrying handbags. Erskine Childers, who would go on to become President of Ireland in 1973, is there representing his father who was later shot by the Free State forces in 1923, Childers' appearance in the ceremony is a further reminder of the continuing dominance of republicans in Irish politics during this period.

This mixture of real footage from 1914 and the re-enactment in 1961 is a very effective means of making the past meaningful in the present. Seeing the Old IRA men and the women of Cumann na mBán at the pier in Howth and witnessing the emotion that the event obviously stirs up for them brings home the immediacy of these events almost half a century later and makes it impossible to downplay its real importance for contemporary Irish political life. Fianna Fáil's Lemass government is often described as a changing of the guard in Irish politics from the de Valera era of politicians but it is quite plain in this film that many of the old guard were still alive and well, and making their presence felt at events such as this, while the new guard was not necessarily new at all. In fact, Lemass was just as much a member of the old guard as de Valera before him. Lemass fought in the 1922–23 Civil War and his brother Noel was one of its victims. So, this reminder of the importance of the Irish Volunteers to Irish nationalist history is once again presented to the cinema audience through a distinctly Republican lens. Of course, the importance of commemorations like this one for the government in power must also be noted. It was in Fianna Fáil's interest to remind the public constantly of its historic importance as the "Republican Party," a fact unlikely to be forgotten with the showing of newsreels such as this one in Irish cinemas.

Reigniting the Phoenix Flame

The events of 1913 and 1914, the formation of the Irish Volunteers and the landing of the Asgard led directly to the Easter Rising of 1916 in Dublin, the climax of which was the "blood sacrifice" of these national martyrs at the hands of the British authorities. Popular revulsion at their executions turned an unpopular revolt centred in Dublin into a national movement for Irish independence. Their subsequent "resurrection" in the 1960s at the hands of the Irish state took place as part of the official gearing up for the fiftieth anniversary of the Rising. The republican themes of blood sacrifice and rebirth are associated with Patrick Pearse in the context of the 1916 Rising but actually date back to Wolfe Tone himself. Condemned to death for his part in the 1798 rebellion, Wolfe Tone attempted to commit suicide but failed to cut himself correctly and instead took several painful days to die. The blood sacrifice of 1916 that Pearse correctly predicted was necessary in order to guarantee the ideological success of a revolt that was logistically and militarily doomed to fail. For Pearse, the sacrifice itself was the most important aspect of the Rising, serving as the spark that would provoke the revitalization of the nationalist movement. The 1916 Rising was thus the catalyst for this "rebirth" of the Republican nationalist tradition of sacrifice and resurrection that began with Wolfe Tone.

The commemoration of 1916 at the Garden of Remembrance, Ireland's monument to the 1916 martyrs, at the Arbour Hill cemetery was an annual affair and the site was also a frequent showpiece destination for foreign dignitaries of post-colonial states[16] but Arbour Hill's significance to Republicans as a symbolic location and a repository of national memory began much earlier than the Easter Rising, during the period surrounding the 1798 rebellion. The land was owned by Christ Church Cathedral and was used to store corn, from which it gets its name, Cnoc an Arbhair (Corn Hill). The area around Arbour Hill was the site of many bloody events

16    "Dr. Nkrumah in Dublin" #51: 27 May 1960; "President of Pakistan in Dublin" #268: 19 July 1964.

including the yeomen massacre of Irish croppies by order of Cornwallis, the Lord Lieutenant. A gallows overlooked Arbour Hill itself, which was used as a place of execution, and is associated with two burial grounds, the Croppies' Acre and Arbour Hill cemetery. Behind the Croppies' Acre Memorial Park is Collins' Barracks, and behind this lies Arbour Hill cemetery. A former school playground was amalgamated with an exercise yard for prisoners to form the large space that is now the Garden of Remembrance, comprising a lawn area with a variety of trees, where the remains of leaders of the 1916 Rising lie. Arbour Hill is thus a site for republican commemoration, from 1798 to 1916, and this theme is strongly emphasized in the *Amharc Éireann* films covering Fianna Fáil's Easter Week commemorations.

"Arbour Hill: Easter Week commemoration"[17] opens with a shot of Lemass entering the area, being greeted by General McKeown and O'Kelly, the army chief of staff. Soldiers march in and de Valera follows, on inspection. The Irish tricolour flag flies high over the cemetery and the Garden of Remembrance below, where mass for the dead is being said. Close-ups focus on their names, carved in Gaelic script into large stone slabs, lying side-by-side and inlaid in the ground in the memorial area. Although the names of the dead are engraved in both languages, they names are not shown in English. Emer Muldowney, easily identifiable as an Easter Week survivor from the medals that adorn her coat, is in attendance representating the contribution of republican women through Cumann na mBán (The Women's Society).[18] Next to her is de Valera himself, similarly adorned. The film closes with a shot of the crowd standing on either side of the priest who stands at the head of the memorial area, his hands together in prayer, reminiscent of images of Jesus surrounded by his faithful flock. By focusing on the various shots on the Irish tri-colour flag, the Gaelic script on the memorial, the veterans' medals, and the priest and his flock, the film represents Irish nationalist identity as a combination of the Celtic

---

17 "Arbour Hill: Easter Week commemoration" #49: 13 May 1960.
18 See Margaret Ward and Louise Ryan, eds, *Irish Women and Nationalism: soldiers, new women and wicked hags* (Dublin: Irish Academic Press, 2004) on republican women.

and Gaelic past and its Republican and Catholic present. It brings together various elements of the republican narrative with traditional symbols of Irish identity, combining Celtic and Gaelic elements (the Irish script) with military references (the medals) and the Easter Rising/republican revolt, but also adding that element of republicanism that is unique to Ireland – the priest. Here the twentieth-century Irish adaptation of republicanism is clearly visible, in the faith and fatherland combination that de Valera enshrined in his 1937 Constitution, which had yet to suffer the effects of the Second Vatican Council.

In "Arbour Hill: ex-servicemen lay wreath"[19] the same old warriors are there again to commemorate the dead ex-servicemen. The line-up comprises de Valera, the army leadership, government ministers, and representatives of Cumann na mBán and the Old IRA. The commentator describes the occasion as Fenians' Day, an unusual variation on the more normal Arbour Hill Day, which calls attention quite frankly to the republican significance of this event. The martyrs being commemorated here are not just the product of 1916, but also descendants of the Fenians of the 1860s and the original Irish Republican Brotherhood, thus symbolizing the entire history of Ireland's revolutionary heroes and martyrs. This time, however, there is a significant addition in representatives of the Citizen Army, James Connolly's workers' army formed in response to the 1913 Dublin lock-out. Connolly is not often mentioned in national commemorations because, as a socialist, he did not fit neatly into the official canon of heroes as easily as devout disciples like Patrick Pearse. In death, however, Connolly was as much a martyr as any. After his leg was badly injured in fighting he was kept at Dublin Castle, in the room formerly used for royalty, and had to be tied to a chair because he was unable to stand for the firing squad.

A re-enactment of sorts takes place in the film, as Counsellor Joseph Dowling reads the same proclamation that was read outside the General Post Office on Easter Monday 1916. The Local Defense Force – contemporary volunteers rather than army reserves – serves as the guard of honour and Commandant Lenihan, the Chairman of Oglaigh Naisiúnta na hÉireann

---

19    "Arbour Hill: ex-servicemen lay wreath" #267: 12 July 1964.

(National Servicemen and women), lays the wreath. As the film closes, the commentator notes that it is time for the last post and the raising of the flag and reminds viewers that under the green sod lie Pearse and other heroes of the revolution, with whom many of the people present at the ceremony stood shoulder-to-shoulder forty years ago. Thus, as in the *Asgard* ceremony, this event is about revitalizing memory through the re-enactment of key events in the past that are important to the republican narrative of Irish history. The audience of former revolutionaries' participation in the event by listening to the reading of the proclamation serves as a reminder that this is not just ancient history but still an important part of Ireland's present. Once again, it is the reenactment of this key event – and the audience's participation in it – that makes the film a didactic tool. This is not simply commemoration – this is the redoing, the reliving, of the event. It is the element of participation that will reignite the "Phoenix flame" and keep it alight for future generations of republicans; and this is, of course, exactly the purpose of such ceremonies.

## Reliving the end

The same motivation underlies the commemoration of the victims of the War of Independence that followed a few years after the 1916 Rising. The execution of the 1916 martyrs by the British authorities transformed a minority radical cause into a nationwide movement for independence. Growing popular unrest grew into the War of Independence in 1919, which lasted until 1921 and resulted in the signing of the peace treaty between Britain and Ireland that established the Irish Free State in 1922. The War of Independence created many more martyrs to the Irish nationalist cause, including the members of the Dublin brigade and the Four Courts garrison, and those held and killed in Mountjoy Prison by the British authorities, chief among them the young Kevin Barry, the 18-year-old University College Dublin medical student and Irish Volunteer.

In response to growing unrest, the British government had imposed the Restoration of Order in Ireland Act (ROIA) in August 1920, allowing the British authorities in Ireland to bypass the jury system of the civil courts by substituting courts martial run by British army officials in their place. These courts martial heard capital offences and the first conviction in this regard was Kevin Barry, who was used as an example to others of the harsh punishments now available to the courts under the ROIA. Barry had taken part in a raid on a British ration party, which was collecting bread for its barracks at Monk's Bakery on 20 September 1920. The attack went wrong and three British soldiers were killed, one from particularly gruesome wounds resulting from the use of flat-nosed bullets. The rest of the raiding party escaped but Barry was caught hiding under the lorry and was captured.[20] Barry was tried and found guilty, but rather than fighting the charge he refused to recognize the jurisdiction of the court and echoed Wolfe Tone's stance in his refusal to recognize the legitimacy of the British government. He was found guilty and sentenced to death by hanging. Appeal for clemency were rejected by the British authorities on the grounds that Barry's guilt was clearly established, that he was not much younger than any of the three British soldiers, and "for the sake of example, given 'that it was precisely young and irresponsible men of this type who were the main cause of the present disturbance in Ireland.'"[21] General Macready wanted to demonstrate that it was possible to bring the IRA to justice through legal means under the ROIA, which meant going ahead with Barry's execution no matter what. His death was marked in masses all over the country and is remembered in nationalist ballads. Thus Kevin Barry passed into republican folklore as another martyr who sacrificed his life for Ireland.

The *Amharc Éireann* series captures a key moment in the rebirth of the Republican nationalist mythology surrounding Kevin Barry. On the fortieth anniversary of his execution, University College Dublin students

20  John Ainsworth, "Kevin Barry, the Incident at Monk's Bakery and the Making of an Irish Republican Legend" *History* 2002, 87 (287), pp. 373–87.
21  Ainsworth, p. 377.

marked his death in pilgrimage fashion by marching in his honour to the site of his death, Mountjoy Prison. "UCD students honour Kevin Barry"[22] records what would become an annual commemoration by the students and is the first of three such films in the *Amharc Éireann* series. The film opens with a close-up shot of the flower wreath with a card addressed to Barry attached, then pans out to a crowd of students approaching, carrying similar arrangements as they parade down the street. They stop at the General Post Office, the centre of the 1916 Rising, gathering in front for a silent "honour break" and holding tall flag poles with the Irish flag. They then march to Mountjoy Prison, where Barry was held and later hanged. Two students approach the front entrance, where they get permission to leave flowers at the young martyr's grave. That they were granted permission to enter Mountjoy Prison and visit the grave is extraordinary. Once the violence began in the North in the early 1970s, this type of potentially inflammatory action would never have been allowed in the Republic.

Two later films, both entitled "Kevin Barry remembered,"[23] record the then-established annual commemoration of Barry's death in similar fashion, following the students' journey as they march from the university through Dublin city to the General Post Office. In each case, students are allowed into Mountjoy prison to lay a wreath at the place where Barry died. The students' march to Mountjoy is represented as a pilgrimage, in which the laying of the wreath at Mountjoy is the final destination and perhaps a means to make up for the fact that Barry's family and friends were not allowed to attend his funeral when he died. The ritual is thus a corrective action to compensate for the events that took place in 1920.

The filming of this annual event is an important addition to the nationalists' catalogue of events, in that it involves the youth of the early 1960s. While all the other films on national commemoration feature the aging veterans of the revolution, the Kevin Barry remembrance is presented as a means for the Irish youth to express the significance of his martyrdom

---

22   "UCD students honour Kevin Barry" #78: 2 December 1960.
23   "Kevin Barry remembered" #179: 3 November 1962; "Kevin Barry remembered" #231: 2 November 1963.

to them as well. Thus the revolution and its heroes are not confined to the geriatrics – rather, it is embraced and commemorated by the new generation of leaders as well, and will be constantly renewed in this fashion with each new cohort of UCD students. The visibility of this active re-birth and renewal of republican nationalist sentiments must have been a gratifying sight for those viewing such events of the continuing strength of the sacrificial tradition – and a disturbing reminder for others of the power of this ongoing re-opening of old wounds in an era of supposed reconciliation.

The theme of martyrdom is continued in "Mountjoy Prison: President unveils memorial to patriots,"[24] to mark the unveiling of a memorial to Barry and another nine men hanged in Mountjoy Prison during the War of Independence. These men are now known as "the forgotten ten,"[25] as their names subsequently disappeared into history, only to resurface in the 1960s in the context of preparations for the 1966 celebrations of the fiftieth anniversary of the 1916 Rising. In 1960, Sean Kavanagh, the Governor of Mountjoy Prison, wrote to Oscar Traynor, the Minister for Justice, asking on behalf of the prison staff for permission to erect a memorial to Barry and the other nine men hanged in Mountjoy and in 1961 the government decided to erect the memorial.

The film records the unveiling of a memorial to those hanged for their alleged part in ambushes or attacks on British forces in Ireland as part of the guerrilla warfare tactics that characterized the War of Independence. On 8 October 1961 the ceremonial unveiling took place for the memorial to the ten "forgotten" martyrs. Of the ten, only four actually took part in attacks (Barry, Flood, Traynor, Foley) and of these, only two (Barry and Traynor) were armed. Moran and Whelan were innocent of the charge of having taken part in the Bloody Sunday attacks orchestrated by Michael Collins' "Squad" of assassins on 20 November 1920, in which 14 of Britain's "Cairo gang" of intelligence officers were killed. Some were certainly innocent,

24    "Mountjoy Prison: President unveils memorial to patriots" #124: 20 October 1961.
25    The 'forgotten ten' are Kevin Barry, Thomas Whelan, Patrick Moran, Patrick Doyle, Bernard Ryan, Frank Flood, Thomas Bryan, Thomas Traynor, Edmund Foley and Patrick Maher. See Tim Carey, *Hanged for Ireland: the 'forgotten ten' executed, 1920–21: a Documentary History* (Dublin: Blackwater Press, 2001).

others were guilty, but technically, as political prisoners of war, they should not have been hanged. Nevertheless, under the ROIA they were sentenced to die as criminals guilty of treason to the British king, and to be buried in the Patriots' Plot in Mountjoy prison.

The film simply records the Fianna Fáil government's ceremony, which echoes the traditional republican rejection of the British government actions in Ireland during this period. A shot of the exterior of the prison is followed by one of the men with medals. De Valera inspects the honour guard as the commentator instructs the viewers to think about the part played by Mountjoy Prison on this occasion of the president's visit to the location. Once again the audience is being instructed to reflect on the past, to re-open the old wounds inflicted on the Irish by the British. De Valera visits the grave where the ten men's remains were buried together and unveils a large cross that stands in their honour. In his speech that day, de Valera said:

> This is sacred ground. Here the bodies of ten young soldiers of the Army of the Republic who, 40 years ago, gave their lives and all that those lives promised, in order that the nation might survive and be free. The older ones amongst us here remember the universal anguish when these young lives were taken, but the pride, too, that the ruthlessness of the enemy was unable to break the spirit of our people.[26]

Instead of simply making peace with the past, his words are a reminder of the pain and suffering endured by the Irish republicans in the conflict. While the event might be seen in some senses as a positive, cleansing and unifying national commemoration, in another it was an incitement to anger in the present. It reflects the continuing dominance of the hard-line republican narrative of Irish history, with de Valera himself serving as a constant reminder of the past. However, there were even in the context of commemorations such as this one, reminders that the dominant narrative was not equally and necessarily shared by all – not even by some of the victims' families. When the "forgotten ten" were later re-interred on 14 October 2001, the family of Patrick Maher requested that rather than

---

26  Quoted in Carey, p. 188.

have his remains interred in Glasnevin cemetery with the rest of Ireland's heroes he be buried at home in Ballylanders, Co. Limerick.[27]

The Bloody Sunday attacks for which some of the "forgotten ten" were punished provoked an unofficial and unacknowledged response from Britain. In "Dublin Castle: Dublin brigade volunteers honour executed comrades,"[28] the former members of the Old IRA. The Auxiliaries had retaliated that same night by killing three men in their custody, Dick McKee, Conor Clune and Peadar Clancy. The film opens with martial music and a full shot of Dublin Castle – the old centre of British administration in Ireland – setting a rather grim scene. De Valera is first seen arriving for the ceremony. The Old IRA men, wearing long overcoats and armed with rifles, march solemnly toward the castle entrance holding the Irish flag, as the commentator recites the names of the three men who are being remembered here today: Dick McKee, Peadar Clancy, Conor Clune. As is the case with all of these films on national commemorations, there is no explanation of who these men were or the event that is actually being remembered. Rather, it is assumed that the audience is still sufficiently close to the events – a full forty years later – that no such explanation is necessary; that the audience will understand that McKee, Clancy and Clune were the three men in custody who were killed by the Auxies in retaliation for the Bloody Sunday operation conducted by Michael Collins' men. It is telling, too, that no mention of Collins himself is made. The Dublin Brigade took part in the guerrilla war directed by Collins while de Valera was in the United States but in the government's commemoration ceremony no reference is made to Collins.

A close-up shot follows of the sculpture over the entrance of King's Chapel of a hand holding a large key. Inside the church people kneel at the pews while the priest says mass. A shot of a flag, embroidered with the words "1916–21 Dublin battalion, Oglaigh na hEireann", referring to the Old IRA, the Irish Volunteers who are here today to commemorate their

27   Carey, p. 195.
28   "Dublin Castle: Dublin Brigade volunteers honour executed comrades" #129: 24 November 1961.

executed comrades. Outside again, the men are pictured lined up in formation, alternating with a shot of another flag, this time reading "IRA Association, 4th battalion, Dublin brigade." The men in formation then shoot their rifles in the air in a unified salute. De Valera is pictured looking up to the sky as they shoot, captured as he presumably ponders the fate of his lost comrades. The three names are repeated once more – Dick McKee, Peadar Clancy, Conor Clune – as the sight of the Old IRA men in their gun salute is followed by a shot of the medals on the men's overcoats.

These Old IRA men are the remaining heroes of the War of Independence. The sense is that for them and for de Valera, the event being commemorated could have taken place only yesterday. The solemnity with which the memorial service is held, the ritualistic gun salute, the marching Irish Volunteers, all call to mind the film on the return of the Asgard to Howth Harbour, in which the Old IRA men and women are extremely earnest in their participation in the event. There is no hint of cynicism or hesitation on the part of these old Volunteers – if anything, they appear to take their role more seriously than ever, as reminders for the next generation of the conflict that they still remember so clearly.

## Reinforcing the split

The War of Independence ended with the signing of the Anglo-Irish Treaty on 6 December 1921. Sadly however, after signing the treaty Irish nationalist politicians and the army split between pro-Treaty and anti-Treaty forces, with de Valera and his hard-line republicans on the anti-Treaty side[29] and the more moderate Free State supporters of the Treaty, including Michael Collins and Arthur Griffith, on the other. This, then, is a crucial period for Irish republican history, which saw the formerly united nationalists split into two armed camps. In June 1922 the Irregulars stepped up their

---

29    This group was known as the "Irregulars."

opposition to the pro-Treaty government and occupied the Four Courts, the centre of the legal system in Ireland. They thus imitated the doomed strategy adopted by the Irish Volunteers and the Irish Citizen Army when they occupied the General Post Office and other key buildings in April 1916, apparently learning nothing from that stunning failure in military tactics. After a couple of days of delay on the part of Collins' Free State forces, who were reluctant to fire upon their erstwhile nationalist comrades, the Civil War began in earnest with the firing on the Four Courts on 28 June 1922 by the pro-Treaty forces. Eight days later, the Four Courts garrison surrendered and two hundred anti-Treatyites were taken prisoner by the Free State government forces. For the next decade, a moderate government led Ireland and outlawed the IRA, which then went underground, but in 1932 de Valera's Fianna Fáil party took office, marking the beginning of an almost uninterrupted tenure as *Taoiseach* until 1959 (with the brief exception of two Inter-Party Governments in 1948–51 and 1954–57) when Lemass replaced him and de Valera became President. Thus the memory of the Civil War and of the Four Courts garrison being presented here in the *Amharc Éireann* films is very much a Fianna Fáil one, a republican version of events.

"Four Courts garrison: 42nd anniversary"[30] records a commemoration of the battle and the deaths of Rory O'Connor, Liam Mellows, Richard Barrett and Joseph McKelvey. The four were executed on 8 December 1922, in reprisal for the assassination by the anti-Treaty forces of Sean Hales, and are thus the martyrs to the Irregular, anti-Treaty, Republican side of the Civil War. While the earlier films commemorate the nationalist martyrs from 1798 to 1922, once the country split in the aftermath of the Treaty, it was apparently only the Republican martyrs that counted. Unlike the "forgotten ten," who are the "entire" nation's heroes from the War of Independence, "Rory, Liam, Dick and Joe" are the martyrs to the Republican side of the Civil War, the only side commemorated by the state at this juncture and the only side recorded in the *Amharc Éireann* series.

30  "Four Courts garrison: 42nd anniversary" #184: 8 December 1962.

This film opens with a shot of the familiar exterior of Dublin Castle followed by the interior of the King's Chapel and the congregation inside as the commentator introduces the event. The same location and the same sequence of events are used as in the commemoration for the victims of the War of Independence, reinforcing the fact that despite the 1922 split between moderates and hard-line republicans, in 1960s Ireland republican mythology was still the predominant version of Irish nationalist history. Outside the chapel after mass, Lemass stands with other Civil War veterans including Kevin Boland and Todd (C.S.) Andrews. Lemass and Andrews are both wearing their medals. Kevin Boland, a hard-line republican himself, is representing his father, Harry Boland, who was shot attempting to escape from the Grand Hotel in Skerries on 31 July 1922 and later died on 2 August in hospital. Todd Andrews was Ernie O'Malley's clerk in the Four Courts and was wounded while fighting in Dublin. Lemass, for his part, was Captain Adjudant of the Four Courts garrison. Having escaped from Jameson's Distillery, where he was held after its surrender, he became Director of Communications from July 1922, but was captured in December and imprisoned before being released in December 1922. The scene of Dublin Castle and the soldiers-turned-politicians closes with a shot of one of the towers of Dublin Castle, reinforcing the Castle's significance as a symbol of captivity and authority.

The event resumes at Glasnevin cemetery, announced by the opening shot of the familiar round tower standing inside the high walls, from the gates. Glasnevin cemetery is situated two and half miles from Dublin city centre and is the resting place of numerous national heroes, many of whom spent time in Kilmainham Gaol, including O'Connell, Parnell, Collins and many others. The O'Connell Tower was built in 1847 as a memorial to honour Daniel O'Connell, the constitutional nationalist responsible for bringing Catholic Emancipation to Ireland in 1829 and the founder of the cemetery. Interestingly, it was O'Connell's wish that the cemetery be non-denominational, a stance more in the tradition of Wolfe Tone's non-sectarianism that O'Connell's own brand of Catholic nationalism. Designed by George Petrie, the antiquary, it rises 160 feet and dominates the entrance area of the cemetery. The opening shot of the round tower is thus not only instantly recognizable to Dublin viewers, serving to locate the next scene of the film, but more importantly, refers viewers back to an earlier "Liberator" – if not a specifically Republican one – than those being celebrated here.

Veterans walk in carrying the Irish flag and a wreath is laid for the four dead men, followed by shots of gravestones and inscriptions which read: "Pray for Joseph P. Dowling, Casement Brigade, 1916–18, Died August 1st 1932" and "Cathal Brugha 1922." At this point, the film conflates the heroes of the War of Independence with those of the Civil War. Joseph Dowling, a former member of Roger Casement's Irish Brigade, landed from a German submarine on 12 April 1918. The "German Plot" fabrication was conceived by this incident; the alleged communications between Ireland and Germany in April-May 1918 were used to justify wide-scale arrests and deportations. He was arrested, court-martialed and sentenced to life imprisonment, of which he served six years, and thus took no part in the Four Courts garrison or the Civil War. Cathal Brugha, on the other hand, was part of the anti-Treatyite Four Courts garrison, as well as a major player in the War of Independence. When the Dáil split after the debate on the Treaty in January 1922, Brugha, one of the most hard-line republicans and a vehement enemy of Michael Collins, went with de Valera. From this point onwards Brugha was thus associated with the republican Irregulars. In the Civil War, he ordered his garrison to surrender in O'Connell Street on 5 July 1922 but refused to surrender himself. He was shot and died two days later. Brugha is thus the symbol of republican intransigence – opposed to the Treaty, an enemy of Collins, and a hard-line republican to the bitter end. The shot of his grave following that of Dowling's serves to reinforce the narrative of the wronged Republican, be it by the British before 1922 or by fellow Irish after the split.

These graves both form part of the "Republican plot" at Glasnevin cemetery, located to the right of the O'Connell Tower, where the remains of many of those killed in the War of Independence and the Civil War were interred. The plot includes many other famous revolutionary nationalist names, including Thomas Ashe, John Devoy, Michael Joseph O'Rahilly, Jeremiah O'Donovan Rossa, Countess Constance Markievicz and Maude Gonne MacBride. Other earlier heroes include John O'Leary, the Fenian and journalist, and James Stephens, co-founder of the Irish Republican

Brotherhood. Thus, the shots of the gravestones at this occasion in Glasnevin cemetery are not specifically referring to the republicans lost in the Civil War, but to all republicans, from the entire revolutionary period and its ancestors in the nineteenth century. The names mentioned evoke emotion and nostalgia, rather than to referring to a factual chronology of events or identifying the actual members of the Four Courts garrison and participants in the Civil War. It links the Civil War veterans to earlier martyrs, just as other films evoke the memory of 1798. This rather hazy representation of events, then, better suits the purpose of the series as a whole as by focusing on emotion rather than intellect, the purpose of commemoration is fulfilled.

The men in the crowd include flag-carriers and a trumpeter – the so-called "boys" of the brigade – and family members. The film ends by returning to the republican victims of the Civil War as the wreaths are laid by surviving members of the Four Courts garrison in memory of their lost "boys": Rory, Liam, Dick and Joe, referring to Rory O'Connor, Liam Mellows, Richard Barrett and Joseph McKelvey, whose grave is in Belfast. They are referred to only by their Christian names, once again assuming the viewers' familiarity with their names and relevance to Irish history.

The other side of the Civil War, the pro-Treaty forces, is only mentioned once in all of the *Amharc Éireann* films dealing with national commemorations and symbolic locations. Michael Collins and Arthur Griffith are the subject of "Collins and Griffith remembered,"[31] filmed again at Glasnevin cemetery. Collins was the leading figure in the War of Independence, as the President of the Irish Republican Brotherhood, leader of the Irish Volunteers and Minister of Finance in the first government. Collins is a celebrated figure now in Irish history but this was not always the case. Throughout de Valera's tenure as Taoiseach, very little was done in the way of commemorations in his name.[32] Arthur Griffith, the founder of the Sinn Féin party that won the December 1918 election

---

31 "Collins and Griffith remembered" #221: 24 August 1963.

32 Anne Dolan, *Commemorating the Irish Civil War, 1923–2000* (Cambridge: Cambridge University Press, 2003).

and constituted the first self-proclaimed Irish Government in January 1919, replaced de Valera as President of Dáil Éireann on 10 January 1922 after the split following the Treaty debate. He was the leader of the negotiating team in London, who along with Collins, signed the Anglo-Irish Treaty and brought the Irish Free State into existence. He died on 12 August 1922, just ten days before Collins was killed in an ambush by Irregular forces at Béal na mBláth (Mouth of Flowers), Co. Cork. Both men were thus giant figures in the history of Ireland and their noticeable absence from the *Amharc Éireann* films reflects the lack of activity on the part of the Fianna Fáil government to commemorate the state's heroes on the pro-Treaty side during this period. In the film, after mass in Dublin city a procession makes its way to their graves, where Professor Liam O'Brian leads the prayer at Collins' grave and Piaras Béaslaí lays a floral wreath at Griffith's. Béaslaí was a journalist who had served as Vice Commandant at the North Dublin Union during Easter Week 1916, as the Liaison Officer between the government Department of Publicity and IRA headquarters in 1919, and as the editor of *An t-Oglach* (The Volunteer). He helped draft the constitution for the first Dáil and was the IRA Director of Propaganda. He also wrote the first official biography of Michael Collins in 1926.[33]

This film is unusual in that it highlights the importance of the pro-Treaty or Fine Gael side of Irish nationalism, which is generally ignored in these overwhelmingly Republican films. In attendance at the memorial is W.T. Cosgrave, first prime minister of Ireland (as President of the Executive Council of the Irish Free State) from 1922–32. Cosgrave was ruthless in his defense of the state against the republicans and was never forgiven for the execution without trial of republican prisoners between November 1922 and May 1923, including Liam Mellows and Rory O'Connor, featured in the previous film commemorating the Four Courts garrison. Also present is his son Liam Cosgrave, Minister of External Affairs from 1954–57 (who went on to become Taoiseach from 1973–77), and General Richard

---

33   Piaras Béaslaí *Michael Collins and the making of a new Ireland* (Dublin: Phoenix Publishing Co., 1926).

Mulcahy, head of the Dublin brigade of the Irish Volunteers and Minister of Defence during the Civil War (1922–23). In that capacity he directed the fight against the anti-Treaty forces, introducing Special Emergency Powers on 10 October 1922, which gave enormous scope for suppressing anti-Treaty activities. General Mulcahy, Arthur Griffith, Michael Collins and W.T. Cosgrave were all, thus, very important names in Irish national history, but not names that Republican nationalists would have tended to glorify. In closing, the commentator begrudgingly notes that even after forty years, the memory of Griffith and Collins lives on and will for a long time to come, obviously avoiding the more personal and moving tributes that were given in the name of the Four Courts garrison members or the martyrs to the British during the War of Independence.

The *Amharc Éireann* series was first and foremost a cultural nationalist project, sponsored by an organization whose mandate was the promotion of Irish language and culture, and produced by a member of a family with strong republican ties. The representation of Ireland's political history in the *Amharc Éireann* series in terms of the apostolic succession of national martyrs and their sacrifice for the cause of freedom was entirely in keeping with republican mythology. While in other topics the series displays a progressive tendency in choice of topic and outlook, the representation of national commemorations and symbolic locations in 1960s Ireland is quite the opposite, recreating instead the traditional republican narrative of Irish political history.

It is unfair, however, to blame Ó Laoghaire or Gael Linn completely for this decidedly one-sided perspective. Although the choice of topics and the Irish-language commentary that accompanies the films was chosen by them, the events were staged – for the most part – by the state, so they are guilty only of mirroring state-sponsored events and failing entirely to address the glaring lack of balance in the representation of Ireland's national history. In this sense the makers of the films are guilty of perpetuating an image of Ireland as a backward-looking political society, more concerned with its revolutionary past than its present, rather than the reality of the Lemass era politics and economics. These films thus represent not only the contradiction that runs throughout the entire series, between a forward- and backward-looking nationalism that is not unique to Ireland, but perhaps more importantly, they reflect the ambiguous message being transmitted to the Irish public by the Fianna Fáil government itself, which is on the one hand seen to be embracing and directing political and economic change, while simultaneously trumpeting the old republican cause.

# CHAPTER FIVE

# Decolonization and diaspora

While in terms of national commemoration, Ireland was presented as a rather inward- and backward-looking place in the *Amharc Éireann* series, on the international stage it was quite the opposite. Ireland's transition "from independence to internationalism"[1] was an important element in the country's modernization process, which among other things meant active contribution to the work of international organizations. Ireland joined the United Nations in 1955 and was from the beginning a vocal member of the organization. As a former British colony and the first "post-colonial" nation, Ireland's UN representatives saw the country's role as an important one.[2] Irish involvement in the Congo crisis of 1960–64 represents an important chapter in the country's maturation process, which despite the tragedy of losing a number of Irish soldiers did not dissuade the government from sending forces to Cyprus shortly thereafter. The mood surrounding the Congo expedition is overwhelmingly hopeful, ambitious, and ultimately, naïve – while the few Cyprus films speak to an Irish population that had suffered the losses that peacekeeping work entails, and is much more focused on practicalities than high-minded ideals.

The other significant international element in the Gaelic News films is the growing importance of the American presence in Ireland, which is manifest in its influence on popular culture, as well as in state visits and the visibility of the United States ambassador in Ireland. It was during the Congo crisis that Ireland's increasingly western/American orientation

---

1   See Michael Kennedy and Joseph Morrison Skelly, eds, *Irish Foreign Policy, 1919–66: From Independence to Internationalism* (Dublin: Four Courts Press, 2000).

2   See Joseph Morrison Skelly, *Irish Diplomacy at the United Nations, 1945–65: National Interests and the International Order* (Dublin: Irish Academic Press, 1997).

became evident but it was President John F. Kennedy's visit and his death only six months later that prompted the nation-wide mourning that is reflected upon and recorded in the *Amharc Éireann* series.

Finally, the European presence in the Gaelic News films is a small but significant indication of the other direction in which Irish international relations were to head as the 1960s progressed. While Frank Aiken, and later Kevin Boland, concentrated on the United Nations, Lemass turned his attention to Europe. Ireland made its first application to the European Economic Community in 1961 and its second in 1966, before finally being admitted on its third attempt in 1973. Although the films make no reference to the application, they do note the relevance of the idea of European integration to Ireland during this period through their attention to the Common Market.

## The Congo crisis

The guiding principles of Ireland's foreign policy at the United Nations were a product of its own colonial history. The terms of Ireland's participation in the Congo mission (1960–64) and in Cyprus (1964–73) were determined by the country's national political tradition, which supported the two basic principles of self-determination and anti-partitionism in international affairs. The Congo crisis and the Cyprus conflict both involved the actual or potential partition of a country. In the Congo, the province of Katanga had seceded from the rest of the country, while in Cyprus the threat of Turkish intervention included the potential for an imposed solution in the form of partition of the island along ethnic lines. Ireland was, not surprisingly, supportive of the post-colonial nation's right to self-determination. In the case of the Congo this meant that Ireland, at least theoretically, supported the Congolese right to be free to conduct its own affairs independent of foreign, particularly Belgian, influence in Katanga. In the case of Cyprus, Ireland was predictably sympathetic to the Greeks rather than to the former colonial power, Turkey. Ireland opposed partition in both of these cases and supported the UN missions to re-integrate Katanga into the Congo and to prevent the division of Cyprus into two divided communities.

The *Amharc Éireann* series captures the extent of Ireland's military, diplomatic and psychological involvement in the Congo crisis. A sense of the magnitude of the Irish effort in the Congo is evident in the sheer number of films on the topic, which record the details of all arrivals and departures of troops, officials and diplomats. The Gaelic News reels express the feelings of excitement, loyalty and apprehension of those left at the "home front," celebrating the Irish troops' achievements with their families and, when tragedy strikes in Niemba in September 1961, mourning with them as one national family. A strongly anti-colonial theme runs throughout the series, which draws viewers' attention to the bond between Ireland and other newly independent African and Asian states. The accompanying Irish-language commentary repeatedly stresses Ireland's important role as a mentor to postcolonial nations that have much to learn from the country's experience as Britain's first ex-colony.

The Congo gained independence from Belgium in June 1960. This left the new government ill prepared for and unable to cope with the practicalities of governing a huge multi-ethnic state. With over 200 different tribes, there was no coherent sense of Congolese national identity; instead, regional and tribal identities were the norm. More importantly, the Belgians in the Congo refused to accept the implications of independence, that they would be replaced by Congolese in positions of authority. When the black "force publique", or Congolese National Army, mutinied against its white Belgian officers, Belgian paramilitaries were sent in to control the situation. In the midst of the upheaval, Tshombe, head of the most mineral-rich province, Katanga, declared independence from the Congo. Katanga was, however, in reality still controlled by Belgian financial interests and Tshombe was merely the stooge of the Union Minière company, a subsidiary of a larger Belgian group that maintained 80% of the costs of secession throughout the period. Thus, the Katanga secession was merely an attempt on the part of the Belgians to maintain control over the sources of wealth in the province.[3]

Lumumba, who had become the first Prime Minister of the Congo on 23 June 1960, requested aid from the United States but the reluctant Eisenhower administration quickly passed the problem on to the United Nations to solve. The UN issued resolutions on 14 and 22 July 1960 calling for troops to restore order to the area. Dåg Hammerskjöld, the UN Secretary-General, was strongly anti-interventionist and keen to create a multi-national force that would not be deemed threatening by the Congolese. Unfortunately, the issue of color never occurred to Hammerskjöld and the fact that the multi-national force was composed of all whites undermined the UN's objectives, as Lumumba objected strongly to a force devoid of Africans. The anti-colonial status of the US-backed UN mission was not entirely clear at the outset either, when it was supported by the pro-colonial and pro-Belgian Eisenhower administration. It was only once Kennedy replaced Eisenhower in early 1961 that American policy toward the Congo took on a distinctly anti-colonial stance, which in turn invoked European anger over what appeared to be a cover for the substitution of Belgian financial interests with American and Swedish ones.

As a non-aligned middle power, Ireland was believed to be well suited to lead the new nations in the UN because of its anti-colonial record and its neutral status.[4] The guiding principles of Ireland's foreign policy at the United Nations were a product of its own colonial history and the terms of Ireland's participation in the Congo mission from 1960 to 1964 were determined by the country's national political tradition. The Irish opposed partition and supported the UN missions to re-integrate Katanga into the Congo. Ireland was, not surprisingly, supportive of the post-colonial nation's right to self-determination in all senses. In the Congo, this meant that Ireland supported the Congolese right to be free to conduct their

3   See David Gibbs, *The Political Economy of Third World Intervention: Mines, Money and U.S. Policy in the Congo Crisis* (Chicago: University of Chicago Press, 1991).
4   See Nina Heathcote, "Ireland and the United Nations operation in the Congo," in *International Relations* 3, no. 11 (1971): 880–902.

affairs independent of foreign, particularly Belgian, influence in Katanga. The extent of Ireland's involvement in the Congo crisis was significant given its history of neutrality. The Irish forces contingent was out of proportion, both in terms of the numbers of forces contributed to the mission and the visibility of Irish figures in high places. The leader of the UN forces was General Seán McKeown and the representative of the UN Secretary-General Hammerskjöld in Katanga was Conor Cruise O'Brien.[5]

The first resolution requesting troops was issued on 14 July 1960. McKeown recalled his response to an urgent request that came for a battalion: "I was at first taken aback about the Congo: I was just wondering where the hell the Congo was for a start (like a great many other people, during the course of that particular Sunday)."[6] It appears that it was rather mundane factors that prompted the dispatch of Irish troops: "The emergency of the second world war was long over; we were living from hand-to-mouth, from day-to-day and from week-to-week, running courses and trying to keep our officers abreast of things. It was the sense of lack of purpose in our minds at the time that prompted me to say 'yes' to a battalion."[7] Special legislation was passed to send Irish troops abroad and the first battalion left thirteen days later, on 27 July 1960. The consequence of this urgent call for Irish troops was that there was very little time to prepare for the practicalities of the mission. There are a number of films on the departures of various battalions to the Congo, all of similar format and substance, none of which address any of the real problems they faced, including the lack of briefing on the political situation or appropriate uniforms for the climate. The uniforms were a public relations disaster but no negative publicity of this sort was included in the series. Instead, the mood depicted in the Gaelic News films surrounding the expedition is overwhelmingly hopeful and

---

5   His story is told in full in his memoirs: Conor Cruise O'Brien, *To Katanga and Back: a UN case history* (London: Hutchinson & Co., Ltd., 1962) and recounted in less detail in Conor Cruise O'Brien "The Congo (ONUC): the political perspective" in *Irish Sword* 20, no. 79 (1996): 37–42.

6   Sean McKeown, "The Congo (ONUC): the military perspective," in *Irish Sword* 20, no. 79 (1996): 43.

7   Ibid.

ambitious. Rather than calling attention to the understandable yet dangerous lack of preparation, the pomp and circumstance of the departures dominates coverage of the departure of Irish troops.

The first film on the crisis is "'Operation Sarsfield' gets under way,"[8] which records 350 soldiers being seen off by government ministers and other dignitaries, as well as hundreds of relatives and friends. Lemass is there as well to inspect the guard of honour before they board the planes that await them on the runway. The planes are donations from the United States, and the UN mission was overwhelmingly US-supported. A few weeks later, the number of soldiers departing has already doubled. In "Congo airlift: Taoiseach inspects 33rd battalion,"[9] General Bunworth, the Army Chief of Staff, is present with Frank Aiken, Minister of External Affairs and Kevin Boland, Minister of Defense, to inspect the 700 guards of honour that are leaving that day on another six planes.

Three months after the Irish troops arrived, nine of eleven of a platoon of Irish troops on routine patrol died in a Baluba ambush in Niemba and a tenth soldier went missing.[10] The Baluba were an educated minority in Katanga, persecuted because they posed a threat to Tshombe's regime. In the early stages of the Congo crisis the UN forces were ineffective in ousting the Belgians, which may have been construed by the Baluba as implicit UN support for Tshombe. When the Baluba saw the all-white UN force, of which the Irish were a part, they equated them with the Belgian mercenaries that the Irish were in fact there to oust. The issue of colour in the composition of the UN forces was a contentious one from the start. Lumumba was opposed to an all-white European-based UN force, favouring instead an African and Asian contingent. Due to the lack of foresight on the part of the UN, which had not considered the perception on the part of the Congolese of an all-white force, the Irish soldiers were placed in a dangerous situation. It was this case of mistaken identity that led to the

---

8    "Operation Sarsfield gets under way" #61: 5 August 1960.

9    "Congo airlift: Taoiseach inspects 33rd battalion" #64: 26 August 1960.

10   See Tom McCaughren, *The Peacemakers of Niemba* (Dublin: Browne and Nolan, 1966) for a first-person Irish propaganda/journalistic account of the Niemba ordeal.

ambush of the Irish troops in Niemba in November 1961, and was the first major lesson in the complexities of postcolonial peace-keeping for the Irish.

The deaths resulting from the Niemba ambush are covered in a news film entitled "Our Congo Dead,"[11] made on the occasion of the funeral for the nine servicemen, and recording the outpouring of grief and collective mourning in Dublin. While an active debate on the topic ensued in the newspaper press,[12] the *Amharc Éireann* series reverted to a tone of sacrificial martyrdom and the funeral provided the perfect opportunity for the type of glorification and commemoration of national heroes that it specialized in. The film is split into three parts: the arrival of the nine bodies at Baldonnel military airport and the mass; the parade of the dead in Dublin centre; and the funeral proper at Glasnevin cemetery. It reveals the sadness with which the Irish population greeted the news of their deaths and depicts the soldiers as national martyrs. The soldiers' deaths are described as yet another blood sacrifice in the same spirit as the 1916 Rising, the War of Independence and the Civil War, hammering home the message about Ireland's role as mentor to newly independent former colonies.

The film opens with a scene in a large garage or aircraft hangar at Baldonnel military airport, in which a lone soldier stands guard over the coffins of his nine dead comrades. It then switches to the interior of a church, showing the large congregation from the rear balcony. After mass the people file past the coffins, paying their last respects to the young soldiers. Next is the collective grieving of those in the streets of Dublin: A flag flies at half-mast from the top of the General Post Office and people line the streets to watch the procession of military men that precedes the coffins. The parade of the dead proceeds from the General Post Office at College Green, the site of the 1916 Rising and across from Trinity College, and down Dame Street before crossing the River Liffey, which divides north Dublin from south, then along O'Connell Street. The parade includes all of the major military representatives of Ireland, past and present. The coffins are draped with UN flags and the tricolour of the Irish Republic, followed

11  "Our Congo Dead" #77: 25 November 1960.
12  From 15–20 September 1961 in *The Irish Times*.

by trailers overflowing with flowers and wreaths. After the names and ages of the dead are recited, the music fades out and the commentary ends. Only the shuffling sounds of the mourners in Dublin remains, accompanied by the military band and rhythmic steps of the procession as it passes. The final phase is the burial of the coffins of the dead soldiers in Glasnevin for the military and family members. Approaching Glasnevin cemetery, the gates frame the tall round tower monument to Daniel O'Connell, Ireland's famous "Liberator."

As the military jeeps turn into the entranceway, the commentator proclaims: "After their long tiring journey of life the national martyrs are home to Glasnevin. Peace was their mission. Peace and friendship between blacks and whites. But a *misunderstanding* happened." This characterization of the ambush deliberately avoids the fact that the Baluba identified the white UN soldiers as colonial forces supporting the Katangese secession. The Baluba attacked what they saw as an enemy force in Niemba because they believed the Irish to be in league with the Belgian mercenaries.[13] Although the UN mission became officially anti-colonial with the new Kennedy administration in the United States, the Baluba presumably did not know the difference between an all white UN force that implicitly supported Tshombe, their persecutor, and an all white UN force a year later that did not.

The commentator encourages viewers to focus on forgiveness rather than vengeance: "We will forgive them on behalf of the nine who made a blood link between Africa and Ireland." This favorite theme of Irish nationalists – of the blood link, which recalls the original blood sacrifice that eventually gave birth to the independent Irish Free State – is broadened in order to extend the hand of friendship to a fellow post-colonial nation suffering the birth pangs of independence. The Congo is now divided after newly acquired independence in the same way that Ireland was during the Civil War over the terms of the Anglo-Irish Treaty. In this sense then, Ireland and the Congo are brothers as postcolonial nations, dealing with

---

13    See McCaughren for the Irish soldiers' accounts of Baluba perceptions that they were Belgians.

similar birth pangs of independence. In this sense, the loss of the Irish soldiers joins rather than divides the Congo and Ireland, both victims of international forces more powerful than themselves.

As a result of events like the Niemba ambush, there is a growing sense of the danger that the mission poses to the Irish soldiers in the *Amharc Éireann* news films. This is perceptible in the commentator's assurances to the cinema audience of the Irish troops' increased capabilities, and in his frequent references to their new personal weapons and clearly marked Irish/ UN uniforms. When the "3rd Congo airlift: 34th leaves"[14] in January 1961, the 700 Irish soldiers being seen off by Cardinal Haley and Kevin Boland are pictured with the shamrock insignia proudly displayed on their jackets. Viewers are assured that "each man is carrying a personal weapon, which did not happen before – it will no doubt give them protection and defense." This comment is obviously meant to reassure those at home that the Irish soldiers were being properly identified as friendly forces and equipped to defend themselves in the event of future attacks. Now armed, "they will follow the example of the heroes who went before them and they won't fail them or us." By the time that the "35th battalion leaves for Congo"[15] six months later, the group of 500 soldiers made up from Company A, B and C from all over the country are presented as experienced peacekeepers. In December 1961, the "Taoiseach reviews 36th battalion,"[16] accompanied by the priest who blesses the flag specially made for this tour of duty; by 1962[17] the Irish have been abroad for some time, and finally in 1964 yet another group of soldiers is at "McKee Barracks: Taoiseach reviews 2nd infantry group,"[18] this time under the supervision of Lt. Col. O'Sullivan.

Some films also feature civilians going to the Congo to support the troops. Before the ambush, in "Dublin: Red Cross doctors leave for Congo,"[19] Dr. Joseph Barnes is seen off by General MacSweeney and

---

14  "3rd Congo airlift: 34th leaves" #85: 20 January 1961.
15  "35th battalion leaves for Congo" #108: 30 June 1961.
16  "Taoiseach reviews 36th battalion" #132: 15 December 1961.
17  "Dublin: 38th battalion fly out" #180: 10 November 1962.
18  "McKee Barracks: Taoiseach reviews 2nd infantry troops" #232: 9 November 1963.
19  "Dublin Airport: Red Cross doctor leaves for Congo" #63: 19 August 1960.

Mrs. Hackett, the Vice-Chair of the Red Cross. Such volunteer work was not a novelty for Irish doctors, as indeed "Dr. Barnes has spent 12 years working in Africa already." This sort of work would have been seen as a continuation of the national tradition of missionary work that Irish civilians and priests had been carrying out in Africa for decades. Others went to the Congo to entertain the Irish soldiers, such as those featured in the film, "Irish entertainers leave for Congo,"[20] in which well-known figures in Irish entertainment, including Edmund Brown, Harry Bailey, Monica Bonnie, Jackie Farren and Dolly McMahon, one of the finest traditional singers in the country, set off to the Congo, where "no doubt they will be well-received in that wounded land." This sending of the Irish entertainers, as much as the peacekeeping mission itself, is a sign of the extent of Irish psychological involvement in the Congo. In mood and intent, it mirrors the accepted practice of other erstwhile wartime nations attempting to bolster their troops' morale by sending entertainers from home.

The Congo effort, then, is portrayed as a national one in every sense, and while the Irish population did not necessarily know what to expect from a UN peacekeeping operation, the country was certainly not shown to be half-hearted in its commitment. Troops and leaders returning from their six months in the Congo were greeted as national heroes. In the "Congo: 34th battalion return,"[21] three planes return after six months in the Congo. The men from Company A literally run down the gangplank off the plane, only to be restrained by a sharp grab on the sleeve by officers waiting on the ground. As each of four young soldiers introduce themselves to the nation and wave to the camera, the shot focuses again on the shamrock on their sleeves and the ONU decal, proudly displaying the Irish national emblem alongside that of the UN's Congo mission. The greatest reception, however, was reserved for General Seán McKeown, the leader of the UN forces in the Congo for a year and a half. In "General McKeown: his homecoming,"[22] the audience is treated to a glimpse of "Daddy" as he

---

20   "Irish entertainers leave for Congo" #146: 23 March 1962.
21   "Congo: 34th battalion return" #109: 7 July 1961.
22   "General McKeown: his homecoming" #148: 6 April 1962.

greets his wife and children, Frank Aiken, the Minister of Foreign Affairs, as well as media and photographers, all eager to get his stories. McKeown is presented as the father figure to the entire nation – a military leader to the young soldiers and a family man at home.

In February 1961, the Kennedy administration had backed a UN resolution that allowed for the use of force in order to remove the stubborn Belgian mercenaries backing up the Tshombe regime in Katanga. This political intervention in the internal affairs of a sovereign state explicitly violated UN values and brought about a distinct and controversial change in the character of the UN mission from peacekeeping to enforcement.[23] Ireland was directly involved in the consequences of the February resolution as Cruise O'Brien, seconded as personal representative to Hammerskjöld in Katanga, utilized the February resolution when he called on the UN to remove the Belgian mercenaries by force in September 1961. This use of force was a major gaffe in the UN mission and received much negative press. O'Brien was accused of acting on his own initiative, which he denied and "Dr. Cruise O'Brien arrives from New York,"[24] is the only film in which Irish concerns over the course of events in Katanga are even hinted at.

Shown arriving from the US on an Irish plane, Conor Cruise O'Brien was greeted by family, friends and Patrick Lynch, Chairman of the Board of Aer Lingus, and the media, which viewers are told only received a written statement. O'Brien then promptly "headed home to Howth but told everyone he would have lots to say," which certainly proved to be the case. In the film, the commentator refers rather obliquely to Cruise O'Brien's whistle-blowing and his initiation of military action against the Belgian mercenaries, saying simply that "Cruise is the big man famous throughout the world because of the fortnight he spent in the Congo" but adding, importantly, "He let the cat out of the bag regarding the hypocrisy of Belgian and French financial interests in Katanga." After being reprimanded by Hammerskjöld, Cruise O'Brien resigned from both the UN and the Irish diplomatic service

---

23    See Trevor Findlay, *The Blue Helmets' First War? Use of Force by the UN in the Congo, 1960–64* (Clementsport: The Canadian Peacekeeping Press, 1999).

24    "Dr. Cruise O'Brien arrives from New York" #132: 15 December 1961.

and recorded his grievances in his memoirs, *To Katanga and Back* (1966). David Gibbs has pointed to the veracity of Cruise O'Brien's accusations with regard to the financial interests as the motivating and driving force in the conflict over Katanga[25] but at the time he was assumed to have made a mistake in authorizing the use of military force to oust the Belgian mercenaries from Katanga. Although his public accusations of wrongdoing did not endear him to the Irish government, he went on to enjoy a distinguished career as a politician, academic and author.

The *Amharc Éireann* series took full advantage of all available opportunities to present Ireland's involvement in the UN system, and in the Congo crisis in particular, as a source of national pride and as inspiration for other former colonies. Indeed, most Irish politicians saw the UN mission as an opportunity to gain influence, increase the country's international prestige, and as a means of legitimizing the country's independent status by virtue of its participation within the UN system. The country's military leaders also saw participation as a unique and practical opportunity for the inexperienced Irish soldiers to gain valuable international experience in the field. As it turned out, the Irish got more than they bargained for in the Congo, as the glorious aspirations of national politicians and the naïveté and inexperience of the army personnel were rapidly rectified.

Even once things went downhill on both the military and diplomatic fronts, the series – in classic propagandizing newsreel style – fails to address the situation as it was, presenting instead an almost apolitical picture of Ireland's involvement. This refusal or inability to deal with the facts and details of the Congo situation is, however, entirely in keeping with semi-factual tone of the nationalist pride-boosting project of the *Amharc Éireann* series as a whole. Instead of criticizing the Irish effort, the films gloss over the disturbances and controversies that took place over issues such as troop preparedness and the disputed role of Conor Cruise O'Brien, focusing instead almost exclusively on the tremendous importance of the role that

25   See David Gibbs, "Dag Hammarskjöld, the United Nations, and the Congo Crisis of 1960–61: a Reinterpretation," in *The Journal of Modern African Studies* 31, no. 1 (1993): 163–74; Gibbs, 1999; Cruise O'Brien, 1966; and Cruise O'Brien, 1996.

Irish troops were playing for the UN mission. This rather proud representation of Ireland's role as a postcolonial peacekeeper and key player in UN
politics is very much in keeping with the tone of the *Amharc Éireann* series
as a whole, the purpose of which was to promote Ireland to cinema audiences at home. The amount of real international influence Ireland gained
from its involvement in the UN system, however, is another matter. While
at the outset, Ireland was justifiably proud of the independent position it
adopted as a relatively new, yet increasingly high-profile player, but by the
end of the Congo crisis, Ireland's position had moved from an independent, non-aligned and neutral stance in the early 1960s to a noticeably more
pro-Western, US-aligned position.

## The Cyprus conflict

Ireland learned its lesson from the military and diplomatic casualties it
suffered in the Congo crisis, so when the UN appealed for troops to go to
Cyprus in March 1964, the country was much more cautious in its response.
The Irish attitude to the Cyprus mission was determined by its experience
in the Congo, where they sustained significant military losses and dealt
with the political complexities of an ideological superpower rivalry and
the reality of European financial interests in Katanga. The descent along
the slippery slope from peacekeeping to enforcement was a journey that
Ireland did not want to repeat, and as a result, it asked for specific guarantees from U Thant, the UN Secretary-General, regarding the nature and
extent of its UN commitment. The Irish stance in Cyprus was similar to
its position on the Congo in one important respect, however, and that
was the country's adherence to the principles of self-determination and
anti-partitionism. This stance tended to make the country more sympathetic to the Greek than the Turkish cause and the Irish were afraid that,
as part of a UN mission in Cyprus, they might be compelled to enforce
partition. Lemass stressed that, if that were the case, Irish troops would be

withdrawn from Cyprus. The government also stressed that the UN force must be better equipped than previously, that it not be responsible for the enforcement of any political decisions, and that it be under UN control. To quell Irish fears U Thant produced two documents that placed limits on the UN force, stipulating that the Irish were only responsible for the prevention of the recurrence of violence, guaranteeing freedom of movement, and would use force only in self-defence.[26]

The Irish hesitancy borne of its Congo experience is evident in the Gaelic News films on the Cyprus mission. In "Curragh Camp: 40th battalion in training for Cyprus,"[27] 600 men from the Collins barracks are seen doing military exercises. This fact alone appears to be a significant advance from the complete lack of preparation the Irish troops had for their Congo mission. The training is practical for Cyprus and the soldiers obviously have an indication of the specific tasks they will be completing. Road blocks were a major source of stress in the Congo, as the Baluba regularly cut down thirty to forty trees on the road between one town and another, to slow the UN force's progress or halt it entirely. It was at these points that the Irish forces felt themselves vulnerable to attack from the Baluba hiding in the forest around them.[28] Although a different situation, this film acknowledges that the conflict in Cyprus is an inter-communal ethnic one, in which dealing with angry mobs was to be expected. "Another danger will be crowds like this one. You need training to handle a big crowd like this," says the commentator as a rather amusing Irish version of a menacing "Cypriot" crowd approaches the soldiers-in-training, brandishing broken bottles and pipes. The seriousness of the exercise is more than a little eroded by the fact that the crowd is laughing and hardly looks threatening, but the lessons of the Congo are clear: "Even though our boys are going on a peace mission it is possible that they will meet with violence – we learned that in the Congo." In the end, as always, confidence in the Irish soldiers prevails: "There's no

26    See Norman MacQueen, "Ireland and the United Nations Peacekeeping Force in Cyprus," in *Review of International Studies* 3 (1983): 95–108.
27    "Curragh Camp: 40th battalion in training for Cyprus" #254: 12 April 1964.
28    See McCaughren for accounts of the difficulties experienced by the Irish troops as a result of Baluba road blocks.

doubt that our soldiers will be standing at the mouth of danger but they are ready. They are a credit to us and have experience from the Congo."

The men are ready to leave for Cyprus a week later, in "40th battalion away."[29] All of the dignitaries are there and in recognition of the danger the mission poses to the troops, the new addition this time around is Panhard armoured cars from France. The UN force is again an international one, made up of soldiers from Sweden, Finland, Britain and Canada, as well as some Greeks and Turks. The name of the Irish camp is – significantly – Wolfe Tone, a reference to Tone's wish for peace among Irish Catholics, Protestants and Dissenters, and equally applicable in the Cypriot case to the Turks and Greeks as different ethnic groups sharing a common Cypriot identity. In a bizarre comment, perhaps meant to assure audiences that their troops would be more comfortable this time around than they were in their bull's wool uniforms in the tropics, the commentator mentions that "they have tax free goods available, so cigarettes and beer will be cheap" before returning to a more sober note, in which he reminds audiences that the soldiers' mission will be hard work. Now that viewers have witnessed the mixture of training, sensitivity and eagerness to hit the duty-free, the commentator closes with what can only be described as a cartoon-like gesture: "But no worries, the Irish army is on its way!"

## Diaspora

Irish support for postcolonial nations was expressed through more than military means in the early 1960s. *Amharc Éireann* news films on cultural events and state visits highlight the presence of the postcolonial diaspora in Ireland and draw attention to the status of their homelands as independent states. "The ancient dancers of India,"[30] featuring women in Indian dress

29   "40th battalion away" #255: 19 April 1964.
30   "The ancient dancers of India" #191: 26 January 1963.

performing traditional dance, the "Nigerian independence ball," "Malayan students celebrate 'Mardeska'" and "Malayan independence ball"[31] also remind Irish viewers of the value that other nationalities place on traditional culture. Each film opens with a shot of the Irish flag hanging alongside that of the newly independent nation, a sign of their mutual solidarity.

There were also examples of support for the colonies from everyday Irish people. A popular protest against the system of apartheid in South Africa is recorded in "Students stage boycott march,"[32] in which some three hundred university and college students participated from Trinity College Dublin, University College Dublin, Monalee College and the Vocational Schools. "They are out today because," the commentator states bluntly, "the black people in South Africa are not free." The blame for this situation is clearly placed on Ireland's former colonizer: "South Africa is still a colony of England."

This solidarity is expressed much more explicitly in the coverage of state visits by leaders of postcolonial nations – most clearly in "Ireland's warm welcome for Dr. Nkrumah,"[33] when the president of Ghana came to Dublin.[34] Africans and Irish, as well as Lemass and army personnel, are gathered at the airport to meet Nkrumah, who had been president since Ghana gained independence from Britain in 1956. At the Irish United Nations Society meeting, Nkrumah had spoken of African liberation movements and the example that Ireland had been on them, making an explicit reference to Ireland's role as mentor for newly independent African states. "Dr. Nkrumah said that Ghana's struggle for freedom had to some extent been

31  "Nigerian independence ball" #73: 28 October 1960; "Dublin: Malayans celebrate independence anniversary" #24: 20 November 1959; "Malayan students celebrate 'Mardeka'" #76: 18 November 1960; "Malayan independence ball" #128: 17 November 1961.

32  "Students stage boycott march" #37: 19 February 1960.

33  "Dr. Nkrumah in Dublin" #51: 27 May 1960. This script is in English.

34  Other state visits include Sukharno's, covered in "Prime Minister of Indonesia arrives in Dublin" and Khan's in "President of Pakistan in Dublin," during which he was brought, significantly, to see the 1916 memorial Garden of Remembrance at Arbour Hill, where he thanked Lemass for Ireland's readiness to help the UN regarding the Kashmir question.

influenced by Ireland's struggle. Dr. Nkrumah was a symbol of a struggle we Irish understand and for which we have sympathy. For Ireland, unique among the nations of Europe, shares common experience with the new nations of Africa!"

The commentary does not, however, dwell quite as much the statement Nkrumah made earlier that day to a group from the Association of African Students, when he reminded students that liberation in Ghana was about pan-African rather than national identity: "The Ghana constitution was unique in that Ghana was prepared to surrender her sovereignty, in whole or in part, for the greater good of the African people; no more do we think of Africa in terms of Ghana or Nigeria; we think of Africa as a continent." While the Gael Linn commentator is happy to publicize the positive influence of Ireland's experience on Ghana, he is less willing to apply this comment to the Irish case and take the comparison to its logical conclusion – that is, that Ireland might have surrendered its sovereignty willingly for the sake of all Irish people and thus avoided the violence in the North between Catholics and Protestants. For of course, as republican nationalists saw it, Ireland *did* in fact surrender part of its sovereignty when it agreed to the partition of the country in the Anglo-Irish Treaty of 1921. Thus the mutual influence of Ghana and Ireland was only useful, as Nkrumah himself said, "to a certain extent," because although Ireland's border issue was also a religious-ethnic issue, there was no greater "Africa" to speak of in the Irish case, there was only the island of Ireland. There was to be no giving up sovereignty because in Ireland's case it would not be to another Irishman but to the British, the former colonial power.

## The US presence

The ties between Ireland and the United States are another strong sub-theme in the Gaelic News films. These ties take a number of forms, including historic, commercial and diplomatic, and while the Americanization

of Irish culture is not perceptible at this stage, popular culture from across
the Atlantic is given attention in a small number of films. The high profile
of the American ambassador, who appears numerous times in films highlighting the ties between the two countries, makes the importance of the
American presence in Ireland for diplomatic and commercial purposes
crystal clear. Most striking, however, is the film about President John F.
Kennedy, which pays tribute to him as a son of Ireland.

American popular culture appears through the coverage of the odd
celebrity visit, such as when "Bob Hope visits Ireland"[35] to play golf, where
he was greeted by the US ambassador Grant Stockdale and his wife. The
latest dance craze is introduced in "Doing the Madison,"[36] which had taken
over from the Twist. From Hollywood, "Disney in Dublin"[37] records the
visit to promote the opening of *Darby O'Gill and the Little People*, in which
the requisite references to leprechauns and banshees are made, and Mickey
and Minnie Mouse are introduced in Irish as "an tUasal Mickey agus Minnie
MacLochlan." A number of tourist and holiday films feature American
visitors to Ireland, of which "US postman on goodwill visit"[38] is surely the
most odd. It features Bernard O'Connolly from Oakland, California, the
American postman who left his home three months previously to deliver
a goodwill message to the Irish Ministry for Posts and Telegraphs and to
learn some Irish on the way. Other visitors include "US students enjoying
Irish holiday,"[39] who are shown enjoying three weeks of camping and canoe-
ing in Co. Cork. Other visitors inspire Irish jealousy of American wealth,
such as the early film, "Luxury liner docks at Dublin,"[40] shown carrying
500 passengers to Dublin for a one-day visit en route to a tour of Europe.
When the "US coastguards visits Dublin,"[41] the ships are opened to thousands of Irish who are curious to get a glimpse of the big guns on board.

35   "Bob Hope visits Ireland" #127: 10 November 1961.
36   "Doing the Madison" #182: 24 November 1962.
37   "Disney in Dublin" #4: 3 July 1959.
38   "US postman on goodwill visit" #58: 15 July 1960.
39   "Co. Cork: US students enjoying Irish holiday" #63: 19 August 1960.
40   "Luxury liner docks at Dublin" #2: 19 June 1959.
41   "US coastguards visit Dublin" #264: 21 June 1964.

In each of these films, the sense is that the Americans are being shown the best side of Ireland so that they will be suitably impressed, while the Irish are clearly in awe of American success and wealth.

When the "New American embassy opened"[42] in May 1964 in Dublin, all of the government officials were out in force. There had been some controversy over the building, whose circular design prompted its description as an architectural monstrosity, but the commentary draws attention instead to the use of Connemara marble for its interior, praising the combination of the traditional and the modern in one building. Matthew McCluskey was retiring from the position of ambassador, soon to be replaced by Grant Stockdale, who arrived on a luxury liner in Cobh, Co. Cork with his wife and four children a month earlier, as featured in "Cobh: new American ambassador arrives."[43]

Most indicative of the Irish-American relationship in the Gaelic News films is the tribute paid to the American president in "JFK: 1917–63 – A Remembrance."[44] Irish ties to the United States are presented very personally through the figure of John F. Kennedy, the embodiment of Irish emigration during the Famine. The film is a compilation of footage from Kennedy's visit to Ireland six months previously, juxtaposed with shots of newspaper headings announcing his death and people receiving the bad news in Dublin. It emphasizes the contrast between the present danger in the United States and the safety he felt six months previously in Ireland, as if to drive home the message that Kennedy was better off in Ireland among his own ancestors than in the United States. Indeed, this was the opinion of the Irish security forces, who previous to his visit were concerned that the American press might take liberties common in the US but forbidden in Ireland.[45]

The film opens with a shot of Kennedy, followed by news headlines and people reading them. The next shots are flashbacks to JFK's visit. "It was only

42 "New American embassy opened" #260: 24 May 1964.
43 "Cobh: new American ambassador arrives" #102: 19 May 1961.
44 "John F. Kennedy, 1917–63 – A Remembrance" #234: 23 November 1963.
45 Ian McCabe, "JFK in Ireland," in *History Ireland* 1, no. 4 (1993): 39.

six months since he visited. We welcomed him heartily – was he one of our own?" An extra stop was added to JFK's tour of Ireland at Limerick, once it was discovered that his ancestor had visited the Fitzgeralds in 1938.[46] The closeness of the contact between the president and Irish public is empha-sized in the shots of him being greeted at the airport by crowds of people and shaking hands with him. Returning to the present, the next few scenes are of flags at half-mast in Dublin and a shot of Lemass with JFK boarding a helicopter going to New Ross, where he spoke to the crowds, followed by a photograph that appeared in the papers of him being kissed by an Irish woman. JFK's visit to New Ross was a homecoming of sorts, where he visited his second cousin once removed for tea. The informality of the meeting was said to have touched Irish and international audiences.[47] As well as the visual juxtaposition between danger now in the United States and the safety six months ago among the people of Ireland, the language throughout the film stresses JFK's identity as "one of us" and celebrates him as the living embodiment of the historic connection between the USA and Ireland. "Six months previously there was jolliness and hand-shaking. He brought the modern world to us but it was the old world he sought." Returning to the present, the film shows the photograph of JFK in the car where he was ambushed, followed by his funeral. "How could such a thing happen? What sense or meaning did it have? A man who was respected throughout the world, north and south, a man who brought reason and intelligence to world affairs, a man who gave hope for justice and rights, who spoke loudly for what he believed in but who also understood the other man's causes." JFK is shown in the Four Courts and in Dublin city streets, always smiling, shaking hands, connecting with people; then at the Arbour Hill memorial to the 1916 revolutionaries, laying wreaths for the martyrs. "Yes, he had the respect of the world but we had a special love for him. He understood us too. We'll never know what he might have achieved but we'll treasure his visit. He paid attention to what he saw in Ireland. He was proud of our history and our literature." Finally returning to present,

46   Ibid., 42.
47   Ibid., 41.

the film closes with shots of men looking at the photograph of the face of JFK that opened the film and these emotional words: "Yes, the Fitzgerald Kennedy son came among us and we'll remember him as long as we live. May the Lord have mercy on his noble soul!"

## Europe

Europe does not figure largely in diplomatic terms in the series, but some films showcase cultural and artistic events, such as the "Swedish ceremony of light" and "Old Nordic feast: 'Santa Lucia' visits Ireland."[48] Others deal with industry and technology, where trade with the Continent is important in the context of the growing Common Market. The only significant coverage of political events on the Continent is by way of "Dublin: 'Berlin Wall' exhibition,"[49] which comments on the events taking place in Germany. This film was made in 1962, at the height of the anti-communism that was soon to be exacerbated by the Cuban Missile Crisis. Ireland helped the United States, by insisting on the inspection of Soviet planes before leaving Shannon airport. The exhibit at the Goethe Institute consists of pictures of children and old people trapped behind the barbed wire dividing the city, while the commentator freely expresses his sentiments: "The display shows the barbaric wall made by the communists in the city of Berlin. Young and old have to spend their lives in a military state." Shots follow of soldiers on patrol in Berlin and crowds of people out in the streets in protest. "There have been protests but the wall still stands in the centre of the city. The damage is done and will last a long time." Again, the Irish objection to partition of any sort is made clear.

48 "Swedish ceremony of light" #238: 21 December 1963; "Old Nordic feast: 'Santa Lucia' visits Ireland" #30: 1 January 1960.
49 "Dublin: Berlin Wall exhibition" #156: 1 June 1962.

Although Ireland lodged its first application to join the European Economic Community (EEC) in 1961, there is no mention of this at all in the Gaelic News films. The application was shelved along with the British one thanks to de Gaulle's veto but the lack of coverage is more likely a reflection of the fact that many Irish nationalists tended to be opposed to Irish membership of the EEC. Just as the films tend to ignore the reality of partition in the North, they also ignore the political implications of European integration for Ireland. There is an awareness of the growing importance of the Common Market to Ireland but this appears – not surprisingly – more in the context of industry than international diplomacy. The only acknowledgement of the importance of the Common Market occurs in "Dublin: Mr. Aiken attends economic conference,"[50] in which Frank Aiken, Minister for External Affairs, is seen with Walter Hallstein, the president of the European Commission. European integration at this stage was strictly economic, and although it was in the early 1960s that extension of cooperation to include the political sphere was being considered by EEC members via the Fouchet Plan, this would not have been seen as particularly relevant to the average Irish citizen at this point.

Britain and Canada also appear very rarely in the Gaelic News films, unsurprisingly given Gael Linn's "Ireland for the Irish" mandate. Britain is only mentioned in the reporting of the arrival of new ambassadors to Ireland[51] and in "Lord Mayor of London visits Dublin,"[52] on the visit of Frederick Hoare to Ireland. The latter was unlucky enough to be overshadowed somewhat by the coincidence that Peter Ustanov, the famous actor, was also on the plane, which prompted the photographers' interest – and presumably the Irish audience's too – much more than Hoare's arrival. The dignitaries were brought on the same tour that "Princess Rainer and Princess Grace in Ireland"[53] were treated to – a visit to the National Stud Farm and the Japanese Gardens – apparently the staple "show-off" tour

50   "Dublin: Mr. Aiken attends economic conference" #8: 31 July 1959.
51   "Dublin Airport: British and Japanese ambassadors fly in" #245: 8 February 1964.
52   "Lord Mayor of London visits Dublin" #145: 16 March 1962.
53   "Prince Rainier and Princess Grace in Ireland" #106: 16 June 1961.

for non-political dignitaries (in comparison to the Arbour Hill memorial site for the sympathetic post-colonials and Americans). Canada also makes a very brief appearance in the "Prime Minster of Canada arrives in Dublin,"[54] which features Diefenbaker breezing through, en route to England, and "Dublin: Canadian fleet in,"[55] featuring Canadian sailors on the HMS Lauzon Atlantic 1944 who were in Dublin for just a week and allowed the public onto the boat in the same way that the Americans did. But Britain and Canada are very obviously not presented in the series as friends to Ireland in the way that the United States and postcolonial African and Asian nations are.

Although Ireland's visibility in the international arena was greatly increased due to its activities on behalf of the UN in the early 1960s, by 1964 Ireland was identified much more closely with the United States. Although Europe was very much in the minds of some Irish politicians and economists during the early 1960s, it barely makes an appearance in the *Amharc Éireann* series, despite the fact that Ireland submitted its first application for EEC membership during this period – and received its first rejection. The focus is clearly on postcolonialism and the re-orientation of Irish international policy towards other members of the British Commonwealth.

54 "Prime Minister of Canada arrives in Dublin" #92: 10 March 1961.
55 "Dublin: Canadian fleet in" #164: 27 July 1962.

President John F. Kennedy leaving the US Embassy in Dublin after a meeting with Taoiseach Seán Lemass. 27 June 1963.
*Reproduced with permission from the Irish Photo Archive.*

# CHAPTER SIX

# Industry, urbanization and architectural heritage

The over-arching theme of the entire *Amharc Éireann* series is progress, modernization and national growth. The beginning of the Gaelic News phase of the series in 1959 coincided with the reign of Seán Lemass as Taoiseach (1959–66), and the launching of the first Programme for Economic Expansion, covering the years 1959–63.[1] This period brought the formal end of protectionism in Irish economic policy, which had lasted since 1932, and the beginning of more outward-looking policies that accompanied the "take-off"[2] in modern Irish industrial development. The 1961 application to the European Economic Community (EEC) began the move toward free trade, which would begin officially with the Anglo-Irish Free Trade Agreement of 1965 and continue after Ireland joined the EEC in 1973 as part of the common market. The first programme focused on productive investment in Ireland and the inducement of foreign investment by way of a zero rate of corporation tax on exported goods.[3] Foreign companies were only allowed to manufacture within Ireland for export, so as to prevent

---

1   See Brian Girvin, *Between Two Worlds: Politics and Economy in Independent Ireland* (Savage, Maryland: Barnes and Noble Books, 1989); J.J. Lee, *Ireland, 1912–85* (Cambridge: Cambridge University Press, 1989); Garret FitzGerald *Planning in Ireland: a P.E.P. Study* (Dublin: Institute of Public Administration & London: Political and Economic Planning, 1968).

2   See John Kurt Jacobsen, *Chasing Progress in the Irish Republic: Ideology, democracy and dependent development* (Cambridge: Cambridge University Press, 1994): chapter 4.

3   See John Bradley, "Changing the Rules: Why the Failures of the 1950s Forced a Transition in Economic Policy-making," in *The Lost Decade: Ireland in the 1950s* (Cork: Mercier Press, 2004): 105–17.

competition with domestic producers and in order to aid Ireland's balance of trade, thus preventing further balance of payments crises.

While measures taken earlier in the 1950s had already indicated a change in policy direction under the second Inter-party Government, the continuing existence of the Control of Manufactures Act, as well as bureaucratic lack of vision, had hindered concrete development. During the period of the first programme, these controls were relaxed and then removed entirely, and it was due to the rapid growth in manufacturing and industry that the country hit a 4% growth rate for the period, twice the target figure. It has been stressed that it was not so much the content of the first programme that was responsible for Ireland's dramatic economic turnaround, which was also attributable to international trade patterns, but rather its psychological impact. The setting of specific targets, such as the 2% growth rate in four years, was more motivating than previously vague advice about tightening belts and living frugally. The Gaelic News film coverage of various aspects of Ireland's industrial development during this period can only have increased this positive psychological impact on Irish viewers. Ireland's rapid economic growth was a major feature of the *Amharc Éireann* series, which focused on the wide range of national progress taking place as a result of state and foreign investment.

The name Sean Lemass has become synonymous with Ireland's economic development and nowhere is his influence on Irish affairs more obvious than in the promotion of national industry. He is omnipresent in these films, in the same way that de Valera is in those on the celebration of republicanism. Lemass appears time after time, at each and every event of any importance to the national economy – opening new factories, research facilities and industrial enterprises of various kinds, cutting ribbons and preaching the gospel of industrialization and progress. Government visibility in this context is logical as Ireland's is a mixed economy, in which state-sponsored (or semi-state) bodies form an important part of the public sector. The work of some of these state-sponsored bodies has already been seen, in the short documentary films on Bord na Móna (the Turf Board) and Bord Iascaigh Mhara (the Fisheries Board). In the news films that coincided with Lemass's time as Taoiseach, the role of the semi-state bodies is publicized more forcefully by sheer repetition, drawing attention to the energetic promotional efforts of the government. The makers of the *Amharc Éireann* series are clearly supportive of these efforts on the part of Fianna Fáil. Just as the nationalist commemoration films focused on the heroes of the so-called republican party, paying little attention to the legacy of Michael Collins, Arthur Griffith or General Mulcahy, the films on industry focus on efforts of Fianna Fáil in office. Many of these films thus function as quasi-government publicity films, highlighting the rapid progress that is underway thanks to the work of the semi-state bodies. They pay only minimal attention to private enterprise or to the fact of foreign investment, although this reality is implicit in many of the films. Instead, the series consistently underlines the nation-state's contribution to development, through its attention to the quality of Ireland's resources and the state-sponsored bodies that support industrial growth.

The representation of events in the North of Ireland is dramatic as well, but in a completely different way. The shipping industry, once the cornerstone of the Northern economy, now appeared to be on an inexorable path to decline as the shipyards of Harland and Wolff suffered the effects of sporadic contracts and underemployment, resulting in worker unrest. In contrast, the airline industry in the Republic was literally taking off, fueling growth most spectacularly in the tax-free development area around the Shannon airport, as well as the building of a new regional airport in Cork. The Shannon Free Airport Development Company was the success story of the decade, building upon the success of the tax-free airport. Other Irish industries were prospering too, including one of the more potent national symbols, the Guinness brewery, and the service and hospitality industries in general. This highlighting of Ireland's successes and failures in geographical terms thus draws attention to the reversal of fortunes in the North and in the Republic. But surprisingly, in spite of these reminders of the relative decline in Northern industry, the series does not in fact acknowledge partition at all. "Ireland" refers to the entire island, and events and locations highlighted in the films are not mentioned as being part of the North or the Republic, but are simply part of Ireland as a whole. This refusal on the part of the filmmakers to acknowledge the fact of political partition is a strong, albeit silent, statement of their republican sympathies.

As with any success story, however, there are casualties and it was the role of *Amharc Éireann* to draw attention to what was lost as well as gained during the hey-day of Irish industrial growth. In the transport industry, the old regional railways lines were closed and the historic routes that they took were sacrificed in the name of economy and efficiency. Due to the rather one-sided emphasis on increasing productivity, the state chose to cut back its funding for social services and housing, thus ignoring the necessities of daily life for many of its citizens. The series also acted as the country's social conscience, paying unflattering attention to the darker side of Ireland's rapid industrialization and speaking up for Dublin's marginalized poor. The rise of Liberty Hall, Dublin's architectural symbol of progress, is mirrored by the collapse and demolition of numerous parts of old inner-city Dublin – in particular, some of the more notorious tenement housing areas as well as other, more precious buildings constituting the heart of Georgian Dublin. The disappearance of other key buildings symbolized the end of the lifestyle and culture of old Dublin, epitomized by the closing of the Theatre Royal – the old music hall, and the old Abbey Theatre – the best-known symbol of the late nineteenth-century literary and cultural revival. The Abbey was rebuilt but the Theatre Royal was gone for good. All of these changes are recorded and reflected upon in the Gaelic News films, providing a unique step-by-step visual chronicle of the decline and disappearance of old Dublin and its simultaneous replacement by the increasingly shiny, new, modern city.

## Openings, energy and exports

The perception of Lemass as the primary instigator of Irish economic growth is echoed in dramatic visual form in the Gaelic News films. His appearance in practically every film related to the state's economic development efforts creates the inevitable association of one with the other. Although agriculture made some progress in the context of the first economic programme, manufacturing exports were the main source of Ireland's economic growth in the early 1960s. New research and development initiatives were also part of this development. When Lemass was not present, another member of the Fianna Fáil government was, usually Erskine Childers or Michael Hilliard.[4] The films serve as a visual showcase of Irish progress, acknowledging the importance of international investment, but always emphasizing the superiority of the Irish contribution in terms of natural resources. This is the series' way of reconciling its nationalist tendencies with the reality of Ireland's outward-looking economic policies. The more open Ireland's economy became, the more susceptible it would become to the vagaries of the international economic climate, so it was important to continue to stress the unique and valuable nature of the Irish contribution to its own destiny.

The events for which the government delegates turned out were the official openings of various factories and industrial and commercial enterprises. In "Irish-American enterprise: opening of bubble-gum factory,"[5] Michael Hilliard and Richard Briscoe, the Lord Mayor of Dublin, were there with Scott McLeod, the American ambassador, for the opening of the factory in Kilcock. American corporations played a vital role in Ireland's transition from a largely agricultural economy in the 1950s to industrial status in later decades.[6] While the American contribution is acknowledged for the 30,000 pounds a year it generates in income for Irish farmers, the commentator is quick to point out the quality of the Irish product. As the camera focuses on McLeod chewing the gum, the commentator notes, "that's the Irish sugar that they are tasting, without a doubt." Comhlucht Siúicre Éireann Teo. (Irish Sugar Company Ltd.) was established in 1933

---

4  Throughout the 16th Dáil (from March 1957 to September 1961), Michael Hilliard was the Parliamentary Secretary to the Minister for Industry and Commerce (Sean Lemass). Erskine Childers was the Minister for Lands. Throgout the 17th Dáil (from October 1961 to March 1965), Michael Hilliard was Minister for Posts and Telegraphs. Erskine Childers was Minister for Transport and Power.
5  "Irish-American enterprise: opening a bubble-gum factory" #17: 25 September 1959.
6  Dermot McAleese, "American investment in Ireland," Chp. 14 in *Irish Studies 4: The Irish in America: Emigration, Assimilation and Impact* (Cambridge: Cambridge University Press, 1985): 329.

under the Sugar Manufacture Act. By 1959, Sean Lemass was able to boast that "in recent years, approximately 20,000 tons of sugar has been exported annually as a component of Irish-manufactured goods,"[7] which had far-reaching effects on the national economy. The company also conducted research on beet cultivation and processing, control of pests and weeds, and was engaged in experimental work on the reclamation and cultivation of bog land. Thus it had far-reaching effects in many areas of the Irish economy, and it was in the national interest to make sure that it was profitable. Schemes such as this bubble-gum factory would ensure that this would remain so.

In the film it is evident that for public perception the native product had to be seen to be the crucial ingredient in this recipe for Irish economic success. It was the Irish sugar that made the product what it was, not the American financial input; this was the means by which foreign investment in the national economy was made digestible to the national audience. It was quite clear that the policy of protectionism had not worked, but after decades of "sinn féin-ism,"[8] the opening of the Irish economy to foreign investment was presumably considered something that should be presented to viewers in the most positive light. As in the case of the early short documentary films, increasing investment from overseas in the early 1960s was presented merely as the catalyst for development, while it was the natural resources of Ireland that made the crucial difference in terms of quality.

While support for international investment in Ireland might not appear to mesh very well with the nationalist bent of much of the *Amharc Éireann* series, it is the involvement of the semi-state bodies that makes this development more palatable. The Irish mixed economy did not arise out of any sort of state socialism in the Soviet sense. Rather, as Lemass noted, it "developed in this country in a ... haphazard way to meet particular needs and opportunities as they arose, when no other course appeared

---

7    Sean Lemass, "The Role of State-sponsored bodies," in *Economic Development and Planning* (Dublin: Institute of Public Administration, 1969): 184.

8    "Sinn féin" is Irish for "ourselves" – it refers to the protectionist economic doctrine of self-sufficiency, in the sense of "ourselves alone" or "standing alone."

to be practicable. Industrial development in Ireland is based on private enterprise and the profit motive."[9] The priorities and concerns consistently expressed in the *Amharc Éireann* series similarly point to a very real sense of the importance of the national community, its needs and its ideals. By stressing the government's role in the economy, the fears of all-out free trade liberalism and its potentially harmful consequences for the Irish economy at this still vulnerable juncture are negated or at least minimized.

The role of Bord na Móna (the Turf Board) has already been discussed in the context of the "Eyes of Ireland" short documentary films made from 1956–59.[10] Events involving the role of state-sponsored bodies are also featured in Gaelic News films including a "Senators and TDs tour: Bord na Mona works."[11] The peat industry had been growing since modern techniques were imported with machinery beginning in the 1930s and was by this time very efficient, bringing in 1.5 million pounds worth of revenue per year. This film features a factory that produces briquettes rather than the milled peat featured in the short documentary film.[12] Milled peat was used to power the ESB's power stations, which in turn supplied power to the country and its industries, while briquettes were another form of domestic fuel, meant to replace either coal or wood in a fire. Since Ireland did not have a wealth of coal resources and had long since felled most of its forests, this import substitution of a domestically produced source of fuel was deemed vital by Lemass, who estimated that this would result in the avoidance of imports of other forms of fuel valued at 5 million pounds.[13] This film, then, shows the development of the peat industry to the extent that the technology is literally bringing the sod back into Irish homes again, but in new form and on a grand scale. Viewers are assured that the work done here and all over Ireland is "more than just a modern turf spade and wheelbarrow – our forefathers would be astonished at the change."

9   Lemass: 178.
10  See Chapter Two: Industrial and rural development.
11  "Senators & TDs tour Bord na Mona works" #114: 11 August 1961.
12  "Bua na Móna" (Milled Peat Production) #13: June 1957.
13  Lemass: 180.

Later, in "Co. Offaly: Bord na Mona briquette factory opened,"[14] Erskine
Childers opens the factory officially. Here, the use of turf in briquette form
for home-heating is illustrated and the commentator informs viewers that
the factory would produce 100,000 briquettes a year and provide employment for one hundred people, thanks to the growing market for this type
of fuel at home and abroad.

Between the 1930s and 1960, the growth in the energy contributions
of oil to Ireland's energy needs rose from 10% to 27%.[15] In "Co. Cork: An
Taoiseach opens Whitegate refinery,"[16] this is described as "a great step forward for industry." The Whitegate oil refinery was established in 1959 in Cork
Harbour, the only refinery in the country. The choice of location reflected
government policy, which favoured development outside of Dublin, as well
as other factors including local political influence and market distribution.
It was built by the Irish Refining Company, a consortium of Esso, Shell, BP
and Texaco, partly in response to government pressure on the oil companies
and partly as part of the tendency to locate refineries in market countries.
According to the film's commentator, the refinery's facilities were the most
advanced in Europe and cost 11 million pounds to build. It would, it was
claimed, produce 30,000 gallons of oil a day. When the "First tanker at
Cork refinery"[17] arrived, there was a crowd of dignitaries present for the
occasion, including Scott McLeod, the US Ambassador, and Jack Lynch,[18]
along with guards and drummers. The captain demonstrated the workings
of the machinery to the Lord Mayor of Cork, who then turned the wheel
to get the oil flowing ashore. Meanwhile, the camera switched to the rather
incongruous scene of a group of Indian sailors playing with another sort of
pipe – the traditional Irish uilleann pipes – who, viewers were told, "had

14 "Co. Offaly: Bord na Mona briquette factory opened" #126: 3 November 1961.
15 Desmond A. Gillmor, *Economic Activities in the Republic of Ireland: A Geographical Perspective* (Dublin: Gill and Macmillan, 1985): 82.
16 "Co. Cork: An Taoiseach opens Whitegate refinery" #17: 2 October 1959.
17 "First tanker at Cork refinery" trial issue: 5 June 1959.
18 Jack Lynch was Minister for Education from March 1957 to September 1961 (16th Dáil), and Minister for Industry and Commerce from October 1961 to March 1965 (17th Dáil).

their own tune"! This sort of bizarre and humorous touch at a completely unexpected and unrelated point in the films is a regular occurrence in the Gaelic News films, and was presumably another awkward attempt to make the films more interesting for cinema audiences.

"Co. Liex: open-coast mining with world's largest excavator"[19] shows the beginning of another new enterprise. The novelty is the engine that cost 4,000 pounds, stands at 25 feet tall and is capable of removing 4,000 tons of anthracite a year. The anthracite was, interestingly, destined for Continental and English markets – a noteworthy reversal of fortunes – and the mining venture employed some 150 men. The commentator notes disapprovingly that although this activity is very valuable to the country, "it gets no state grant" and is rather a private enterprise. No reason is given for the absence of state support, nor is the name of the company providing the funds given. Viewers are simply left with the impression that the lack of state presence is regretted. A week later, in "Coolkeeragh, Co. Derry: Ireland's first oil-fired power station,"[20] the relationship between this advanced industrial technology and international investment is made clear by the comment that thanks to its huge storage capacity, it can not only supply power to the city of Derry, but also the companies in the North – including the American Du Pont factory. This was the second power station of its kind in Northern Ireland, while the Republic still had none. There is no sense of this in the film, however, and no comment is made to that effect. The silence on the subject of comparison between the two parts of Ireland is in keeping with the tone of the series as a whole, in which the political division between Northern Ireland and the Republic is completely ignored.

All private enterprise in Ireland was not created equal, however, and one with great national symbolic, and well as economic, value was the Guinness brewery. The importance of the brewing industry to Irish identity is celebrated in the 1959 film, "Bi-centenary of Irish firm,"[21] which celebrates the "200 years of a lovely long drink!" Lemass is there with Lord Iveagh, the

19   "Co. Leix: open-cast mining with world's largest excavator" #74: 4 November 1960.
20   "Coolkeeragh: Derry's first oil-fired power station" #75: 11 November 1960.
21   "Bi-centenary of Irish firm" #7: 24 July 1959.

Chairman of the Board, to lay the foundation stone for a new playground, as three generations of Douglas family Guinness employees are congratulated for their commitment to the company. In another film, a "Foreign trade body visit Dundalk brewery,"[22] which opened in 1960, as part of a nation-wide factory tour that aimed to increase the export trade, and in "Dublin: barmen visit Belfast brewery,"[23] three hundred barmen visit from Dublin to enjoy something of a busman's holiday. In "Taoiseach opens new Guinness laboratory,"[24] Lemass uses the occasion to stress the importance of science and research in Ireland, adding that there was a great need for manufacturing to continue the country's economic progress and growth, and to further research of the kind published by the attached library, which published the results of the lab's work. Guinness was both an example of a long-standing successful national industry and one that was embracing the modern age through research and development.

Other openings include the "New Ireland assurance building"[25] in Dawson Street, Dublin, attended by Sean Lemass, Dr. James Ryan[26] and Donogh O'Malley.[27] When the New Ireland Assurance Company was founded forty years earlier by Michael Collins, while he was interned in Frongoch, its income was only a thousand pounds. It was created to keep some of the money being sent out of the country for English insurers in Irish hands and was to become one of the country's largest insurance businesses.[28] "Now it's over 3 million," says the commentator, as Lemass praises the contribution it made in savings and economic development. Despite the theme of the importance of international investment to Irish industry, this

---

22    "Foreign trade body visit Dundalk brewery" #216: 20 July 1963.

23    "Dublin: barmen visit Belfast brewery" #199: 23 March 1963.

24    "Taoiseach opens new Guinness laboratory" #266: 5 July 1964.

25    No issue number or date available.

26    James Ryan was the Minister for Finance throughout this period (16th and 17th Dáils: 1957–65).

27    Donogh O'Malley was Parliamentary Secretary to the Minister for Finance (Ryan) from 1961–65 and was to become famous for his tremendous work in overhauling the Irish education system in the late 1960s.

28    Tim Pat Coogan, *Michael Collins: a biography* (London: Hutchinson, 1990): 55.

film presents an example of economic "sinn féin-ism" – self-sufficiency – in practice; not in the sense of closed-off protectionism from the rest of the world, but simply the use of Irish money for Irish development. The new building is proof for the public of the success of national enterprise and stands as an example to others of the progress that is possible with national investment.

The opening of the ERI (the Economic Research Institute, later to become the ESRI, the Economic and Social Research Institute) was another milestone in Ireland's modernization. In "Taoiseach opens economic research unit,"[29] Lemass is accompanied by Grant Stockdale, the US ambassador, along with a number of other important figures. Stockdale's presence represents the American investment from the Ford Foundation that is to thank for the opening of this research unit, while the audience is a veritable who's who of all major Irish management and development figures of the time. Those present at the opening include T.K. Whitaker,[30] Ivor Kenny,[31] Patrick Hillery,[32] Jack Lynch[33] and Lord Mayor Dockerel of Dublin. Lemass is welcomed by J.J. McElligot,[34] while the camera zooms in on Senator and Professor George O'Brien.[35] All were gathered in the garden to hear McDaniel of the Ford Foundation speak and as Lemass thanked the Foundation for the 100,000 pounds donated for the venture. It is clear that the Ford Foundation is the main investor in the ERI, and though the Irish Government was involved, not much is made of this in the film except when in closing, when the commentator adds, "Indeed, the government is helping too!" While the Ford Foundation provided the funding and foreign expertise for the first few years of the ERI's activities, the Irish state

29   No issue number or date available.
30   Secretary of Finance and author of *Economic Development* (1958), upon which the government based its first economic programme (1959–63).
31   Later to become the Director of the Irish Management Institute (IMI).
32   Minister for Education during this period and later to become the President of Ireland.
33   Minister for Industry and Commerce.
34   Former Secretary of Finance and Governor of the Central Bank.
35   Distinguished economic history professor.

was actually very much involved in the activities of the Institute – unfortunately, this comes across more as an afterthought than an indication of any significant gesture on the part of the state in setting up the Institute.

## The airline and tourism industry

The Irish Tourist Association was established in 1925 as a voluntary body and in 1939 the Tourist Traffic Act established the state-appointed Irish Tourist Board, but it was not until the 1950s that a more serious commitment to tourism was made. In 1955 the Irish Tourist Board was consolidated with another organization into one statutory body, Bord Fáilte Éireann, and a major revision of its methods was conducted in 1955–56. The Council for Education, Recruitment and Training, a national training organization for the tourism industry, was established in 1963. Lemass stressed that Bord Failte Éireann had an important role to play in the development of the industry that brought in a gross income of 30 million pounds annually and constituted a substantial factor in the country's balance of payments, which the extension of the Aer Lingus network would help to develop.[36]

This growth in the Irish airline industry in the early 1960s is documented in the openings of new airports, the announcement of new flight paths and the publicity for new airplanes, all reflecting and stimulating the growth of leisure and international tourism. Aer Lingus was founded in 1936 and expanded its services rapidly after the Second World War, first to Britain and later to Europe. In the 1960s, the Shannon Free Airport was continuously touted as a major success-story for Irish enterprise, attracting foreign companies and factories to the new tax-free development zone and providing jobs for thousands of Irish workers. New regional airports were also built in Cork and Belfast. In "Cork airport: inaugural

36  Lemass: 182.

flight,"[37] Lemass and his wife are seen flying from Dublin to Cork for the inauguration of the 1 million pound Cork airport. The new airport would serve regional commuter traffic between the two cities with five flights a week from Dublin to Cork, as well as flights to London, Cardiff and Bristol, which would contribute to tourism and development of the area. A couple of years later in "Belfast: new airport at Aldergrove,"[38] Mr. Dempsey, the CEO of Aer Lingus, is there to meet the new arrivals. The increase in visitors to the area prompted the overhaul of the former military airport, which now sports a "nice, modern look" compared to the old airport at Nutt's Corner.

Jet aircraft were introduced to Ireland in the 1950s, and new destinations included New York and the Continent. "The 'Caravelle' jet at Dublin airport"[39] had been used for years in France but was new to Ireland in the early 1960s. It arrived in Dublin complete with a huge crowd on its way to a rugby match. The growth in international travel had obviously not made much headway yet in the provincialism of Irish perceptions of "abroad," however, as the commentator introduced the captain and the "nice coloured girl" from France who accompanied him on the flight. The "First jet service via Shannon to Europe"[40] records the journey of the US Pan American airline as it stopped in Shannon en route to Düsseldorf, Germany. American airlines continued to take advantage of Shannon's tax-free status even after the need to stop over was eliminated by the arrival of jet aircraft. The DC8 in the film carries 168 passengers, some of whom are Irish, and the commentator notes that there will be a weekly service from Chicago and Detroit via Shannon to London, Düsseldorf and Frankfurt. He also draws attention to the comfort and safety of the plane, while the camera focuses on passengers reading magazines and relaxing. Once Düsseldorf appears outside the windows, it is time for the tour of the city: A little history – "Düsseldorf, one of the big towns on the Ruhr, was bombed during WWII

37  "Cork airport: inaugural flight" #125: 27 October 1961.
38  "Belfast: new airport at Aldergrove" #231: 2 November 1963.
39  "The 'Caravelle' jet at Dublin airport" #98: 21 April 1961.
40  "First jet service via Shannon to Europe" #54: 17 June 1960.

by the British and the United States, but has risen beautifully again" –
is followed by shots of cafes, the centre city and people at a fountain, all
drawing attention to the attractions that the city offers.

The Costa del Sol was the destination of choice for Irish holiday-
makers in the 1960s. "Dublin-Malaga: Aer Lingus start winter sunshine
flight"[41] is half airline promotion film and half tourist film for Malaga.
Shots of Dublin airport on a rainy day are contrasted with the destination,
sunny Malaga on the Spanish Costa del Sol. Passengers are shown relaxing,
reading magazines and generally enjoying the short trip on the comfortable 4-engine Viscount airplane, St. Ciarán. Upon arrival at the airport
in Malaga, a Spanish man and a female flight attendant greet them, and
whisk them away to the beaches, hotels and swimming pools that await.
These twice-weekly flights from Dublin reflect the increasing interest in
Ireland in winter holidays in the sunny south, where the contrast between
climates, people and architectural surroundings is a novelty for the Irish
travelers. Shots focus on the geographic features of the area – the beach
in front and mountains behind the rapidly rising apartment building, the
group of young Spanish children running through the narrow streets, and
the signature white-washed houses.

Along with commuter flights and short tourist flights to European
holiday destinations, the major development during this period was the
start of trans-Atlantic travel. The inauguration of North American service
was delayed until 1958 and later became a major burden on the company.[42]
Aer Rianta's first flight to New York City was the source of much excitement, as reflected in "Dublin – New York jet-liner: inaugural flight."[43] This
film, again, is part national aircraft industry promotion and part tourist
information. Government figures, including the Lord Mayor of Dublin,
and journalists were all there for the send-off, described as "an historic
moment," while the Lord Mayors of Cork and Birmingham went on the
actual journey. The film traces the entire 3,000-mile journey, from the food

41   "Dublin-Malaga: Aer Lingus start winter sunshine flight" #232: 9 November 1963.
42   Gillmor, 1985: 114.
43   "Dublin – New York jet-liner: inaugural flight" #81: 23 December 1960.

and drink provided by the "nice Aer Rianta girls" to the first glimpse of Manhattan from the air at 2 a.m. The commentator reminds viewers that this Manhattan skyline was the first sight seen by thousands of European immigrants to America – many Irish among them – before turning to the sights and sounds of the New York City. What follows is a short tour of Manhattan, complete with shots of skyscrapers, 5th Avenue and Rockefeller Plaza and the incredulous comment that "eight million people live here in the middle of the city!" Spotting a sign for Brendan Behan's play, *The Hostage*, the commentator adds that "there were lots of friends from Europe who got here before them" before concluding that "it's a wonderful sight to see the huge numbers of people, the lights and the unending traffic."

A follow-up film was made, "New York: Irish airline opened on 5th Avenue,"[44] to record the actual opening of the Aer Rianta offices. Again, the theme of Irish emigration to New York is brought up with shots of Ellis Island and the Empire State Building. Proud of the Irish commercial presence in this metropolitan centre, the commentator says that "now that there's a direct link between the US and Ireland it's only fitting that there would be an office. It's located on the most fashionable street in New York." How times have changed – the Irish are no longer entering the States as poor, half-starved immigrants but now as equals with something to offer, and are able to stake their claim on the most sought-after commercial property in the city. The chair of Aer Rianta, Patrick Lynch, does the official opening and, just in case anyone might fear that the Irish have forgotten themselves entirely, there is a priest present to bless the offices before they officially open. The Irish International Airlines sign appears in lights and the commentator note approvingly, "we are proud of the progress that Ireland is making."

The presence of the priest in New York was not a one-off event. Rather, the involvement of the church in Irish commercial activities was as apparent in all sorts of industry-related areas as it was in the films on national commemoration and Ireland's international involvement in the Congo. One of the more peculiar of these events was the annual blessing of the

---

44  "New York: Irish airline opened on 5th Avenue" #82: 30 December 1960.

Aer Lingus fleet. Two such occasions are recorded in the Gaelic News films, the earlier "Dublin airport: Aer Lingus fleet annual blessing" and a later "Annual blessing of the Aer Lingus fleet."[45] The visual imagery in these two films is quite incongruous: With a huge aircraft hangar in the background, the planes sit on the tarmac. The priest stands at an altar beside the hangar, specially erected for the occasion, with the altar boys in all their regalia. The commentator informs the viewers that there were two jets and three DC3s present, before asking the priest to "pray to keep them safe from foul weather and other dangers to all who travel in them." The closing shot has the altar boys standing in front with the plane in the background, a striking juxtaposition of the Catholic tradition and modern machinery combined in the one image, and the statement "Aer Lingus has a very good safety record and please God let it stay that way."

With or without God's blessing, the Shannon industrial zone continued to expand throughout this period. The success of the world's first duty-free airport shop, opened there in 1947, was the subject of an earlier short documentary film.[46] Unfortunately for Ireland, the coming of long-range jets that did not require refueling at Shannon resulted in a decline in international traffic in the late 1950s. In response to the potentially damaging regional impact of this decline, the airport was promoted through tourism, manufacturing and warehousing through the state-sponsored Shannon Free Airport Development Authority, established in 1957. After 1965, the decline was reversed and use of the airport tripled. In 1961, "Shannon Free Airport: industrial boom"[47] draws attention to the dramatic industrial progress already being made due to international investment in the area. Beginning with a view of the airport, the commentator exclaims, "the tax-free area at Shannon Airport is booming!" There were 250 acres of available space, thirty of which were nearly ready, with space for fifty factories in total. These factories were expected to

---

45   "Dublin airport: Aer Lingus fleet annual blessing" #157: 8 June 1962; "Annual blessing of the Aer Lingus fleet" #210: 8 June 1963.

46   "Aerphort na Sionainne" (Shannon Airport) #2: July 1956 – see Chapter Two: Industrial and rural development.

47   "Shannon Free Airport: industrial boom" #84: 13 January 1961.

provide work for 1,500 men and women. All are foreign companies geared towards production for overseas markets: Japanese, German, American and English. Focusing on a large sign that reads "progress," followed by a scene of men working on various machines, the commentator assures viewers that the factory is "up to international standards." The biggest international company there is the German SPS – a manufacturer of precision steel, which also had eight factories in the US, two in England and one in Germany. As the view of men and women working attests, it employed one hundred workers and the numbers were increasing all the time. "There's a big industrial scheme growing in Shannon. Good luck to the new city!"

The second film on the area boasts of the "Continued expansion at Shannon industrial zone,"[48] where by 1964 the Shannon Free Airport is also growing as an industrial zone and manufacturing area. The occasion for this film was the visit of a trading association to see its progress. By now there are twelve factories and seven other businesses at Shannon. The manufacturing company they are visiting is the Rippen Piano factory, which employs 2,000 people and serves as an amazing demonstration of the power of the tax-free area to extend beyond the more usual small luxury items like Irish whiskey and jewelry, to goods with a much heavier weight-to-value ratio. Here, raw materials were apparently flown into Shannon, the pianos constructed on site and then flown out fully made. As a result of enterprises such as this one, the Shannon industrial zone had by now grown to include two hundred houses and over 130 flats for employees, as well as a new hotel. As the commentator says, "its great progress from the one little airport that could only hold five people!"

48 "Continued expansion at Shannon industrial zone" #263: 14 June 1964.

The shipping industry

In contrast to the airline industry's apparent "up and up" story, the picture
of the shipping industry in the North is of a much bumpier ride punctuated
by strikes, lay-offs, short-term contracts and worker unrest in the Harland
and Wolff shipyards. Meanwhile, the new Verolme dockyard in Cork is the
centre of new activity in the Republic. For Irish Shipping Ltd., the general
objective of developing a fleet of merchant ships was widely understood. As
in the films on the airline industry, in which the growth of Shannon stands
in dramatic contrast to the new airport at Aldergrove in the North, those
on the shipping industry highlight the reversal of fortunes in the North
and the Republic as a result of foreign investment.

Two films trace the evolution of the new Cork dockyard,[49] which will
produce a number of ships in this period thanks to the investment of the
Dutch Verolme Company. "New Cork dockyard: Taoiseach lays first keel
of ship"[50] marks the beginning of a new industry for the Republic, thanks
to foreign investment. The opening shot is of a member of the volunteer
Irish navy, which supplied the guard of honour for the occasion, pictured
with his cap spelling "Éire", the visual reminder of the national importance
of such a venture. Lemass is here to lay the keel of a fifteen-thousand ton
boat that will take two years to build and be the biggest one made in the
Republic so far. At this point it is only known as ship number 645. Four
hundred other people are here, among them Erskine Childers and the
Bishop of Cloyne, who does the blessing. The next scene is of the ship's
plating shop, where another ship is being built for Irish Shipping Ltd. The
sign above the front reads "Verolme Cork Dockyard Ltd." and the commentator reminds viewers, "at last, workers are making ships in Ireland for
Ireland, thanks to Cornelus Verolme!" There is no irony in this statement –
only gratitude for the fact that, thanks to Dutch financing, the Irish are

49   The dockyard is new in the sense that it used to be a repair site but is now a fully
     fledged building yard.
50   "New Cork dockyard: Taoiseach lays first keel of ship" #73: 28 October 1960.

now seeing domestic industry make some progress. The second film on this topic, "Cork dockyard: new Irish fishing vessel launched,"[51] made nine months later, records the ship's completion. De Valera is there with his wife, Sinéad, and greeted by Lemass. The ship is now the Irish Rowan, upon which one thousand men have worked.

The other major site for Irish shipbuilding was Belfast, the home of Harland and Wolff. However, the Belfast shipbuilding industry is not portrayed as doing as well as the dockyard in Cork. In fact, in contrast to the happy picture presented in the south, several films about Belfast draw attention to worker unrest resulting from the instability of their contracts with the major ship-builders and the stop-and-go nature of the industry in the north. "Belfast: shipyard builds novel liner"[52] introduces the liner being built, which will cost fifteen million pounds and carry two thousand passengers. This is not the only ship being built at the shipyard – twenty-five thousand men are currently working on thirty different ships for Harland and Wolff. In "Belfast: 15 million pound 'Canberra' completed"[53] viewers are presented with an example of the finished export as "at the Belfast docks after three years of construction a British liner is finished." The completion of the task is no cause for celebration, however, and the film ends on an ominous note, pointing to the trouble ahead now that "sadly the thousand workers have nothing to look forward to." Happily, in "Belfast: shipyards busy again,"[54] "it's a good story at the shipyard in Belfast that there's enough work for all as a tanker is being built for Britain." The tanker is the biggest built outside of Japan and employs the two thousand men who would otherwise be out of work. The noise of the shipyard is described as "sweet music to the workers' ears" but this does not distract from the knowledge of what will inevitably follow once this project is complete. "Now the shipyard is alive again but there's always the question; will the work last?"

51 "Cork dockyard: new Irish fishing vessel launched" #132: 15 December 1961.
52 "Belfast: shipyard builds novel liner" #35: 5 February 1960.
53 "Belfast: 15 million pound 'Canberra' completed" #100: 5 May 1961.
54 "Belfast: shipyards busy again" #212: 22 June 1963.

The terms of continuing employment are spelled out for the workers in "Belfast: shipyard closedown averted,"[55] in which a dispute between the union and Harland and Wolff is brought into the spotlight. The argument "came close to having the whole shipyard closed down and ten thousand men out of work". Two thousand workers were let go, and negotiations between the principals and the union were not looking good. Harland and Wolff made a statement promising that "jobs would be found for anyone out of work". This rather surprising turn of events apparently meant that all future job losses would be compensated – an unlikely, if not impossible sounding scenario – while the commentator admitted that although a sort of peace had been found, "things remain unsettled in the industry." Thus, while Belfast's Harland and Wolff shipyards are languishing, the Verolme dockyard in Cork is thriving. And although the shipping industry in Cork would have been susceptible to the same fluctuations in international trade cycles as that in Belfast, pessimistic comments never appear in the films on Cork as they do in those on Belfast.

There is one important film on a strike in the Dublin docks, "Dublin docks: ships idle – strikers march,"[56] in which the 1963 trade dispute between the Marine Port and General Workers Union is documented. Shots of ships and goods stuck in port alternate with scenes of men sitting around, killing time. Scenes of marchers holding up banners and posters reading "lock-out of MPGWU" are interspersed with others of Liberty Hall under construction. The reference to the 1913 Dublin lockout is clear, as dockers from Belfast, Cork, Dublin and even Liverpool are pictured protesting in front of the GPO. This protest is unusual because it unites the workers of the entire island in their discontent, and includes some from Britain. It is thus one of the rare instances of international working-class solidarity that is featured in the Gaelic News films, which tend to focus on more specifically national issues.

Overall, however, both the shipping and the airline industries in the Republic of Ireland are portrayed as doing far better than its counterparts

55    "Belfast: shipyard closedown averted" #235: 30 November 1963.
56    "Dublin docks: ships idle – strikers march" #224: 14 September 1963.

in the North. The films never make any reference to the fact that Northern Ireland is under British rule – they simply point to the northeastern part of Ireland as one that is suffering in comparison to the rest of the island – which constitutes implicit criticism of the British government and the degree of its support for ailing industries in Northern Ireland. The reliance on British contracts in Northern shipyards is evident in "Belfast: commissioning of Indian aircraft carrier 'Vikrant',"[57] in which the completed carrier is celebrated by the Lord Mayor of Belfast, Villiers, the Lord of the Admiralty, and Madame Pandit, an Indian dignitary. Viewers are told that the ship was first made in 1945 for the English fleet but is being re-commissioned now by Harland and Wolfe for the Indian navy. As the camera zooms in on the Indian captain of the ship, who is wearing a turban, the commentator gives a brilliant display of life before political correctness, volunteering that "there isn't much similarity between the captain of the Vikrant and Villiers!" – clearly a reference to the turban-clad Indian captain versus the British Lord of the Admiralty.

Other evidence of the degree of activity in the Irish shipping industry during this period appears in "'Irish Cedar' launched in Holland", "New B+I ship launched" and "21 years of Irish shipping."[58] The Irish Cedar was another of the ships made in the Cork dockyard, along with the previously mentioned Irish Rowan. The occasion of the boat's launching in Holland presents another opportunity for a short tourists' view of the country. Beginning with views of Rotterdam, "the second largest city in Holland and one of the biggest port cities in the world," viewers are told that it was badly damaged by the war but has been completely rebuilt around the port area and docklands. Cliché views of traditional Holland abound in shots of clogs and cyclists, but the overall message stresses the modernity of the rebuilt city: "When all of the restoration work is done it will be one of the most modern cities in Europe." The ceremony to launch the Irish Cedar was marred by bad weather but this did not interrupt the festivities,

---

57 "Belfast: commissioning of Indian aircraft carrier 'Vikrant'" #92: 10 March 1961.
58 "'Irish Cedar' launched in Holland" #150: 20 April 1962; "New B+I ship launched" #23: 13 November 1959; "21 years of Irish shipping" no issue number or date available.

as a woman from Cork is pictured breaking the bottle while the people applaud. The reverse slide of the massive ship off its launching pad into the river is quite dramatic but, in spite of worries about the narrowness of the Maas River, the launch goes off perfectly, representing another triumph for Irish engineering.

The "New B+I ship launched" in Dublin was part of the British and Ireland line of ferries. The "Meath" was the biggest ship in the Liffey dockyard, worth half a million pounds, and the directors of B+I were there for the occasion, along with Mr. and Mrs. Lemass and Jack Lynch. Mrs. Lemass baptizes the ship, the supports are removed and off it goes into the River Liffey. The significance of this film is not, however, the ship itself but rather what it will be used for. Rather than the usual passenger ferry service, viewers are told that this ship will be used to transport cattle to England. Such use of a ferry of this size gives some indication of the continuing size and importance of the livestock industry to Ireland, even in the context of rapid industrialization and new economic growth. The commentary closes with the assertion that "the men are very proud of it. It's a monument to their courage and a sign of hope." The hope is presumably that the export of cattle in such large numbers to England will continue. During the 1955 balance of payments crisis that resulted in massive cutbacks in government spending in the 1956 Budget, the "real problem lay in a slump in our cattle trade to Britain and our displacement from the British egg market." Their optimism would be rewarded in 1965 when Anglo-Irish Free Trade Agreement "returned Ireland to the close economic ties with the United Kingdom that had characterized the period 1800–1922."[59] Thus the two economies were brought even closer together, partly as a reaction to two refusals of entry by the EEC and partly in preparation for eventual membership in the early 1970s.

59   Brendan Walsh, *Ireland 1945–70* (Dublin: Gill & Macmillan, 1979): 29–33.

# Transport

Córas Iompair Éireann (known as the CIE) is Ireland's national transportation organization. It was created in 1945 with the amalgamation of the Great Southern Railway Company and the Dublin United Transport Company, and became a public enterprise in 1950 when it was amalgamated with the Grand Canal Company. Under the 1958 Transport Act CIE had been set the task of an internal reform. This meant the transport industry was also visibly undergoing the effects of industrialization and modernization, most obviously in its fleet, as well as in the cut-backs and closures to some of the traditional rail routes, mourned for their contribution to cultural history and resulting status as quasi-heritage sites in Irish popular history. The over-lengthened railway system was subject to state control, which resulted in the contraction of the network of lines and stations. Under the 1958 Transport Act, financial relief was given to the CIE to reorganize and rationalize the transport system, in order to provide an efficient transport system position and eliminate much of the economic waste attributable to an excess of transport facilities. The period of network contraction actually began in 1953 and most of the light railways were closed by 1960. Of those remaining, small stations and shorter lines were closed, supposedly to reduce costs and traveling time. However, the result of these measures was that the average length of journey actually increased.

Two films chronicle the closure of the old railway lines and mourn the loss for national heritage of these historical routes. "Branch lines close: Kenmare's last train"[60] draws attention to the down side for the remote region of Co. Kerry, on Ireland's southwest coast. The men on the platform look down forlornly at the empty railroad. "It makes one lonely to see the railways no longer used". The stationmaster Frank O'Brien was here for forty years but now it is feared that the engines "will only be used for children's entertainment," as the CIE is replacing them with buses. In another isolated part of rural Ireland, the "West Clare railway: the last

---

60   "Branch lines close: Kenmare's last train" #32: 15 January 1960.

run"[61] takes place. The commentator explains that this famous train route is also being replaced by buses because of the expense of keeping them going. The route is only fifty miles long but Todd Andrews, the CEO of CIE, says it is losing 23 million pounds a year. "After eighty years this train went from Ennis to Kilkee but now it is at an end. The station master is sad at the waving of the flag for the last time." As traditional Irish music plays in the background, the film follows the train from Ennis to Kilkee through Ennistymon, tracing the historic route used in the 1950 John Ford film, *The Quiet Man*, a portrait of rural Irish life in the 1920s.[62] Percy French[63] also wrote "Are you right there Michael, are you right?" about the West Clare railway. The regional route is thus a significant monument to Irish popular and traditional culture, appearing as it does in both domestic song and international film. The film ends on a rather upbeat – if not necessarily constructive – note, as "the passengers understand what is needed and race into the pub" to mourn the loss of the West Clare railway over a pint of stout. This way of commemorating the end of an era says less about the significance of the route itself than the rural population's reaction to the problem of uneven development. While it is entertaining to see and in one sense just another lighthearted conclusion to an otherwise weighty topic, this was hardly the solution to the regional problem of underdevelopment and the closing of routes.

The path to modernization and efficiency was literally closing off other routes to development, forcing the population to take one route to prosperity, both literally and metaphorically. Meanwhile, new diesel engines later imported from the United States for the CIE were noted in two films, "Detroit diesels for CIE" and "New 1,000 horse power diesel engines for CIE."[64] The first film consists simply of views of the ship as the six new engines from General Motors arrive, and the crane as it removes

---

61    "West Clare railway: the last run" #88: 10 February 1961.
62    See William C. Dowling, "John Ford's Festive Comedy: Ireland Imagined in *The Quiet Man*," in *Éire-Ireland* 23, no. 1 (2002): 190–211.
63    Percy French was a writer of humorous Irish songs, b. 1854 – d.1920.
64    "Detroit diesels for CIE" #182: 24 November 1962; "New 1,000 horse power diesel engines for CIE" #188: 5 January 1963.

the large machinery. There would be twenty engines in total arriving from the US. "CIE is always improving the railways" and "this is the kind of progress that is being made all the time", the commentator notes approvingly. As the rest of the diesel engines arrive they are put on display but would soon be put to work in Irish vehicles. Irish transportation thus cannot be criticized for not keeping up with the times, in terms of the utilization of imported new technology.

Evidence of giving up on rural areas was hardly encouraging to those who preferred to stay there and now faced the necessity of reorganizing their daily lives, but at least the old ways would not be forgotten. "Steam locomotives back at work"[65] records the outing taken by a group of four hundred locomotive-philes from England and Ireland who made a ten-day journey of 2,500 miles, for which the CIE put an old train at their disposal. This sort of nostalgia for a by-gone era echoes the mourning for the lost rural railway lines but, rather than drowning sorrows in a pint of bitter, suggests that – like many other sites of national historic interest – the regional railways could be put to good use in the name of heritage tourism.

## Urbanization and architectural heritage

One of the major corollaries of industrialization is urbanization, and while Ireland's rapid economic growth was hailed as progress within the actual industrial sectors themselves, its social repercussions were not as easily dealt with. The Dublin area grew rapidly from the early 1960s onwards, but because of the state's focus on productive rather than redistributive investment, social welfare measures were neglected and the human cost of economic growth became obvious, often dramatically so. While the rebuilding of Liberty Hall and the Abbey Theatre symbolized Ireland's economic and cultural rebirth, other buildings fell to ruin. Parts of Georgian Dublin

---

65   No issue number or date available.

either collapsed or were thoughtlessly demolished, while other landmarks of old Dublin were simply destroyed.

Although the Irish state pursued a policy of decentralization during this period, Dublin grew faster than anywhere else in the country, and the city's skyline was transformed. Rapid growth combined with poor urban planning created the circumstances in which the architectural eyesore, Liberty Hall, was erected. The building of Liberty Hall, hailed as "a beacon of modernity,"[66] the symbol of industrial development and national rebirth, was also a reminder of the turbulent national past. In "New Liberty Hall: foundation stone laid,"[67] the site where the old Liberty Hall had stood before it was burned to the ground in 1916 was blessed by a priest, in preparation for the building of the new building in its place. The audience is reminded by the commentator of the historic significance of the location and the building to Irish national history: "The Young Irelanders used to meet there in 1848 and this is not the first time that Liberty Hall has risen again," referring to the Easter Rising when the original Liberty Hall was burned out. Years later, "Liberty Hall: Ireland's highest building goes up and up"[68] draws attention to the fact that it will not only be the tallest building in Dublin, but that it was also the birthplace of the Irish workers' movement and the centre of the 1913 Dublin Lockout. "Our history is there – the history of freedom. It was originally the Northumberland Hotel but was taken over in 1912 by the ITGWU.[69] The 1913 strikes started there." The building – or its site anyway – serves as a symbol of both national freedom and workers' rights. Neither James Connolly nor Jim Larkin are mentioned – as the names of socialists rarely are in the series – but Larkin's activities in the name of Irish workers are more than alluded to by mention of the Irish Transport and General Workers' Union, which he founded in 1909. Indeed,

66   Frank MacDonald, *The Construction of Dublin* (Dublin: Gandon Editions, 2000): 40. "It shone like a beacon of modernity, a symbol of the transformation of Dublin from the black-and-white era of drab tenements in the Georgian slums to an almost blinding Technicolour future, laden with all sorts of possibilities."
67   No issue number or date available.
68   "Liberty Hall: Ireland's highest building goes up and up" #226: 28 September 1963.
69   Irish Transport and General Workers' Union.

the commentator makes it clear at the end of the film that Liberty Hall is not just a building but "a symbol of the freedom and well-being of our workers." Finally, in "Dublin's changing skyline"[70] viewers are treated to a bird's-eye-view of the city from the top of the almost-completed building. The earlier incarnations of the building saw the prelude to nationhood in 1848, the lock-out of Dublin workers in 1913 and the birth of the nation in 1916. Now Liberty Hall's resurrection is a symbol of Dublin's rebirth as the centre of modern industry.

While Liberty Hall was rising ever higher another piece of old Dublin's architecture was being demolished. The Theatre Royal,[71] once a home to stage shows, big musicals and the burlesque style of live entertainment, was now outdated. The films on the Theatre Royal point to the succession of this era by the technological age, in which television and cinema are king. In "Skyscraper to replace Dublin theatre,"[72] the end of the thirty-year-old Theatre Royal is announced by Sir Thomas Bennett, accompanied by John Davis of the Rank Organization and Dublin Mayor Robert Briscoe. The commentator's conclusion is simply that "Yes, Dublin is rising!" – a pun on the fact that a skyscraper would be replacing the theatre, with all of the associations that come with the new building in terms of Ireland's march into modernity. "Theatre Royal: final scene"[73] stresses more strongly the impact of the coming of television on traditional entertainment in Dublin. Mickser Reed, one of the famous names associated with the old theatre, was on site for the demolition as the wrecking ball tore into the building. The commentator explains: "The owners of the theatre thought it was better to close – they would be losing money because the numbers were down. Now that we have television in homes people don't want to go out in the evening for that kind of entertainment." Thus the changes to Dublin's skyline signify more than mere architectural evolution – they also point to the evolution of Irish popular culture. Liberty Hall is no longer the site of the

70   "Dublin's changing skyline" #256: 26 April 1964.
71   Hawkins House, the headquarters of the Department of Health, now stands on the
       site of the Theatre Royal.
72   "Skyscraper to replace Dublin theatre" #160: 29 June 1962.
73   "Theatre Royal: final scene" #174: 29 September 1962.

workers' or the nationalist struggle – instead it is the symbol of economic growth and industry. Similarly, Theatre Royal, a hangover from earlier forms of popular entertainment, is now antiquated and serves no purpose in a city preoccupied with growth and new technology.

Keenly aware of the human side of development, other news films in the *Amharc Éireann* series highlight some of the less-publicized shortcomings of the first programme and its consequences for the people of Dublin in particular. While all energies were directed towards productive investment, the redistributive elements of the state's development policy were left aside. In fact, the cut-backs in the level of social or "non-productive" spending were the main source of funds for new areas of government spending. Thus government spending on the public housing programme, health services and further improvements to the social system was postponed until economic recovery was underway. Manufacturing and industry occupied the front and centre positions, while housing and construction projects were abandoned. The result was a housing shortage in Dublin and a number of tragic accidents in the old inner-city tenements. It was not recognized that there were many poorly housed families living in slums or in houses in danger of collapse, even though there were many vacant publicly owned houses in the city and suburbs, and the housing programme was scaled down. Some of Dublin's inner-city poor died as a consequence of this lack of attention, and the state's shortsighted attempts to rectify the situation through the provision of temporary and low-income housing projects.

Georgian Dublin suffered the most from this shortsighted policy. The films capturing the effects of the collapse of tenement houses were a powerful means of protesting government neglect of the urban decay and poverty that accompanied the other, supposedly more glamorous developments in the city. While the building of shiny new monstrosities like Liberty Hall was being celebrated, some of the most precious parts of the city were destroyed or allowed to collapse with little thought to their heritage value or to the lives of those who lived in them. In "Dublin tenements collapsing: growing alarm,"[74] the "conscience of Dublin and of the whole

---

74   "Dublin tenements collapsing: growing alarm" #211: 15 June 1963.

country was pricked" when two little girls were killed by the collapse of their houses near Fenian Street. The film provides close-ups of the kind of housing problems that should not have continued to exist in the Ireland of the early 1960s, and served as a wake-up call to government ministers to act. It follows the funeral of the girls as it passed through the streets of Dublin, stopping for a moment at the site of their deaths. "It takes a tragedy of this sort before people will wake up to reality and realize the conditions these buildings are in." A TD[75] is pictured as he speaks to the people of the area, answering their questions as to what will be done to remedy the terrible situation. Three generations of mothers stand on a small doorstep in front of one of the buildings, looking pitifully undernourished. This image communicates very effectively the extent of overcrowding in tenement housing, in which generations of families all lived in one or two rooms, and a large number of families occupied one building.[76] "These buildings are not fit for animals, much less for people and children starting out their lives," says the commentator. While other parts of the city are being attended to, this area still suffers from state neglect: "Buildings are being knocked down on the north side of the city, near Blackhall Place, where there are a lot of these condemned houses, but there are still people and children living here." The camera focuses on a building, the side of which has fallen clean off, exposing the interior of former rooms. "Despite props and scaffolding and the tragedy that happened, these walls are coming down." Another building like this one, in Bolton Street, had also recently collapsed, killing a woman and a man. The moral of the story, of course, is that "there is only one cure for the situation, which is to knock them down and rebuild." The commentator goes further, suggesting as a remedy that the people should be re-housed in modern residences in the suburbs and the next scene shows these brand new buildings. This paternalist attitude and the action suggested is similar to that adopted by urban planners in Britain, Europe and North America during this period. There is no sense

75  TD stands for "Teachta Dala" or Member of Parliament in Irish.
76  See Kevin Kearns, *Dublin Tenement Life: An Oral History* (Dublin: Gill and Macmillan, 1994).

of awareness or curiosity as to what the residents themselves might prefer, but rather a condescending certainty born from knowing what is best for them. It was this type of attitude that also decided what was best for marginalized people in Ireland, that created public housing projects like the fifteen Ballymun towers completed in 1969, billed as "Ireland's greatest housing scheme," which would go down in history as the State's worst urban planning disaster.

The follow-up film is "Dublin: dangerous buildings' demolition continues,"[77] which focuses on the demolition of the tenement buildings at Kings Inn and Blackhall Place. These were old Georgian houses, tragically not cared for, so that now "old Dublin is disappearing." As in the earlier case, there are still some people living here, but not for long. "There is a new scheme for houses and apartments for these people." According to the commentator, the new buildings cannot be completed quickly enough to meet the need, so in the meantime the residents are to be housed in prefabricated caravan-style homes. There is no mention of an availability of the housing in the suburbs in corporation dwellings or housing estates for these slum-dwellers.[78] Incredibly, in the film these caravans are presented as "modern cottages", which although temporary, "still have electricity and every comfort in them – water, cooking facilities – and are decorated very nicely. Another benefit is the space." This last sentence approaches a joke made in very poor taste, with the accompanying shot of a matchbox-sized caravan in which there is no room at all to move. Still, the presumption is that the residents will be at least less likely to be killed by falling buildings here and the commentator does admit that "this is another concern of the city council" before reassuringly if not quite credibly closing with the assertion that "it has the problem firmly in its grasp."

Problems such as these were the underside of Dublin's rapid modernization. With the increase in wealth and prosperity for some, others were inevitably left behind. The rising tide failed to lift quite all boats and some

---

77   "Dublin: dangerous buildings' demolition continues" #245: 8 February 1964.
78   The availability of these types of housing is referred to by Garret FitzGerald: 23–4.

were simply swallowed up by the swell. Another instance of state paternalism in response to the dislocation resulting from modernization surfaces in "Taking census of the travelling people."[79] In this case the Travellers are being driven to areas where they would not otherwise choose to live, such as the outskirts of urban areas, because their traditional rural livelihoods are being eroded. The result is that they are living in unsanitary conditions, without proper amenities, and their presence is apparently causing discomfort for the permanent population. In the film the police are described as descending on every camp and halting site of the travellers in order to take a census for the newly established government commission set up to deal with the issues. They speak to a number of Travellers including one who owns a horse and cart and sells iron for a living. The commentator assures viewers that "he is a very intelligent man even though he is not formally educated." The camera follows the police as they ask questions about their way or life, in order to learn "how they can do more for them and their families." The Travellers respond by asking not for suburban homes but simply for "proper halting sites," presumably so that they can continue with their traditional migrant lifestyle. In terms of modern amenities, the "women want clean water and toilets and a chance to send their children to school." No final judgment as to where the Travellers belong is expressed in the film. The commentator is sympathetic and simply asks for the same in the viewers by asking in closing: "People dislike them and the racket they make but do they not deserve the help of God like the rest of us?" He does not, however, question the motivation of the government commission either, which seems to indicate a continued faith in the ability of the state to deal with marginalized populations effectively.

By 1964 the tone has changed, however, from simple concern for the Travellers to outright criticism of the state. Negative judgment of the government's approach to the problem is clear from the title of the film, "Tackling Ireland's Apartheid Problem,"[80] which places the blame squarely on the shoulders of the state for its systematic separation of the travelling

79   "Taking census of the travelling people" #80: 16 December 1960.
80   "Tackling Ireland's Apartheid Problem" #241: 11 January 1964.

community from the rest of the settled population. By now, the Irish public also identifies the Travellers as a community in need of humanitarian support, which is shown in the film in typically Irish Christian terms and echoing the earlier film's plea for God's help, this time on banners that say "No room at the inn?" and "Good will to all men." The film highlights the sympathy on the part of a segment of the general population for the plight of the itinerant Travellers, who see them both as fellow Irish citizens and children of God, and therefore deserving of equal treatment before the state. It focuses on the itinerants' site, where women are shown in their caravan while men are at work pulling apart furniture and scrap. We then move to the family, as Joseph O'Donoghue tells his story to the film crew. They want a school instead of the shed that is there now; a volunteer teacher works there already. The film shows the interior of the shed – a miserable hovel with dirty, badly dressed children sitting inside, listening to their teacher. The commentator tells us that even though they are on the road again the next morning, this is a new beginning: "The public knows about their problems now. We're listening still." The Travellers' main point is simply that they deserve as much state care as the fixed population. The commentator agrees: "These people are right – they are Irish and it's necessary to recognize that."

Sadly, the onward march of modernization also meant the destruction of some very important heritage buildings in Dublin, to which the series drew its audience's attention. The resistance to the destruction of grand old Georgian houses mirrors the protest against the collapse of the tenements. Both of these sets of buildings were products of the Hanoverian dynasty that ruled Britain from the late eighteenth to the early nineteenth century. The coverage of this action in the Gaelic News films was prescient – these films were made before the movement got fully underway and can be credited with raising public consciousness regarding the issue. By the mid-1960s a protest movement that had formed to fight the further destruction of Georgian Dublin received much public support and publicity.[81]

81    See Desmond Guinness "The E.S.B. Buildings: will they survive?" in *Quarterly Bulletin of the Irish Georgian Society* 4 (1961): 29–34.

The protests against the destruction of Georgian Dublin were somewhat successful, although they came too late. In "Georgian society protest to ESB,"[82] some buildings have been used by 1961 to house the offices of the Electricity Supply Board (ESB). Other buildings were under protection and a protocol was being signed to prevent any further changes to them. Two years later, in "Preserve Georgian Dublin,"[83] viewers are instructed as to the area's wider cultural and historic importance: "In the 1800s when European city streets were being designed so was Dublin, with streets going north and south, with nice boulevards and big squares." But some of those buildings were those tragically knocked down to build the new ESB office in Fitzwilliam Street. The film shows the site where half a building was destroyed and the modern one put in its place. "There's a big dispute about the ESB's plans to knock them down", says the commentator, as "the destruction is creating gaps in the façade of the city," illustrated in closing with shots of Lower Baggot Street and Upper and Lower Fitzwilliam Street. Indeed, the modern ESB edifice, entirely undeserving of comment, shown next to these examples of Georgian architecture, was creating more than "gaps" – it threatened to destroy the façade of a portion of old Dublin city.

The mere fact that these buildings are highlighted as needing protection in this series is noteworthy. As a group of films that could be characterized as focusing almost exclusively on the interests of "Irish Ireland," the inclusion of the architectural remnants of the Georgian era in Ireland is somewhat of an anomaly, as their inclusion implicitly acknowledges and even celebrates the architectural feats of the Empire. Indeed, the nationalist mood of the time points to the same conclusion; some even voiced the opinion that Dublin would be better off if all of its Georgian buildings were torn down. However, as is stressed by the commentator in one of the films on the subject,[84] Georgian Dublin is evidence of the city's rightful inclusion as one of the major *European* cities. Seen in this light, it has very little to do with Britain or the Hanoverian monarchs and much more to

---

82 "Georgian Society protest to ESB" #125: 27 October 1961.
83 "Preserve Georgian Dublin" #198: 23 March 1963.
84 "Preserve Georgian Dublin" #198: 23 March 1963.

do with the elevation of Ireland to the same stature of the rest of modern Europe in the context of the early 1960s.

One building that would not be allowed to disappear for good was the old Abbey Theatre, the home of the early twentieth century literary and cultural revival.[85] The Abbey was restored and renovated during the 1960s, as a powerful symbol of Ireland's cultural stature among European nations. Three films on the Abbey Theatre record the end of the old Abbey and the beginnings of what would become the new theatre. In "The new 'Abbey' building starts soon,"[86] the commentator scolds the tardy state: "In 1951 the old Abbey was destroyed by fire. Now, eight years later it is being rebuilt." Architect Michael Scott[87] talks to Ernest Blythe, the former Abbey director, while all that is left of the building is a painting of Lady Gregory and W.B. Yeats and another of Barry FitzGerald. The model of the new building is shown – it will seat six hundred people and be ready in two years. A year later, in "Dublin: the last of the old Abbey"[88] the wrecking ball at the demolition site is all that is left of the old theatre founded in 1904. The Peacock Theatre once housed in the basement, where viewers are told "lots of young actors got their start," went with the old Abbey. Also mentioned is the recently deceased Barry FitzGerald, the famous character actor best known for his role as Father Fitzgibbon in *Going My Way* (1944), for which he received an Academy Award for Best Supporting Actor. Two years later, in "Abbey Theatre foundation stone laid"[89] the "resurrection" of the theatre is celebrated. This is a favorite term for the commentator throughout the *Amharc Éireann* series; it seems sometimes as if Ireland itself was being resurrected from the ashes and presumably this is not accidental for a cultural

---

85    See Mícheál Ó hAodha, *The Abbey Theatre – Then and Now* (Dublin: Sackville Press, 1969); Hugh Hunt, *The Abbey: Ireland's National Theatre, 1904–78* (Dublin: Gill and Macmillan, 1979).

86    "The new Abbey: building starts soon" #30: 1 January 1960.

87    The architect most famous for his design of the Busáras building, the Dublin Bus headquarters. See Paul Clerkin, "Fifty years of Busarus," in *History Ireland* (2003): 38–42.

88    "Dublin: the last of the old Abbey" #91: 3 March 1961.

89    "Abbey Theatre: foundation stone laid" #223: 7 September 1963.

nationalist production. "The renowned theatre is rising from the debris", says the commentator, as was Liberty Hall just down the street. "The two historic buildings will go up together step by step." The foundation stone bears the names of the founders of the original Abbey Theatre, on which written homage is paid to W.B. Yeats, Synge, Lady Gregory, and Frank and William Fay. And so, just as the national martyrs are commemorated at Arbour Hill, Ireland's cultural heroes find their resting place in the new Abbey Theatre, the memorial to Ireland's cultural and literary revival.

The rapid economic growth that Ireland saw as a result of the first economic programme both helped and hurt the country. The one-sided focus on productive investment meant that most of the state's attention was focused on the opening and successful operation of new factories and research facilities, funded through foreign investment and supported by semi-state bodies. The *Amharc Éireann* series draws attention to the national element by stressing the importance of the role played by the state-sponsored bodies, and of Irish human and industrial resources in this growth. However, the neglect of redistributive investment meant that there was a human and cultural price to pay for charging single-mindedly into the future. As the site of the most rapid infrastructural change and the centre of industrial growth, Dublin bore some of the costs of the state's one-sided growth policy. These costs – both human and architectural – are brought to light in the Gaelic News films, which in this sense serve as the country's social conscience. Overall, however, the critical role of state-sponsored bodies in Irish industrial development is celebrated. The series was thus a marketing tool for the economic nationalism still palpable in the series, despite the superficial praise in many of the films for international investment.

Contestants for the ploughing championships.
*Reproduced with permission from the Irish Photo Archive.*

# CHAPTER SEVEN

# Rural life and new technology

The views of Ireland as a proud national, postcolonial and industrializing community in the *Amharc Éireann* series constitute the official, external and public faces of Ireland. These films celebrate Ireland's political history, its international present and its increasingly bright economic future. Meanwhile, Ireland's social identity emerges in the *Amharc Éireann* series through the films that deal with the country's rural communities. The extent to which rural life appears to be entirely untouched by the state and by its policies is striking; this Ireland appears as a distinctly more traditional and community-oriented society than the one concerned with commemorative politics, international relations and economic plans. The films on rural life both capture and mourn the loss of Ireland's rural identity, while documenting various attempts to deal with the challenges and opportunities presented to rural communities in the form of new technology and scientific research. The existence of a separate rural calendar is evident from the coverage of agricultural shows and county fairs, as is the community social life that is connected to the farming calendar and events such as communal sheep-shearing, the ever-popular ploughing competitions, and the Young Farmer of the Year competition.

In spite of the nostalgic tendencies so evident in many of these films on rural life, the forward march of technology is palpable. Research and development is shown to be having an effect on the working of Irish farms thanks to bodies like An Foras Taluntais (the Agricultural Institute) and a number of research facilities around the country. Some rural industries are growing thanks to the work of Gaeltarra Éireann and Gael Linn, never shy of self-promotion and keen to display the positive effects of its development schemes in the isolated Gaeltacht regions of Connemara and Donegal. But the reality was that despite the work of Gaeltarra Éireann, discontent with the state's development priorities was brewing, as farmers felt themselves left behind and out of the government's plans for national prosperity, while the western districts did not seem to count at all. This dissatisfaction appears only briefly in the otherwise completely apolitical view of rural life in the *Amharc Éireann* series, but the small number of films on protests by rural fishermen and farmers gives some indication of the course that events would follow as the 1960s progressed.

## Research and development

Agriculture in Ireland was in trouble in the late 1940s because of soil acidity and low soil fertility due to a deficiency in major and trace elements. Lime and fertilizer use had been inadequate throughout the 1930s and during the Emergency, so crop production and quality was very poor and animal problems were widespread. Before the late 1950s, facilities and funding for agricultural research in Ireland were very limited.[1] In 1945, after the death of the last private owner, Lady Maurice Fitzgerald, Johnstown Castle was presented to the state as a gift, on condition that it be used solely for agricultural research purposes. The estate is composed of one thousand acres of farmland, four hundred acres of wood and amenity areas, and three lakes. In 1949 the first National Soil Testing began in one room in the castle with primitive equipment, under the direction of Dr. Tom Walsh and the Department of Agriculture, using chemicals and procedures imported from the United States. An Foras Talúntais (the Agricultural Institute) was established in 1958 under the Agriculture Act as an agricultural research institute, after an agreement between Ireland and the United States. It was financed from the Counterpart Special Account money from the US

---

1    Michael Shiel, *The Quiet Revolution: The Electrification of Rural Ireland, 1946–76* (Dublin: The O'Brien Press, 1984): 220.

under the Marshall Aid Programme, to facilitate and undertake agricultural research, including horticulture, forestry and beekeeping.

In 1959, "N.F.A. seminar: foreign delegates visit Kildare farms,"[2] visitors come from Canada, the United States, the EEC, the United Nations and one from Tunisia under the auspices of the United Farmers. Juan Green, president of the National Farmers' Association greets them and shows them his one thousand acre farm – an unusually large size in Ireland. That same year, the Castle was passed to Foras Taluntais to be run as a horticultural college, and was in operation throughout the 1960s. Dr. Walsh, also the first director of the Agricultural Institute, focused on soil research on trace elements for crops and animals. The new research facility in Co. Wexford is shown in "Johnstown Castle passed to Foras Taluntais."[3] It consists not only of the castle itself, which would function as an institute for farmers, but also a laboratory which would be used for conducting research on land, animals and crops. "This is the modern way", says the commentator, "the beliefs of our ancestors have been replaced by science."

The application of such research takes place on the other side of the country, in the underdeveloped regions of Mayo and west Cork. One of the major problems suffered by the western districts, as well as small holding size and fragmentation, is the poor soil type and the topography of these areas.[4] A rather striking example of "modern" technology at work appears in "Co. Cork: aerial crop spraying demonstration,"[5] which showcases the attempt to improve the rocky and infertile land. The Goulding Company is employing the latest techniques to administer its product to land that is unworkable – fertilizers sprayed from a plane, which zips back and forth over the fields at an alarmingly rapid speed and at low elevation – just feet over the land and the spectators. The technique is described by the commentator as "the new thing in the twenty-six counties," which company

2    "N.F.A. seminar: foreign delegates visit Kildare farms" #3: 26 June 1959.
3    "Johnstown Castle passed to Foras Taluntais" #34: 29 January 1960.
4    P.J. Drudy, "Land, people and the regional problem in Ireland," Chp. 9 in *Irish Studies 2 Ireland: Land, Politics and People* (Cambridge: Cambridge University Press, 1982): 196.
5    "Co. Cork: aerial crop spraying demonstration" #14: 11 September 1959.

representatives are there to demonstrate to farmers in Ballyvourney. As the crowd of onlookers and businessmen watches, the small plane repeatedly ascends to 30 feet up and descends to 3 feet off the ground to spray the fertilizers onto the fields. There is no comment on the rather dangerous flying techniques – let alone the danger posed to public health – instead, "Isn't it expensive? Yes, but this thing could do what no tractor could do!" This rocky mountainous land is not useful as it is, so aerial crop spraying could improve productivity by opening up areas for cultivation that have been hitherto impossible to work. The commentator assures the viewers that "this is not a new joke or just aerial high-jinks; it's a new way of working that allows farmers to work on the sides of mountains and irrespective of the weather conditions."

Another attempt to improve agricultural land through modern methods is shown in "Ballina, Co. Mayo: Taoiseach opens 3 million pound drainage scheme,"[6] where Lemass, complete with a band, is greeted by army guards for the opening. This drainage scheme, located near the Moy River in Ballina, is the biggest one in the country. "There are half a million acres to be drained and 700,000 acres with rivers and streams to be cleared." After the inspections and speeches, Lemass detonates the explosive that start the work. Two years later, in "Kinsealy: agricultural research centre opened,"[7] Lemass is there again at the opening of a new building belonging to Foras Talúntais near Malahide in north Co. Dublin, where the centre will be used for research on glasshouses, vegetables and soil research. And finally, in "Co. Meath: agricultural delegates see animal research station,"[8] The Grange, another of Ireland's research facilities, is hosting a group of visitors. This institute, unlike Johnstown Castle and Kinsealy, focuses on animal rather than horticultural research. Dr. Moore, the head of Foras Talúntais, welcomes the guests who then tour the farm from a cart pulled by a tractor to see the results of the various trials. Simon Curry explains

6    "Ballina, Co. Mayo: Taoiseach opens 3 million pound drainage scheme" #47: 29 April 1960.
7    "Kinsealy: agricultural research centre opened" #174: 29 September 1962.
8    "Co. Meath: agricultural delegates see animal research station" #56: 1 July 1960.

the importance of the experiments being conducted on accelerated growth in sheep. "This is stock that is worth millions to us each year. Five million pounds worth of wool is bought by the United States each year," an impressive figure, considering the destination for most of Ireland's agricultural exports was still the United Kingdom. The delegates are then treated to an exhibition of farm equipment and modern machinery used to increase hay output.


## Rural industry


The fishery was another major industry in Ireland and the subject of state intervention during this period. In "Bord Iascaigh Mhara: minister sees boat-building at Killybegs,"[9] the fruits of this intervention are visible. This film serves as a continuation of the short documentary films on Dunmore East and Howth[10] in that it demonstrates the expansion of the industry thanks to state funds. "Killybegs is one of the major ports of the country" and the site of this boat-building enterprise. Michael Moran[11] came to visit the shipyard to see the equipment and the new trawler being built. Men are shown working with the machinery to cut and plane the wood. There are customers waiting for these boats, this is just the most recent example of the fifty that have been built so far. One such customer is Padraig Ó Cuneen, a Galway fisherman who, in "BIM: presentation to Galway skippers,"[12] has just bought a boat, presumably with the help of the state. The event is described as a "big day" for the Connemara fisherman, who stands

9    "Bord Iascaigh Mhara: minister sees boat-building at Killybegs" #157: 8 June 1962.
10   See Chapter 2: Industrial and Rural Development.
11   Minister for Lands and Minister for the Gaeltacht during this period.
12   "BIM: presentation to Galway skippers" #131: 8 December 1961.

surrounded by officials including Brian Lenihan[13] and Seamus O'Maolain,[14] looking awkwardly into the camera as Lenihan praises the fishermen.[15]

Sadly, in spite of this sort of investment in research facilities, equipment, new machinery and boatbuilding, there were continued problems in rural industries. "Co. Waterford: bad herring season at Dunmore East"[16] indicates that, while it was once one of the major landing sites for herring in the country, there is very little activity going on there now. "There are now only twenty boats; there used to be two hundred." Apparently the state's boat-building activities are not being felt in Dunmore East. "It's not just the number of boats that have fallen but also the income. Now they only get forty pounds a week and they used to get three to four hundred." The problem is the same as that suffered years ago and covered by the short documentary film: "All the fish are scooped up by the big foreign trawlers." Foreign competitors are still out-doing the Irish fishermen in their own waters but there is a glimmer of hope on the horizon: "The outcome of the recent London conference was a proposal for a six-mile limit." The commentator is justifiably skeptical, however, of the possibilities for implementation of such a regulation: "It's only a recommendation and nobody knows when it will be put into effect." In other words, there is no realistic hope for an improvement to the situation for the fishermen of Dunmore East. There is little point in embarking on boat-building programmes if the bigger foreign trawlers are going to continue to out-compete the Irish fishermen. The commentator's rather cynical conclusion regarding state-driven attempts at helping the beleaguered industry is simply that it constitutes "closing the stable door after the horse has bolted."

Other less traditional methods were employed in an effort to increase the fish catch in Ireland and promote the use of fish by consumers. In

13   Parliamentary Secretary to the Minister for Lands.
14   Chairman of Bord Iascaigh Mhara.
15   Another attempt to increase the fishermen's productivity included the "Galway Bay: demonstration of seine net fishing" #12: 28 August 1959, which was put on by Bord Iascaigh Mhara for young fishermen along the west coast.
16   "Co. Waterford: bad herring season at Dunmore East" #242: 18 January 1964.

"Roscrea: farming with a difference!"[17] new technology is applied to aquaculture at the Fanure Fish Farm, a project of the Inland Fisheries Trust Incorporated. The film shows the hatchery and the injection of tadpoles into buckets, followed by their transfer into larger troughs, before they are moved outside to a row of little pools and then one bigger pool. A shot of the sign reading "Rainbow Trout fresh daily" is followed by the picture of the fish being lifted with a net from the pool and thrown into a bucket, then being packed into a wooden box. The final scene shows the pool being electrified, bringing a rather grim ending to the short life of the rainbow trout.

The increasing demand for fish by Irish consumers was the aim of promotions like the Irish Countrywomen's course in "Louth: ICA members at novel cookery course,"[18] offered with Bord Iascaigh Mhara. One woman from each county was invited to participate in the weeklong course, at the end of which they enjoyed a fish dinner with Michael Moran and other dignitaries. Apparently unwilling to stop at the more traditional forms of promotion, the Fisheries Board even held a national competition, "Bord Iascaigh Mhara's 'Miss Seafood 1964',"[19] a fish cooking competition, the object of which was "to increase the fish consumption amongst the Irish population". There were eight thousand competitors from all over the country but the film records only the final stage, during which the women are described as being "on tenderhooks waiting for the result" and Lemass was there to give out the prizes.

Finally, as well as all of these efforts at increasing the productivity of fishermen and the consumption of fish, there was the increase in rural tourism. In "Kinsale for angling holidays"[20] a new type of holiday was being offered for domestic and international tourists. The scheme, the film shows, was first begun by an Irishman who then went to Canada, and was then taken over by French people who planned to develop it further.

17    "Roscrea: farming with a difference" #20: 23 October 1959.
18    "Louth: ICA members at novel cookery course" #43: 1 April 1960.
19    No issue number or date available.
20    No issue number or date available.

While there are not enough fish for the Irish fishermen to compete with international competition on the other side of the country, there is apparently no shortage for internationally driven tourism. "Three thousand people took up this activity last year and the French hope for more next year." There is, however, no sense of resentment of foreign ownership of the enterprise expressed in the commentary. Simply stated, "it is important that these facilities be here because fishing is a very important part of the tourism industry."

It is a sad comment on the state of the Irish fisheries that it was the international competitors in every field that appeared to be more capable of not only catching more fish, but also marketing the whole enterprise for the purposes of tourism than were the Irish. While the efforts of Bord Iascaigh Mhara were recorded in the *Amharc Éireann* series, they appear to lag behind their foreign counterparts in every way. The only organization that is depicted as having any real success in the field of rural development is – coincidentally – Gael Linn itself. The organization regularly featured films that drew attention to its efforts in and for the Gaeltacht regions of Ireland. The work of state-sponsored Gaeltarra Éireann also appears but is given short shrift in comparison. Although the statutory body was established with the new Department of the Gaeltacht in 1958, it was largely ineffective in its first decade. It was only the early 1970s that the state made a more concerted effort through Gaeltarra Éireann to locate industry in the west but even then there was remarkably little improvement to the western areas since 1960.[21] "New showrooms for Gaeltarra Éireann"[22] is one film in which the new facilities for the showcasing of goods made at Gaeltarra Éireann factories are shown. These goods, increasingly popular overseas, include Donegal Tweed as well as hand-made dolls and other crafts. The other film, "New trademark for Tweed"[23] focuses on the official opening

---

21   P.J. Drudy, "Land, people and the regional problem in Ireland," Chp. 9 in *Irish Studies 2 Ireland: Land, Politics and People* (Cambridge: Cambridge University Press, 1982): 211.

22   No issue number or date available.

23   No issue number or date available.

for the new trademark of "Donegal Handwoven Tweed", the letter D in old Gaelic script.

In contrast, "Teelin, Co. Donegal: vocational officers see Gael Linn project"[24] and the "Gael Linn development scheme in Carna" stress the groundbreaking work being conducted by the organization. In 1958, a 135-acre estate was bought at Teelin in south Donegal, to protect the local salmon fishermen. This included a sheep and pig farm as well as fishing rights to local rivers, lakes and Teelin Bay. The fishermen were allowed to net salmon under license from Gael Linn and a local family ran the farm on behalf of the organization. The occasion for the first film is the visit of the Vocational Education Committee of Donegal to see the woodworking enterprise where young men are employed making souvenirs, crafts, miniature furniture and household items, such as magazine racks and bowls. It is significant that these boys have also made a pleasure boat, for which they are charging only 250 pounds. There is no indication that this is in direct competition with the promotional work of Bord Iascaigh Mhara, but it is noteworthy that in this instance they are learning to make such tools of the trade for themselves, rather than buying them through deals offered by the state.

The other film, "Gael Linn development scheme in Carna,"[25] is a single-item documentary-style film that provides an example of the potential for rural development in the neglected Gaeltacht areas of Ireland. In 1957, Gael Linn had established a fish and vegetable processing plant in Carna, in the Galway Gaeltacht. It also donated five boats for in-shore fishing to local fishermen on a purchase-lease basis. Later on, oyster beds were bought in nearby Bá Chill Chiaráin to support the fish processing. The film opens with a view of Connemara, "a place of beauty where there is plenty of Irish and a dearth of employment", followed by a view of the new factory, which cost five thousand pounds and now provides employment in fish processing and packaging for the local people. Inside, men are unloading

---

24   "Teelin, Co. Donegal: vocational officers see Gael Linn project" #54: 17 June 1960
      – the intertitle for this film misspelled vocational as "occasional."
25   "Gael Linn development scheme in Carna" #250: 15 March 1964.

oysters while women cut fish. The women pack the fish into wooden crates and walk to the freezer, while "the men are at sea bringing in the fish to be processed." The point is made that "Irish only is spoken here – you hear it as they open the oysters" before switching to an exterior shot of a boat in the sea at the end of a small rocky pier where two men pull up a net, spilling oysters through it into the boat. "It is teaming with oysters here" but the crucial factor is not the plentitude of fish – as they sort the oysters, the commentator stresses, "The big plus for these men is the consistent market. They will get a good price from the factory." The men look overboard, smiling, as the lesson to be drawn is hammered home: "The Gaeltacht can be saved and work given to the people of Connemara. This is one scheme that is succeeding brilliantly but lots more like this are needed."

And indeed, a scheme like this is exactly what the fishermen in Dunmore East are lacking. The guaranteed prices that the Connemara fishermen are offered make the difference between a decent livelihood and none at all. While in Dunmore East, their takings are down to ten percent of what they previously made, here in Connemara there is no such danger, thanks to the processing and packing plant nearby in Carna. It is a reminder to the government that, as important as vessels and improvements are to the fisheries, it is markets that are most desperately needed. In the commercial fisheries, the markets do not appear to exist to the same extent that they do overseas, and the technology and equipment is not up-to-date or plentiful enough to compete in any sort of meaningful sense. While efforts like the "Miss Seafood" competition are a novel approach to the attempt to increase the demand for fish in Ireland, they are unlikely to make the necessary impact in time to save this rural industry from dying out in the places that need the economic stimulation the most. By providing the necessary market and guaranteed prices, the fishermen have what they lack elsewhere – security – and this is really the only thing that will keep them working and living in the Gaeltacht, and speaking the language.[26]

---

26　In 1960, Gael Linn had also invested in a seaweed processing factory, Tora Toinne Teoranta, in An Cheathrú Rua, in the Galway Gaeltacht. In 1961, a bee-keeping

## Agricultural shows

One of the major Irish rural industries, as indicated by the obligatory visit of the international delegates to the National Stud Farm, was livestock. There are a number of Gaelic News films on the various bloodstock sales that took place intermittently throughout the year. These sales were an annual event held at the Royal Dublin Show (RDS) grounds that consisted of sales of horses to domestic and international buyers. Usually there are around six hundred horses for sale at each event, with prices going from a few hundred guineas up to a thousand. In "RDS bloodstock sales"[27] the camera focuses on the crowd as the commentator rather pointedly mentions that "here are the types of people who can afford to spend a few hundred guineas on a horse," and again, in "RDS, Ballsbridge: November bloodstock sales,"[28] for which buyers have come from England and Ireland, the commentator remarks that "these are the kind of people who can pay up to a thousand guineas for a horse."

Cow and bull shows were also held at the RDS. In "Ballsbridge: RDS bull show and sales,"[29] displays of hundreds of bulls continued for four days, with buyers from England and the Continent, as well as Ireland. In "RDS, Ballsbridge: Hereford champs on show,"[30] the visitors include the chief-judge from Uruguay, the Minister for Lands and two Russian men who were very interested in the goings on. "There are over two thousand Herefords in the country now," viewers are told, so "this is a very important event for agricultural industry and for economic affairs in general in Ireland."

In Northern Ireland, three Balmoral Livestock and Agricultural Shows take place in Belfast, the equivalent to the RDS bloodstock show and sales

scheme was established in the West Cork Gaeltacht of Cúl Aodha and Corca Dhuibhne in West Kerry.
27   "RDS bloodstock sales" #182: 24 November 1962.
28   "RDS, Ballsbridge: November bloodstock sales" #25: 27 November 1959.
29   "Ballsbridge: RDS bull show and sales" #91: 3 March 1961.
30   No issue number or date available.

in the Republic. The "Belfast Balmoral Show,"[31] the biggest show of stock in Northern Ireland, is the Royal Ulster Agricultural Society Spring Show and Sale, at which various classes of cows and bulls are displayed and sold. The Balmoral Livestock Show is a similar event, marked as taking place in Ulster by the opening shot of the Union Jack flying above the King's Hall, the Royal Ulster Society building in Belfast. There is, however, no point made of this fact beyond the focus of the camera on the British flag; the Balmoral Show is covered as just another agricultural show on the island of Ireland, in the same way that all Northern events are covered as Irish and without overt recognition of partition.

Films covering the various agricultural shows held around the country highlight the function of these fairs as a showcase for new technology, as well as socializing and for the ever-popular horse-jumping competitions. The Balmoral agricultural show again takes place in Belfast, while the Castleblaney, Thurles, Cork agricultural shows and the Tralee county fair represent the activities in the Republic. Rural dwellers are not presented as being slow to embrace the benefits of modernity in the form of new farming technology; these agricultural shows are much more focused on new technology and machinery for farming than on livestock. At the "Balmoral Agricultural Show,"[32] held during the last week in May, a tractor stands suspended sideways in the air as a sort of sculpture and centrepiece of the exhibit. As a novelty amphibious car is featured going backwards and forwards on a sort of roller-coaster, the commentator claims that "anyone would be nuts to climb when a machine like this is available!"

People have come for years to the "Castleblaney Agricultural Show"[33] to display their animals and enter them in competitions, while at the "Thurles Show"[34] one thousand five hundred people arrived on special trains from the early morning from all over to see the tractors and the horse jumping competition in the afternoon because, as the audience is told, "Tipperary

---

31   "Belfast Balmoral Show" #38: 26 February 1960.
32   No issue number or date available.
33   No issue number or date available.
34   "Thurles Show" #64: 26 August 1960.

is a great county for horses!" At the three-day "Tralee: county fair,"[35] farmers came from all over the country to see more new technology on display,
including a huge digger – proof that "the end of the spade has arrived!" – as
well as the obligatory horse jumping competition. Finally, at the summer
"Cork Agricultural Show"[36] a new grain dryer machine is on display. A big
display sign reading "water on tap in every home" also draws attention to
the ongoing demonstration of the benefits of piped water for rural farms
and farm-houses. The closing reference to the unhappiness of the farmers
with some aspects of modernizing is noteworthy: "Don't forget to ask the
farmers what they think about the Common Market," suggesting that they
might not be altogether in support of the idea. It is more than a little ironic
that once Ireland joined the European Community in 1973, it was because
of a perceived trade-off between recognition for the Irish language and
rights for farmers in the context of the Common Agricultural Policy, that
the Irish language was forsaken in the government's negotiations for entry.

## Competitive farming

Other activities important to the rural calendar include the annual ploughing competitions held in every county in Ireland. The representation of these
events in the *Amharc Éireann* series, and the accompanying commentary
in particular, indicate a strong sense of nostalgia for the "old Ireland" that
was perceived as being lost as a result of modernization and technological
advances in the shape of tractors and other machinery. On the other hand,
the appearance of women in many of these events suggests that equality
was increasingly a part of rural work, thanks to these same machines. Thus,
the "price" of technology was not the same for everyone.

35   No issue number or date available.
36   No issue number or date available.

The films on ploughing championships all feature the unlikely combination of progress in the form of women operating the new tractors, and nostalgia for the old ways in the form of showcasing horse-drawn and old-fashioned ploughing methods. In "Roundwood: Co. Wicklow ploughing championships"[37] there were seventy people competing in the Wicklow version of the ploughing competitions being held in every county "under the watchful eye of the local farmers." The active role of women in the work of the rural community is reflected in the appearance of a woman on a tractor. "Muriel Sutton – she's an expert and doesn't need help from anyone. She's a good as any man, God bless her!" gushes the commentator. Such approval and support for the active role of women in the rural community is in keeping with the modern version of the rural co-operative ideal, as exemplified by the work of the ICA, and would certainly have been supported by Gael Linn. In "Thurles: national ploughing championships"[38] men and women compete again on tractors and in the old-fashioned style with horses. There are over one hundred competitors at this competition, in which a man from Kilkenny is pitted against a woman from Kildare. "By the way, she's not married!" offers the commentator.

In "New Ross: ploughing championships,"[39] Co. Wexford is introduced as the biggest county for tillage in Ireland – a somewhat strange comment given that tillage was only introduced by de Valera during the Emergency for crops. "It's the ploughman who is the backbone of the country and they're the ones doing well at the ploughing competition." There were twelve women in this competition, but in this case it was not for the actual ploughing but rather a reversion to more regressive gender roles, for the Queen of Ploughing competition. But the highlight of the event was the old fashioned styles of ploughing – by hand and with horses – that were more and more rarely seen in the Irish countryside. "There's a small number there for the old-fashioned hand-drawn competition but the old style of ploughing with two horses demands skill that will never be achieved by

---

37   "Roundwood: Co. Wicklow ploughing championships" #41: 18 March 1960.
38   "Thurles: national ploughing championships" #180: 10 November 1962.
39   "New Ross: ploughing championships" #76: 18 November 1960.

the engine." The traditional method and accompanying skills will not be entirely lost, however, as "they will continue with old-fashioned horse competition so we can always see this," which presumably cushions the blow.

"Ploughing championships at Athenry"[40] is a long lament for the passing of these old-fashioned methods with horses and by hand. The film opens with a shot of the sign for Athenry, followed by men ploughing with tractors. Although overall attendance was not high, it was noted that each county in Ireland was represented in the competition. As a man is shown ploughing with a tractor with an old-fashioned attachment on it, "there's no doubt that the skill and talent is no longer as important now that the tractor is on the scene." The preference of the commentator is clearly for the old-fashioned and labour intensive approach, if only for the romantic image of the Irish countryside it invoked: "It's certain that there is a special personality to a horse that an engine doesn't have."

There is no recognition in these films of the improvements to lifestyle, working conditions and hours of work the new technology is bringing to rural existence. Again and again, the coming of the tractor is dismissed as nothing more than the supplanting of authentic and traditional rural existence by a modern gadget. This lack of engagement with the positive implications of new technology for rural life constitutes a disappointingly one-sided viewpoint that fails to give due credit for the palpable benefits such improvements must have made in the daily lives of rural workers. It also contrasts quite starkly with implicit praise for the state's activities in horticultural and animal research. Meanwhile, the appearance of women and girls in these films, while glossed over as something resembling a dating game, is important as the introduction of tractors eliminated the need for a man to do work like ploughing, which traditionally required much more physical strength than the average woman had. Now that tractors were on the scene, there was no reason that a woman could not do the same work as a man. This is important in more than symbolic terms, as many women who were left alone because their husbands had to emigrate to find work, or never married, could now – in theory at least – work the farm themselves.

40   "Ploughing championships at Athenry" #233: 16 November 1963.

Other competitions that fostered excellence in farming included the Young Farmer of the Year and an international sheep-shearing competition. The Young Farmers movement was founded in 1944 in Athy during a period of food shortages, high emigration and extremely low rural morale before the Electricity Supply Board's campaign of rural electrification began to transform the countryside. The Emergency highlighted the importance of the agricultural industry in Ireland and the need to provide a proper agricultural education to the young people destined to work the land, as the son inheriting the farm received no formal education beyond the primary school. Rural science teachers held classes and courses in the vocational schools during the winter, and a young farmers' club was started to preserve the contact made between pupils and teachers at these classes. In 1951 the idea of a junior club for twelve to eighteen-year-olds was born, based on the American 4H Clubs.[41] By 1954 there were almost five hundred clubs around the country and the official name had been changed to Macra na Feirme (translated as Young Farmers but the official meaning is "Stalwarts of the Land"). The Young Farmers/Macra na Feirme movement has been described as one of the most positive and constructive movements ever founded in the country, which brought another movement into existence that would play a major part in the politics of Ireland in the 1960s – the National Farmers' Association.[42]

The *Amharc Éireann* films on the subject publicize the good work of the organization by drawing attention to the pride that the winners bring to their rural communities. In "Tuam, Co. Galway: 'Young Farmer of the Year' at home,"[43] Padraig O'Grianan, who has just won the competition, is filmed doing his chores around the farm while being visited by representatives of the vocational school and the head of Macra na Feirme, Michael Moran. In "Kiltegan, Co. Wicklow: 'Young Farmer of the Year' at home,"[44]

41   Michael Shiel, *The Quiet Revolution: The Electrification of Rural Ireland, 1946–76* (Dublin: The O'Brien Press, 1984): 182–4.
42   Maurice Manning, "The Farmers," in *Ireland 1945–70* (Dublin: Gill and Macmillan & New York: Barnes and Noble Books, 1979): 53.
43   "Tuam, Co. Galway: 'Young Farmer of the Year' at home" #33: 22 January 1960.
44   "Kiltegan, Co. Wicklow: 'Young Farmer of the Year' at home" #84: 13 January 1961.

another boy is featured for bringing "fame and fortune" to the area. The boy, who keeps twenty pigs, feeds them vegetables and meal for the camera. "The whole family is very proud of him. He won 100 pounds and a plaque." In comparison to the films on industrial development, which focus on the impersonal aspects of new industries and investments, these films on rural life tend to draw attention to the people themselves, identifying them by name and highlighting the importance of their contribution to the collective well-being of the community.

## Rural protest

Rural life and community revolved around more than ploughing competitions and agricultural fairs. Just as rapid industrialization and urbanization bred discontent in the face of poverty, decay and the state neglect, rural change also gave rise to a new group of demonstrators – the farmers. In the early 1960s post-war trends were visible in the countryside not only in the emigration of the younger farm population and the resulting imbalance in age structure in the remaining population, but also in the rising aspirations of farmers for greater incomes and consumer goods.[45] The rise of farmer activism during this period is the prelude to the more vocal and active politics in which they engaged through the National Farmers' Association (NFA) in the mid- and late-1960s, as part of the trend towards the "direct politics" of protest that took place across the board in Irish life.[46] The beginnings of this sort of activism, while not generally recognized as

45  P. Commins, "Land policies and agricultural development," Chp. 10 in *Irish Studies 2 Ireland: Land, Politics and People* (Cambridge: Cambridge University Press, 1982): 217–40.
46  This "direct politics" was also visible in the Georgian Society protests, women's marches, the language rights movement, the Catholic civil rights movement in Northern Ireland, and the farmers' long marches from 1965 onwards.

being important before the mid-1960s, is recorded in the Gaelic News films in its early stages.

In January 1955 the National Farmers' Association (NFA) was launched, bringing with it Macra na Feirme's expertise on economic policy issues, through which the bulk of the farmers' bargaining would be carried out from now on. Although the NFA's influence spread rapidly though the championing of farmers' issues such as pioneering livestock marts and eradicating bovine tuberculosis, it was not recognized by the government until 1964. By then it was too late to stave off the growing discontent that had been fuelled not only by the perception that farmers were being left behind in Ireland's race for prosperity, but also that Dublin bureaucrats simply did not care about them or understand their problems.

Although the first of the so-called Farmers' Rights marches led by Rickard Deasy did not take place until 1966, it is clear from the number of films on various forms of discontent that the new activist politics actually began in the early years of the 1960s. The farmers in particular were angry at being left behind in Ireland's period of rapid modernization and out of the disproportionate benefits that the first economic programme was dispensing to industry and urban areas.[47] Two examples of this discontent appear in the *Amharc Éireann* series in 1963. The first is recorded in "Farmers demonstrate at Athlone,"[48] when ten thousand angry farmers from two counties assembled outside the Costume Barracks to protest an increase in their taxes. They made a major impact, stopping trains and transport from crossing the River Shannon so that "there was no doubt that the farmers made their case." Later that year, in a second film on the NFA's protests, "Limerick: 30,000 farmers in protest march,"[49] the NFA, led by Tom Maher, is looking for an increase in the price for milk, more representation on committees and more credit from the banks. While the Athlone protest employed simple obstruction tactics, those employed by

47   See Manning and Gary Murphy, "The Irish Government, the National Farmers' Association, and the European Economic Community, 1955–64," in *New Hibernia Review* 6, no. 4 (Winter 2002): 68–84.
48   "Farmers demonstrate at Athlone" #220: 17 August 1963.
49   "Limerick: 30,000 farmers in protest march" #230: 26 October 1963.

the farmers in Limerick are particularly interesting. Tractors and other big farming vehicles are shown draped in red tape, symbolizing the bureaucratic obstacles that the farmers felt they were facing from Dublin.

Another rural protest, this time from the fisheries, is featured in "Galway: Atlantic fishermen join strike; temporary truce announced,"[50] which shows the port in Galway at a standstill. The commentator once again explains the extent of the action, if not its actual motivation: "This is a wide-ranging strike – it's the entire fishing population." Focusing on "Peadar from Aranmore," he continues rather vaguely, "It's the big men who are making the money. This man from the Aran Islands has the same opinion." This comment highlights the animosity towards the government and state bureaucracy, in which the "big men" refers to the government and to Bord Iascaigh Mhara, both based in Dublin. The fishermen, like the farmers, see these men as competing for their share of resources rather than supporting their struggle for a better living. The problem was solved in this case when the fishermen's representatives visited Brian Lenihan[51] and they agreed to place a bar on certain types of fish.

Finally, "Inisturk relieved: supplies by helicopter"[52] illustrates the continuing practical problems suffered by rural populations isolated from the mainland. The eighty people on Inisturk – one of the Aran Islands, off the west coast of Ireland – were short of food for six weeks due to bad weather. Eventually, instead of being helped by the government, they were relieved by the Smithwicks brewery in Kilkenny, which sent its own private helicopter with supplies. Described by the commentator as "a strange story from the most isolated/backward place in the country, which also shows the effects of new technology," the film highlights the incapacity or unwillingness of the government to come to the aid of these regions when they were most in need of help, while simultaneously illustrating the sort of attitude to these

---

50  "Galway: Atlantic fishermen join strike; temporary truce announced" #250: 15 March 1964.
51  Minister for Justice.
52  "Inisturk relieved: supplies by helicopter" #90: 24 February 1961.

regions that perpetuated the situation.[53] The commentator does nothing to change this perception of the Aran Islands. The word used for "backward"[54] in the film is the same as the word for "isolated" in Irish – the two are synonymous. This film, like those focusing on new farming technology and traditional ploughing competitions, illustrates the contradiction inherent in the use of Ireland's rural areas as both the problem and the solution – the source of backwardness and the repository of traditional identity.

The representation of rural life in the *Amharc Éireann* presents a rather surprising contrast to the rest of the series' apparent pre-occupation with Ireland's modernity. While addressing some of the problems of rural development and agricultural decline, the series tends to focus more on the nostalgic and traditional communitarian aspects of rural life. The calendar is still defined by events established in the 1930s and 1940s to battle the isolation and depression that were features of rural life during the Economic War and the Emergency. While it acknowledges the coming of new technology to rural work and life, one does not get the sense that it is particularly welcome from the viewpoint of those more intent on protecting essential "Irishness" than relieving rural workers from hours of unnecessary drudgery. In this sense, it displays a disturbingly similar approach to the state toward the problems of rural Ireland. The western districts appeared to be a lost cause and were treated as such in the context of an economic drive that focused on industrial export-driven growth, while the problems of isolation and the lack of social networks and community facilities were still to blame for the ongoing flood of emigration.[55]

53   In 1953 the last residents on the Blasket Islands left the islands for the mainland. The documents point to a lack of reliable communication with the mainland and of sufficient food supplies as two of their main reasons for leaving. It is startling that eight years later, the same problems persisted in the Aran Islands. See Dermot Keogh, "Leaving the Blaskets 1953: Willing or Enforced Departures?" in *The Lost Decade: Ireland in the 1950s* (Cork: Mercier Press, 2004): 48–71.

54   Iargúlta.

55   See Enda Delany "The Vanishing Irish? The Exodus from Ireland in the 1950s," pp. 80–86 and Tracey Connolly "The Commission on Emigration, 1948–54," in *The Lost Decade: Ireland in the 1950s* (Cork: Mercier Press, 2004): 87–104.

And although dissenting voices were heard, protesting the further peripheralizing of the periphery by the state's modernization policy, depopulation of the west was generally regarded as a positive trend. The cries to "Save the West" that began in Co. Mayo in May 1963 were barely audible yet and would fall on deaf ears.[56] The equivalent to the watershed in Ireland's industrial development in 1958/59 that was so badly needed would not take place in the agricultural arena until 1965, when the Anglo-Irish Free Trade Agreement was signed. When Ireland joined the European Economic Community nearly a decade later, the burden of helping the farmers was placed on Brussels instead, under the Common Agricultural Policy (CAP).

56  See Vincent Tucker, "Images of Development and Underdevelopment in Glencolumbcille, County Donegal, 1830–1970," Chp. 6 in *Rural Change in Ireland* (Belfast: The Queen's University of Belfast, The Institute of Irish Studies, 1999): 109–15.

Opening of Thurles Drama Festival at Premier Hall, Thurles, Co. Tipperary,
organized by Muintir na Tíre and Gael Linn. The Archbishop of Cashel
Thomas Morris arrives at the Hall. 9 April 1961.
*Reproduced with permission from the Irish Photo Archive.*

CHAPTER EIGHT

# Irish language and culture

Gael Linn's concept of Irishness is the underlying subject of the entire
*Amharc Éireann* series and nowhere is it more clear what this entails than
in the films that deal specifically with traditional Irish culture. The representation of various markers of Irish identity in the series is the visible
testament to Gael Linn's Irish Ireland philosophy, which promoted the
advancement of all things Irish. These years may be characterized in hind-
sight as the "years of change" in a very real political, economic and social
sense, but for Gael Linn and Colm Ó Laoghaire, the Ireland in the *Amharc
Éireann* series must also maintain its traditions. While progress and development in domestic industry and the international sphere are applauded
and highlighted throughout the series, it is in the films celebrating Irish
Ireland that the message of Gael Linn is most discernable; the protection
and promotion of Ireland's traditional, Gaelic identity.

The series highlights the work of Gael Linn and other groups that are
actively promoting Irish language education and culture. It showcases the
wealth of Irish talent at the national traditional music and Irish dancing
competitions, draws attention to Irish subjects and players in film and
theatre, and allots extensive coverage to traditional Irish sports – hurling,
Gaelic football and camogie. Irish culture is more than traditional music,
dance and sport, however. The series pays significant attention to rural and
and urban working-class entertainment by focusing on community theatre
in various places. Coincidentally, the Abbey Theatre – that powerful symbol
of the first cultural revival and the Anglo-Irish presence in Ireland – barely
registers in the *Amharc Éireann* series. This is probably mere coincidence,
more to do with the fate of the theatre than a purposeful decision, but
the fact remains that the focus is squarely on community entertainment,
rural and urban, much more in keeping with its Irish Ireland mandate.

Similarly, events in Northern Ireland are treated no differently than those in the Republic, including the Orange Order's 12th of July parade, which is acknowledged as a cultural festival like any other. In the *Amharc Éireann* series, partition might as well not exist – there is no real acknowledgment of the political separation in the films. There is just the island of Ireland with one, shared culture – a strong statement in itself.

## Language education and activism

Gael Linn uses the *Amharc Éireann* series quite unselfconsciously as a vehicle for self-promotion in the area of language preservation and use, unsurprisingly since the promotion of the Irish language and culture was and is its main purpose. There are a number of films in the series that draw attention to the efforts of other bodies to promote the language through other means, but Gael Linn's own programs, along with the state funding that supported many of these measures, are at the forefront. These programs were critical to the survival of the language because they focus on the use of Irish by children of all ages in English-speaking parts of the country, where the language was most at risk of being discarded.

Gael Linn, clearly aware of the benefits of youth for language acquisition, became involved in language education by awarding three-month scholarships for primary school children to attend schools in the Gaeltacht starting in 1955. There are no short documentary films on this early Gael Linn activity, but it is a fairly regular feature in the Gaelic News films. In 1960, "Gael-Linn scholarships: Dublin children off to the Gaeltacht,"[1] sees the train station packed with children heading off to the West and Northern Gaeltachts. Viewers are told, "The government paid half the cost" for the children to go away until Christmas to learn Irish by going to school with

1    "Gael-Linn scholarships: Dublin children off to the Gaeltacht" #68: 23 September 1960.

Gaeltacht children. And later, when "Scholarship children home from Gaeltacht,"[2] some three hundred happy children are shown returning from Kerry, Clare and Donegal. Naturally, "the first presents they got were Irish language books published by the Gaelic National Congress, given out by the Gael Linn trustees there to meet them." Two months later, in "State aid for 'children to Gaeltacht' scheme,"[3] the Minister for the Gaeltacht announced that 50,000 pounds more in grants would be given. The results of this cooperation are shown yet again a few months later, when three months later, more "Dublin children leave for Gaeltacht."[4] These exchanges, which saw young children travelling from the heart of English-speaking Ireland, were critical to the survival of the language outside of the Gaeltacht. Children tend to learn langauges more quickly and easily than adults, but the added element of fun in these exchanges would have been critical in terms of countering the compulsion-oriented state language policy and fostering genuine enthusiasm for Irish in the next generation.

Gaelachas Teoranta (Irish Limited)[5] had also initated a venture in Irish language education, which started well before Gael Linn's. The non-profit company was founded over a decade earlier, in 1944, and opened one of the first Irish Colleges in Garryvoe, Co. Cork. In 1958 it bought Trabolgan House and estate in Midleton, and established a boarding school for boys called Scoil na nÓg (Youth School), which opened in June 1959. Until 1973, 160 pupils each year were educated through Irish at the school. During the summer months, Scoil na nÓg operated a summer Irish college where up to 1,400 boys and girls studied Irish. In "Cork: President opens Trabolgan College,"[6] the new summer school is opened. Viewers are told that Valera is "really pleased to be opening the Gaelachas Teoranta College," as he inspects the omnipresent honour guard. The beautiful grounds are set on two hundred acres with hundreds of chalets that will house seven

2   No issue number or date available.
3   "State aid for 'children to Gaeltacht' scheme" #90: 24 February 1961.
4   "Dublin children leave for Gaeltacht" #98: 21 April 1961.
5   See <www.gaelachas.com> for more information on Gaelachas Teo.
6   "Cork: President opens Trabolgan Irish College" #8: 31 July 1959.

hundred girls and three hundred boys attending summer course, who will "have lots of fun learning Irish."

That might have been the official line on the Irish colleges but some people's recollections are not quite as sunny. In 2013, Ruairi Quinn, Minister of Education, recalled attending the Tabolgan Holiday Centre: "The facilities were so primitive it reminded me of a prison camp. I recall two of my brothers escaping from the camp and they got as far as the Whitegate Oil Refinery before they were caught. I'm always reminded of the film *The Great Escape* whenever I think of my time in Irish college!" On the other hand, Siobhán Bastible, a news presenter on TV3, had rather more positive associations with Irish college: "I was eleven myself when myself and my cousin Jennifer were sent to Coláiste Ciarán in Carraroe, Co. Galway. There was a social element to Coláiste Ciarán, but at the age of eleven, my cousin and I didn't avail of it. We were simply too young – the other girls were mostly in their teens and had a ball, according to the talk at the breakfast table some mornings." But the comment from Luke "Ming" Flanagan, an Independent TD, might be most telling on the issue of who went to Irish college in the Gaeltacht and why. "I would love to have gone to the Gaeltacht when I was younger. Unfortunately, this was the preserve of the more well off. When it came to a choice between feeding us and teaching us Irish, my parents were forced to do as many before had, and that was to choose food. Pity it had to be that way, still is. A bit like brown bread, the poor only get to eat is when the rich didn't want it."[7]

Flanagan's comment highlights the issue of social class and survival of the language from a very different perspective than that suggested by the promoters of Irish. Many of these organizations were composed of the so-called "Gaeilgeoirí" – the educated, middle-class, Irish-speaking intelligentsia, who tended to be better off than those who actually lived full-time in the Gaeltacht. The term "Gaeilgeoir" is often used pejoratively

7    Quoted in "Making the great escape to the Gaeltacht," *The Irish Examiner*, August 2, 2013.

to denote a language fanatic[8] and in the 1960s, some so-called Gaeilgeoirí made the move from Dublin to live in the Gaeltacht full-time. The tension between the "fíor Gael" (a "real Gael" – meaning a native speaker, living in the Gaeltacht) and the "Gaeilgeoir" (referring to an Irish language enthusiast but not a native speaker) is not a new phenomenon,[9] nor is it unique to Ireland – such divisions are part and parcel of cultural nationalism and revival movements. The distinction in Ireland was made explicit in 1926 with the definition of the "true Gaeltacht" as those areas in which 80% of the population was enumerated as Irish speaking, but updated in 1956 to distinguish the *predominantly* Irish-speaking areas from the more Anglicized parts of the country.[10] Thus the very definition of "real" Gael and not-so-real Gaeilgeoir was itself in flux, and expectations of fluency receded, as did borders of the actual Gaeltachtaí (plural of Gaeltacht) over the years.

In 1958, educational opportunities expanded when the Irish-language teaching institute, Foras na Gaelige,[11] was established to organize Irish language courses for adults as well as children. The concrete results of such investments are evident in Gael Linn's other main inititive, the Irish-language debating contest for secondary school students. The debating contests began in 1959 and constitute another success for Gael Linn in terms of maintaining Irish as a living language. They turned out to be very popular and became part of national culture. In 1960, the "Final of school

---

8   Reg Hindley, *The Death of the Irish Language: a qualified obituary* (New York: Routledge Press, 1990): 258

9   See Joep Leersen, *Mere Irish and Fíor Gael: Studies in the Idea of Nationality, its Development and Literary Expression Prior to the Nineteenth Century* (Cork: Cork University Press/Field Day, 1996) and *Remembrance and Imagination: Patterns in the Historical and Literary Representation of Ireland in the Nineteenth Century* (Cork: Cork University Press/Field Day, 1996).

10  Hindley, 258.

11  This teaching institute is not the same as the organization that currently exists, also called Foras na Gaeilge. The latter was founded in December 1999 under the terms of the Good Friday Agreement, for the promotion of Irish throughout the whole island of Ireland. See <http://www.foras-na-gaeilge.ie>.

Irish debating contest"[12] was held in the Shelburne Hotel in Dublin and lots of people from the educational sphere were there for the event. Three years later, the "All-Ireland schools debating contest"[13] had become "the biggest debate competition in the country," in which four teams competed before a large crowd. Tourmakeady, Co. Mayo won the team prize but – significantly – "Dublin had the best talker," a perhaps unexpected result. This would have been a victory well worth publicizing, as those in the west were not always appreciative of the well-intentioned efforts of the Dublin-based Gaeilgeoirí to save the language.

Not all Irish-language activities were based in the Republic either – in fact, one of the most notable was started in Belfast. In "Belfast: exhibition of Gaelic books,"[14] An Club Leabhar[15] (The Book Club) and Queen's University Belfast together put on the exhibition of hundreds of Irish books. An Club Leabhar was set up to promote Irish-language material, and as the only Irish-language book club in the country, its location in Northern Ireland is an example of an island-wide effort to promote the language. The display of books includes Ár Scannáin Féin (*Our Films*) (1953) by Pronsias Ó Conluain, the group's founder and a lifelong champion of the Irish language cause.[16] The event was opened by Ernest Blythe, managing director of the Abbey Theatre[17] and Kevin Darwin, chair of the city council.

Back in Dublin four years later in 1964, the "Let the Language Live"[18] campaign was being promoted at an event in the Shelburne Hotel, where

12    "Finals of schools Irish debating contest" #53: 10 June 1960.
13    "All-Ireland schools debating contest" #200: 30 March 1963.
14    "Belfast: exhibition of Gaelic books" #40: 11 March 1960
15    There is now an online project under the same name, run by Gaelchultúr Teoranta. This company was established in 2004 with the aim of promoting the Irish language and various aspects of Irish culture, including music, song and dance, in Dublin and around the country. See <www.clubleabhar.com> for information.
16    Ó Conluain was born in Co. Tyrone in 1919, son of an IRB member who took part in the 1916 Rising. He is discussed in Chapter 1 in the context of Irish cinema history.
17    Minister for Finance in W.T. Cosgrave's first government and an important figure in Irish language movement, who also invested the initial 100 pounds in the *Amharc Éireann* project.
18    "Let the Language Live" #262: 7 June 1964.

Ó Moráin and other well-known public figures related to the Irish language protection movement, including playwright Brendan Behan's wife, are shown signing the petition in support of the recommendations made by the Commission on the Restoration of the Irish Language. After the opening scene, the film switches to the streets outside, following two people as they collect signatures for the Let the Language Live petition. The final scene is staged: They are welcomed at the door by a man who nods enthusiastically and is very happy to sign, while the commentator urges viewers to take personal responsibility for the revival of the language. The Commission on the Restoration of the Irish Language began its work in 1956 and published its long-awaited report eight years later, its lifespan thus coinciding exactly with that of the *Amharc Éireann* series. The report generated much public interest when it was published, especially from the Irish language contingent, which unsurprisingly stressed the urgent need for the government to take its findings seriously. The juxtaposition of government "action" now versus smaller-scale efforts like the *Amharc Éireann* series eloquently demonstrates the difference between rhetoric and reality at a crucial time in the history of the language. Gael Linn and others has been quietly doing their part to promote Irish, while the government Commission has only just now published its findings.

Indeed, the public call to action from Let the Language Live is part of the larger growth of popular protest movements in many other areas of Irish life in the early to mid-1960s. It is a sign of the growing disillusionment during the Lemass era in many sectors with the (lack of) transformation, which is best represented in the series by coverage of the activism of farmers via the National Farmers Association and efforts from heritage groups like the Georgian Society to save Dublin's architectural treasures. And as with the farmers, it was also a sign of bigger things to come from the language movement in the later 1960s, which would see the birth of the Save the West campaign, the Gaeltacht Civil Rights Movement, and the Plantation of Connacht scheme, to name just a few. These were all in the tradition of community development work featured so strongly in the *Amharc Éireann* series; the same approach promoted by Sir Horace Plunkett, the Irish Countrywomen's Association, Muintir na Tíre, Macra na Feirme, the

work of Father MacDyer in Glencolmcille – based on cooperative principles and the idea of self-help.

The Language Rights Movement in the Gaeltacht areas would take
hold after the *Amharc Éireann* series had come to a close, starting in Ros
Muic, Connemara in 1966. But it would meet government and public
resistance in the late-1960s and early 1970s, as Ireland prepared to join
the European Economic Community and national priorities were
(re-)defined. Again, a particular problem was that the language movement
was internally split between the Dublin-based Gaelgeoirí, of which Ó
Laoghaire and the Gael Linn contingent were members, and those in the
West, who were more interested in bread-and-butter issues like regional
government and political representation. The language movement also faced
opposition from outside – not only in terms of the government's perceived
ambivalence about its fate but also the more purposeful opposition in the
form of Christopher Norris' Language Freedom Movement and the rather
more influential electoral platform of Fine Gael in 1972, which promised
to remove the unpopular compulsory status of Irish. Indeed, Fine Gael
essentially traded the well being of the Irish language for the pacification
of the farmers under the EEC's Common Agricultural Policy by dropping
the language from the list of priorities for accession negotiations in the
run-up to Irish membership in January 1973.

## Traditional music, dance and games

Irish traditional music underwent a revival of its own during the 1950s
and 1960s.

The collection of traditional music began in the 1940s, with the work
of Séamus Ennis, who traveled around the west of Ireland from 1942–47
on a bicycle, collecting songs and transcribing them for the Irish Folklore
Commission and for Radio Éireann from 1947–51. The BBC also began
collecting traditional music in Ireland in 1947, which Ennis joined in 1951.

For seven years, a huge store of over 1,500 recordings from all over Ireland, Scotland and England was built up and played on the BBC radio programme, "As I Roved Out." Ciarán Mac Mathúna, who began presenting traditional music programmes on Radio Éireann in 1955, also traveled around the West collecting music, folklore and song with his Mobile Recording Unit, creating an urban audience for this rural art form.

During the 1940s the status of traditional musicians was still low compared to their "high art" counterparts but in the early 1950s steps were taken to rectify the situation. In January 1951 the Dublin Pipers' Club went to Mullingar, Co. Westmeath, to help set up a pipers' club, and decided to set up an organization for all traditional instrument players. The first Fleadh Cheoil, the traditional Irish music festival, was organized in conjunction with the Midlands feis (an Irish language festival) in Mullingar, which quickly grew into a new forum for musicians, singers and dancers. The Fleadh Cheoil built on existing Irish community traditions – the rural county fairs and the feiseanna (plural) already held all over the country – but injected a new energy.

Indeed, the group that organized the first Fleadh Cheoil subsequently developed into Comhaltas Ceoltóirí Éireann (the Association of Irish Musicians)[19]. By 1956 the Fleadh had grown into a national festival attended by thousands of traditional musicians and dancers from all over Ireland and overseas. The fleadhanna (plural) consisted of parades, pageants and street sessions, as well as music competitions, and attracted a now legendary group of performers, including Willy Clancy, Elizabeth Crotty, Paddy Canny, Aggie White, Peter O'Loughlin, Paddy Murphy, Paddy Carthy and many more. The competition expanded in the 1960s and the Fleadh Cheoil na hÉireann (Music Festival of Ireland) became a meeting place for traditional musicians, singers and dancers from all over the world.

The six films of the various music festivals in the Gaelic News films record the atmosphere and popularity of these events, and their regular

---

19   Comhaltas is now the largest group for the preservation and promotion of Irish traditional music, with hundreds of branches around the world, many of which also teach dance and language classes. See <www.comhaltas.ie>.

appearance in the series enables a comparison between the style and presentation of the festivals as the period progressed. This footage was used to create a television series on Irish traditional music co-produced by RTÉ and the Irish Traditional Music Archive called *Go West Along the Road*.[20] In each of the films the scene is set with an opening shot of the main street in the town, filled with people milling about or pipe and drummer bands parading down the main street. The crowds grow larger as time passes. In the early films in Gorey, Boyle and Ennis from 1960–62,[21] the Fleadh has the atmosphere of a small-town event, attended enthusiastically by the locals. The commentator introduces it while the camera pans across the crowd, focusing on girls looking on and giggling, old country men with wrinkled faces in traditional Irish caps, and the various musicians at the centre of it all. Later on, in the two films made in 1963–4 in Mullingar and Clones,[22] the atmosphere has changed as the popularity of the Fleadh increased. The crowds are bigger, the police are a visible presence, and drinking to excess is noted in a sequence of shots of drunken men in various stages of disarray, passed out at the side of the road and even sitting in a wooden box in the middle of the street. Scenes such as this one illustrate the new mass following for folk and traditional music, which on occasion "tended – literally – to run riot, as anyone who attended the typical Fleadh Cheoil of the period can testify."[23]

The atmosphere is always informal: musicians are never on any sort of stage – the event takes place outdoors, in the shadows of old ruins, in parks, on the streets and in the alleyways of the towns. Traditional instruments featured regularly include the fiddle, bodhrán, pan flute, accordion

20   The RTÉ program began broadcasting in 1994 and is presented and researched by Nicholas Carolan, director of the Irish Traditional Music Archive.
21   "Gorey: 'strange contrasts' at Fleadh Ceoil #159 22 June 1962; "Boyle, Co. Roscommon: Fleadh Ceoil na hEireann" #54: 17 June 1960; "Ennis Fleadh Ceoil" #167: 17 August 1962.
22   "Fleadh Ceoil at Mullingar" #209: 1 June 1963; "Clones: Fleadh Ceoil" #259: 17 May 1964.
23   Brian Fallon, "The Irish Language," Chp. 12 in *An Age of Innocence: Irish Culture, 1930–60* (New York: St. Martin's Press, 1998): 169.

and the spoons. The musicians play in groups of two or three while the crowd looks on, milling around and in between the players, who smile and continue unfazed with their performance to the regularly accompanying hoots and hollers of approval from the audience. Close-up shots of the musicians playing and the audience listening and participating provide a wonderful glimpse of the spectacle itself, as well as the means to enjoy it second-hand. The style of the films themselves also changes as the festivals grow up: the final two films are much more obviously a product of 1960s cinema verité influences, incorporating fly-on-the-wall filming techniques and using the live ambient sounds of the streets. The live music and sounds of people laughing and talking, their feet shuffling in the streets, is carried through to the close of the films, replacing the regular *Amharc Éireann* soundtrack fade-in.

The issue of change within the traditional music scene itself is addressed in one of the films, "Gorey: 'strange contrasts' at Fleadh Ceoil."[24] The festival begins with a procession of historic displays and drummers and pipe bands. The timing of the festival on Easter Week lends a military air to the parade, coinciding as it does with the commemorations of the 1916 Rising. Dancers perform in the street to the sound of a live fiddle and bodhrán, while a group of young people sings in English with a guitar. The appearance of the English-speakers with a guitar indicates that they belong to the ballad movement, an offshoot of traditional Irish music, which reflected the growth in consumer culture in Ireland in the early 1960s. Ballad musicians played professionally in lounge bars, forming trios or quartets of a singer, guitarist, drummer and accordionist. Their repertoire also changed to incorporate the popular ballads that were enjoying a boom in Ireland and North America thanks to television. The English-language lyrics are noticeably out of place in this context and the commentator is dismissive of them, noting simply that "the guitar is getting a new lease on life." This is followed by shots of men in traditional Irish caps, indicating that these are the real traditional singers and dancers, as opposed to the new, trendy ballad singers. The film illustrates the start of the division between the old

24 "Gorey: 'strange contrasts' at Fleadh Ceoil #159 22 June 1962.

versus the new styles that would increasingly emerge in Irish traditional music over the next decade. "Ceoil tradisiúnta" signifies the "sean-nós" (old-fashioned) style of music, while the shortened "trad" refers to the newer, trendy, ballad style of which the commentator so obviously disapproves. In closing, the commentator states his preference clearly: "In the end there is nothing like the old-fashioned music and dance."

Perhaps not surprisingly, the defense of tradition again comes from the North; the sean-nós group featured in this film is Northern and, while the origin of the ballad group is not mentioned, it is presumed to be from the Republic. "Ennis: Fleadh Ceoil,"[25] also features a group from the North, the McPeakes from Belfast at the Co. Clare and the Munster Fleadh Ceoil. "Co. Clare is the county most famous for music in Ireland," says the commentator, a distinction that persists to this day. There were also lots of young Irish dancers, prompting the approving comment, "It's hopeful to see the young at the Fleadh Ceoil." Youth participation in these festivals is a very positive sign for the future of traditional culture, and that is clearly more important than whether they hail from the North or the Republic.

Traditional singing and dancing were part of the same movement to protect traditional culture in the late 1950s and early 1960s. The Cumann Cheoil agus Rinnce (Society for Music and Dance) was formed at the Fleadh Cheoil in Thurles in 1959, and the first dancing festival was recorded in "Oldcastle, Co. Meath: first Fleadh Rinnce."[26] Ten thousand people attended the festival and three hundred dancers took part. The popularity of traditional Irish dancing in Northern Ireland is detectable in the line-up, which features the McKee group from Belfast and another from Cavan formed only one year earlier, while in the "Mansion House: all-Ireland Irish dancing contest,"[27] dancers from all over Ireland again took part. A troop from London added to the dancers from Derry, Belfast and Dublin, who were judged on best in age and grade. According to the commentator, "The competition was fierce and the sharp eyes of the judges missed nothing"

---

25   "Ennis: Fleadh Ceoil" #167: 17 August 1962.
26   "Oldcastle, Co. Meath: first Fleadh Rinnce" #60: 29 July 1960.
27   No issue number or date available.

but the winner of the Irish Championship was a group from Dublin. He reassuringly notes that, "in spite of the foreign dances, it's clear that dancing in Ireland is going from strength to strength." Irish national culture was shown to be more than strong enough to withstand the competition from cosmopolitan influences, thanks to the involvement of youth such as these at events promoting traditional dance and music.

Indeed, Gael Linn itself wrestled with how to accommodate new forms, and the result was not always elegant. In 1956, Oícheanta Seanchais (Traditional Nights) entertainment sessions, consisting of traditional storytelling and sean-nós (traditional) singing, were established in Dublin as part of the An Tóstal (the Pageant) festival, which died out two years later in 1958. The Gael Linn record label was established that same year to fill the gap by providing an outlet for recordings of sean-nós singing and music. But the news film on the "Gaelic 'rock' record released"[28] was an anomaly at best, and unwittingly demonstrated just what strange bedfellows the traditional and the modern could be. It opens very incongruously to the sounds of Séamus Ennis, a very famous Irish traditional music star, playing the uillean pipes, before switching rather abruptly to the scene of a group of people, including Dónall Ó Mórain, gathered in a room listening to the new "rock" record, "Crí Iomlain" (Full Heart). The films consists only of shots of people listening, nodding their heads and generally looking uncomfortable as the "enjoy" the rock music. The song itself is a catchy, early 1960s-style crooning melody, but the context makes for a rather hilarious combination. Overall, it comes across as a bizarre attempt on the part of Gael Linn to shed its old-fashioned skin but this bringing together of the old and the new is awkward at best, and undermines itself from the start by opening with a segment featuring a big, safe name in traditional music, rather than with the rock music it was supposedly promoting.

While the Fleadh Cheoil and the Fleadh Rinnce brought together traditional musicians from Ireland and beyond, the traditional Irish sports played by the members of the Gaelic Athletic Association (GAA) occupied centre stage in the *Amharc Éireann* series. The popularity of Gaelic sports

28   No issue number or date available.

in the 1950s and 1960s was still enormous, as the sheer number of Gaelic News films on the various All-Ireland hurling, football and camogie matches attests. The extent of the coverage of Irish sports in the series, compared to the utter exclusion of (English) football/soccer also underlines the role of these games in defining Irish identity. The GAA, founded in 1884, was closely associated with the growth of cultural nationalism and in particular with the revolution of 1911–22.[29] Gaelic games were still as Gaelic in the early 1960s as when Michael Cusask founded the GAA: Foreigners' (i.e. the English) were still forbidden from playing in the league, a rule originally used as a means to exclude those in the military or police services, which lasted until the 1970s. Gaelic football, hurling and camogie attracted huge numbers of spectators and there are simply too many of these All-Ireland, Railway Cup and National League finals and semi-finals films to discuss them individually. They all follow essentially the same format: The commentator excitedly notes the course of the match, as the huge crowds erupt into applause. These films on GAA matches were quite a selling point for Irish audiences. In the days before television, it was known when the *Amharc Éireann* series would be featuring a certain match, and the appropriate cinema was chosen accordingly. In particular, regular coverage of All-Ireland matches in the *Amharc Éireann* series drew cinema goers, who – until January 1962, when television came to Ireland – would otherwise would have seen no footage of these events.

GAA games helped construct a highly gendered national identity during the period from 1884 to 1916, by stressing the masculinity, violence and skill in the newly invented games, but the exclusion of women from Gaelic games was addressed by nationalist women in 1902 with the invention of a female version of hurling called camogie. The *Amharc Éireann* series paid a great deal of attention to the various All-Ireland hurling and football matches, but also covered women's camogie finals, although less

---

29    See Mike Cronin, *Sport and Nationalism in Ireland: Gaelic Games, Soccer and Irish Identity since 1884* (Dublin: Four Courts Press, 1999); Marcus De Burca, *The GAA: A History (Second Edition)* (Dublin: Gill and Macmillan, 2000); Patrick F. McDevitt, *May the Best Man Win: Sport, Masculinity, and Nationalism in Great Britain and the Empire, 1880–1935* (New York: Palgrave Macmillan, 2004).

frequently. And although the crowds are not as large or as audible in these films, they are present, and the women are represented as strong sportswomen. In fact, it is specifically in the areas of rural working life and in sport that women are represented as anything close to equal in the series, while in the context of urban life, women are depicted as little more than ornamentation in coverage of their participation in beauty contests and modeling jobs. Thus, although the GAA favoured the much numerically stronger male sports, the *Amharc Éireann* series also drew attention to an example of strong femininity through its coverage of the women's version. The focus on the role of rural life and Gaelic sport again underlines the Irish Ireland theme of the *Amharc Éireann* series, but it is interesting that it is in precisely these supposedly more traditional aspects of Irish life that the representation of women presents them at their strongest.

## The North

It might be surprising to find mention of films on the 12th of July parades in Northern Ireland here, in the context of traditional Irish culture and festivals. Some might expect this topic to appear in a section on sectarian violence or urban conflict, especially since the IRA campaign of 1956–64 coincided with production of the newsreels. However, the manner in which this annual event is treated in the *Amharc Éireann* series allows for no such teleological classification of the Orange Day parades. The 12th of July is featured in the *Amharc Éireann* series in a similar manner to all other events taking place in Northern Ireland during this period – as simply another facet of life in the North of Ireland. The 12th of July is represented as a cultural festival peculiar to that part of the country – not as the opportunity for sectarian violence it frequently became from the early 1970s onwards. In the early 1960s "The Twelfth" is simply that – a special day in the Ulster calendar – and no more or less deserving of special mention than the occasion of the Fleadh Ceoil in the Republic.

The festival is covered as an item in the series each year from 1959 to 1963, all of which follow a similar format.[30] "Finaghy: The Twalfth,"[31] opens to marching music and the sights of the Orangemen parading through the streets. The commentator notes that the men of Belfast are "commemorating their ancestry and their brave deeds" without any sense of irony or judgment, indicating that the Orangemen of the North are as entitled to celebrate their heritage and history as any other group of Irishmen. Sixty thousand people are in attendance, most of whom "came to listen to the bands and see the lovely flags and banners, one to every individual lodge." The date is thus not imbued with any sort of political character whatsoever. The crowds have come for the spectacle – for the sights and sounds of the parade – rather than to lend any sort of support to one political creed or another. Shots of little children waving Union Jack flags and smiling underline the importance of the day as a communal festival, rather than a political event. The commentator even goes so far as to say that, "If it weren't for the bands, it isn't likely many people and holiday makers would come and see this display," as the camera focuses on the drummers passing by. This might be a willful statement of ignorance but in the series the 12th of July is represented as a cultural festival, in the same spirit as the Fleadh Ceoil, which also has its parades and flags during events timed to coincide with the anniversary of the 1916 Rising.

---

30   Only three of these films were available for viewing; those from 1959 and 1960 are missing.

31   "Finaghy: The Twalfth" #215: 13 July 1963 - note the spelling of the date, to reflect the Northern accent.

Theatre

Theatre has always been an important part of Irish cultural life and occupies a particularly important space in the public mind, thanks to the association of the Abbey Theatre with the literary revival of the late nineteenth and early twentieth century.[32] The Abbey was founded in 1904 as the Irish National Theatre Company but in July 1952 the building was damaged by fire. A replacement building was designed by Michael Scott – himself a former Abbey actor – and built on the same site. The Abbey Players used the Queen's Theatre until the new Abbey Theatre opened in 1966, then it in turn closed in 1969 and was demolished in 1975.[33] But in its last days there was said to be an air of despondency about the Abbey, thanks to unimaginative productions and shoddy settings under managing director Ernest Blythe. Despite securing an annual grant for national theatre and persuading the government to finance the new building, under his term of office the best Irish plays were produced outside of the Abbey.[34] So the lifespan of the *Amharc Éireann* series coincides with the Abbey's temporary disappearance from the Irish stage. The only real mention of the Abbey Theatre – aside from the films on its rebuilding – is in a reel entitled, "Abbey Players leave for Shakespeare festival,"[35] in which they are seen off by Ernest Blythe as they head for the World Theatre Festival in London to perform Sean O'Casey's "Juno and the Paycock" and "The Plough and the Stars."

Interestingly, the only real attention the Abbey gets in the series is through the person of Mícheál MacLiammóir, the famous actor, poet and dramatist. MacLiammóir, formerly Alfred Willmore, came to Ireland from

32    See Mícheál Ó hAodha, *The Abbey –Then and Now* (Dublin: Sackville Press, 1969); Hugh Hunt, *The Abbey: Ireland's National Theatre, 1904–78* (Dublin: Gill and Macmillan, 1979); Christopher Fitz-simon, "An ancient idealism," Chp. 13 in *The Irish Theatre* (London: Thames and Hudson, 1983).
33    Séamus de Búrca, *The Queen's Royal Theatre Dublin, 1829–1969* (Dublin: Séamus de Búrca, 1983): 1
34    Fitz-simon, 184.
35    "Abbey players leave for Shakespeare festival" #255: 19 April 1964.

England as a touring actor, where he met his future partner and director, Hilton Edwards. Edwards directed most of the plays and MacLiammóir designed for them, as well as appearing in as many as possible.[36] Together, Edwards and MacLiammóir founded the Gate Theatre in Dublin in October 1928, which has been credited with preventing the isolation of Irish theatre from the rest of the western world. MacLiammóir and Edwards also assisted with the first production of Galway's Irish language theatre, An Taibhdhearc. In "Lively banter at theatre symposium,"[37] lots of Ireland's big names are at the Guinness Hall in Dublin, including MacLiammóir and Edwards. Gabriel Fallon – director of the Abbey from 1959–74 – is present-ing, while Alan Simpson is in the audience, along with the "wonderfully odd Brendan" Behan. No reference is made to this in the film but when the Dublin Theatre Festival hosted "The Rose Tattoo" at the Pike Theatre in 1957, director Alan Simpson was charged with presenting a "lewd entertain-ment". The script calls for a condom to fall out of a pocket during the act but knowing its audience, the production simply mimed the act. Still, the authorities objected to its content and on 12 May, the Irish police invaded the theatre and Simpson, as director, was charged. An intellectual revolt followed – led by Brendan Behan, Sean O'Casey and Samuel Beckett – the judge threw the case out of court, the run of the play continued uninter-rupted, and Simpson was released from prison.[38] The commentator makes absolutely no mention of this in the newsreel but the next film, "Dublin University: honouris causa,"[39] shows MacLiammóir receiving his Doctor of Laws in Trinity College Dublin's Big Hall, with Ernest Blythe and Leo MacCabe in attendance. He is being honoured on this occasion for his focus on Oscar Wilde: He wrote and performed his own one-man show, entitled *The Importance of Being Oscar*, based on Wilde's life and work, and in 1954 he erected, along with Lady Dunally, a plaque commemorating the birth

---

36   Christopher Fitz-simon, *The Irish Theatre* (London: Thames and Hudson, 1983): 174–5.

37   "Lively banter at theatre symposium" #122: 6 October 1961.

38   Christopher Morash, *A History of Irish Theatre: 1601–2000* (Cambridge University Press, 2002), p. 322.

39   "Dublin University: honouris causa" #184: 8 December 1962.

of Wilde on 21 Westland Row. So, although there is no explicit mention in either reel of sexuality or scandal, Irish cinema audiences would have been familiar enough with "The Rose Tattoo" production, MacLiammóir's personal life, and his professional focus on Oscar Wilde to understand the oblique reference to the unwelcome interference of the morality police in artistic affairs.

Meanwhile, working-class entertainment was traditionally staged in Dublin's Theatre Royal. There were actually four different Theatre Royals built on Hawkins Street over the centuries – the first was built in 1662, the second in 1820, and the third in 1897 – the home for musical comedy in the early twentieth century before it went out of fashion and was replaced by stage music hall shows, one of which featured Charlie Chaplin as part of an act called The Eight Lancashire Lads. In its final years, the theatre was also used as a cinema, before closing in March 1934 and being demolished. It was replaced by a new building, which opened in September 1935. This Theatre Royal was an art deco building designed for both theatre and cinema audiences of over 3,500 people. It had a resident 25-piece orchestra and a troupe of singers-dancers, the Royalettes. In 1936 Louis Elliman, who owned the Gaiety Theatre and would open Ardmore Studios in 1957, acquired the Royal Theatre and during World War Two he was forced to keep it going with Irish acts, which facilitated the emergence of a slew of performers as staples on the entertainment scene. But the size of the building meant it was never economically viable, so June 1962 saw the "End of an era: Theatre Royal closes."[40] "Every seat was full for closing night" and all of the big names were there for the sad occasion: Paddy Crosbie, Jimmy Campbell, Cecil Sheridan, Mickser Reed, Noel Purcell, Billy Kelly and the Royalettes. "The last show is over, the curtain is down and it won't be long before they level the building."[41] Ardmore Studios also went into receivership in 1963, and Elliman himself died in 1965.

40 "End of an era: Theatre Royal closes" #161: 6 July 1962 – the actual demolition of the building is featured in Chapter 6: Industry, urbanization and architectural heritage.
41 Theatre Royal is covered in Chapter 6: Irish industry, urbanization and heritage in films that deal with its demolition.

The pantomime was also a huge part of working-class culture in Ireland, taking over from the music hall and most popular during this period – a fact only barely registered in a handful of newsreels. Often performed in the poorer districts of Dublin, in local halls and involving the entire community, in "'Panto' time: Cinderella comes to Crumlin,"[42] the local people are the actors in the free show held at the Parish Hall, in "'Puss in Boots' comes to Drimnagh"[43] the people of Crumlin put on the production themselves – the "electricians and painters did their part!" – and the last of the three, "National Stadium: Pantomania!"[44] was staged in a location normally reserved for boxing and wrestling matches.

The ever-present Catholic Church also makes a rather unlikely appearance in popular entertainment, in this instance through the annual staging of so-called moving plays depicting the life and death of Jesus Christ. "Dundalk: moving scenes in passion play"[45] shows the over one hundred people took part in the show. During the Last Supper scene, in which Jesus declares, "there is a traitor among us," Judas crawls out of the darkness, at which point the commentator reminds the audience – twice – that the Jews were to blame for Jesus' death. In another film on the same topic, "Moving production of passion play,"[46] the Dublin City Players put on the show written by Father Eugene of the Order of Friars Minor (Franciscans). There were also moving shows for other religious festivals, as in the "Moving crib tells Christmas story."[47]

Gaelic and rural theatre received attention the sort of attention that one would expect in a series that celebrates traditional culture in all of its forms. The festival now known as the Tipperary Drama Festival[48] opened at the Confraternity Hall in Thurles in March 1960. The festival was organized by Muintir na Tíre (People of the Land), a community self-help movement

---

42    "'Panto' time: Cinderella comes to Crumlin" #31: 8 January 1960.
43    "'Puss in Boots' comes to Drimnagh" #82: 6 January 1961.
44    "National Stadium: Pantomania!" #241: 11 January 1964.
45    "Dundalk: moving scenes in passion play" #96: 14 April 1961.
46    "Moving production of passion play" #201: 6 April 1963.
47    "Moving crib tells Christmas story" #187: 29 December 1962.
48    See <www.tipperarydrama.ie>.

founded by Tipperary priest, Canon John Hayes, in 1937 to improve the political, economic, social and cultural status of the people. It was one of the earlier community organizations to stress a holistic approach, incorporating active citizenship, a spirit of community, neighbourliness and self-reliance.[49] The movement established itself throughout the country, setting up parish guilds and democratically elected Community Councils. Muintir na Tíre pioneered community development in Ireland, encouraging each parish community to take control of its own destiny, providing the necessary power and infrastructural base to improve. In so doing, it helped transform the image of the countryside and the expectations of its people. In this same spirit, the objectives of the Gaelic drama festival were "to provide a meeting place for people, whether they belonged to Muintir na Tíre or not, and to promote a kind of drama that went beyond the Irish stage image so prevalent among rural drama groups at that time."[50] The adjudicator was Dermot Tuohy of the Gate Theatre in Dublin and the director was Joe FitzGerald, who would be the driving force behind the festival for the next two decades. When the "President opens Thurles Gaelic drama festival,"[51] De Valera's presence at the opening, and the fact that his address was broadcast on national radio, speaks to the importance of the festival to politically sanctioned Irish social and cultural identity.

Another rural festival, the Western Drama Festival, began in 1943 in Tubbercurry (Co. Sligo). It is now run under the auspices of the Amateur Drama Council of Ireland, a federation for the whole island of Ireland, which was founded in 1952 with the objective of fostering, developing and encouraging amateur drama in Ireland.[52] Covered in "Tubbercurry, Sligo:

49    See Fr. Mark Tierney, *The Story of Muintir na Tíre, 1931–2001 - the First Seventy Years* Tipperary: Muintir na Tíre, 2004 and Eoin Devereux, "Saving Rural Ireland – Muintir na Tíre and its Anti-Urbanism, 1931–58," in *Canadian Journal of Irish Studies* 17, no. 2 (1992): 23–30.

50    Joe FitzGerald, director of the first festival, quoted on Tipperary Drama website: <www.tipperarydrama.ie>.

51    No issue number or date available.

52    See <www.adci.ie>.

Western drama festival,"[53] the festival was scheduled to take place during Lent, and was looked forward to as a community night out during a season of fasting. The commentator also provides details on a number of plays being performed in various centres, including Bryan MacMahon's "The Bugle and the Blood" in Galway, which had played at the Abbey in Dublin in 1949, and Thomas MacAnna's "Winter Wedding" at the Tuam Theatre.[54]

In Dublin, Irish-language theatre was promoted directly by Gael Linn through the Hall an Damer (known as the Halla Damer or simply the Damer). In 1955, the semi-professional Irish language theatre was established on St. Stephen's Green and in 1957 a series of Irish language drama festivals began, leading to the establishment of An Comhlachas Náisiúnta Drámaíochta (The National Drama Association), an organization dedicated to the promotion of Irish language drama. In "Halla Damer: Taoiseach attends new Irish drama,"[55] Father Victor de Paor's new play, which features hurling being played live on stage for the first time, is being opened to a full house including Éamon de Valera and Dónall Ó Moráin. Later that year, another de Paor work dealing with Irish themes is on at the Halla Damer, this time based on Brian Merriman's 1870 poem "Cúirt an Mheán Oíche" (The Midnight Court) by Eoin O'Tuairiseach, covered in "President attends Irish play"[56]. The poem is a lively, humorous and sometimes explicit exploration of sexuality, gender and marriage in eighteenth-century Ireland, which was featured as part of the Dublin Theatre Festival, as only Irish play in the line-up. The original Merriman poem upon which de Paor's play was based represents the cultural collision between the traditional "natural" Gaelic world and the new "materialistic" English world, and offers "the most complete contemporary vision of the Gaelic world's final cultural battle,"[57] in which the Gaelic order is penetrated by English

---

53  No issue number or date available.
54  MacAnna also produced Irish language plays at the Abbey and served as Artistic Director from 1972–79.
55  "Halla Damer: Taoiseach attends new Irish drama" #141: 16 February 1962.
56  "President attends Irish play" #175: 6 October 1962.
57  Kevin O'Neill, "A Demographer looks at *Cúirt an Mheán Oiche*," in *Éire-Ireland* 9, no. 2 (1984): 143.

concepts of wealth, order, sexuality, gender and marriage. Rather than delving into criticism, however, commentator simply explains rather obliquely: "The play is set in a train station in the west of Ireland and includes lots of references to things and people of the West." The fact that it showcases an aspect of Irish culture and history not generally seen in Dublin theatre is presumably enough information for this audience, and the film closes with the rather superficial observation that the theatre was full and the audience reportedly "happy with the light-hearted production."

## Film

In rather stark contrast to Irish theatre, feature film production had always been a foreign – or transnational[58] – affair, in the sense that it usually involved actors and participants from a number of different locations. The first "Irish" feature films were actually American-made, and the *Amharc Éireann* series would never had made it to the screen were it not for the British Rank Distributors – not to mention the actual processing labs in London used to create the films. The lack of a national film industry had been a subject of discussion for years, and the setting up of the Ardmore Studios by Elliman was attempt to rectify the problem. But Ardmore failed and it would be another twenty years before the Irish narrative filmmaking industry would take off.

One of the most notable English film productions during this period was featured in "Kilmainham Prison: shooting the 'Quare Fella.'"[59] An English film crew was filming and Arthur Dreyfus directing the film adaptation of Brendan Behan's drama, set in Kilmainham Gaol, about a prisoner about to be hanged. Behan's *The Hostage*, about an English soldier being

---

58    See Brian McIlroy (ed.), *Genre and Cinema: Ireland and Transnationalism* (Taylor & Francis, 2007).

59    "Kilmainham Prison: shooting the 'Quare Fella'" #131: 8 December 1961.

held by the IRA, was presented by Gael Linn at Halla an Damer in 1958. *The Quare Fella* (1962) is a compassionate plea for the abolition of capital punishment, which was rejected by Ernest Blythe at the Abbey before being taken up by Alan Simpson at the Pike Theatre. In the film, Hilton Edwards and Leo McCabe are shown among the actors, and Walter Macken (who plays senior warden Regan in the film) is on the set. Behan died in March 1964 and an IRA guard of honour escorted his coffin. His funeral was the biggest since those of Michael Collins and Charles Stewart Parnell.

Another international production of an Irish story was covered in "Co. Wicklow: Rathdrum sees stars,"[60] in which the town of Rathdrum was transformed into an Ulster town for the filming of *A Terrible Beauty* (1960), the story of the IRA in the North. The drama, an adaptation of Arthur Roth's 1958 novel by the same name, was a co-production between the United Kingdom and Robert Mitchum's production company DRM. Actors included Mitchum as Dermot O'Neill, who is recruited into the IRA during World War Two, and Anne Heywood as Neeve Donnolly, his girlfriend. Noel Purcell stars as the priest, with Cyril Cusack as Jimmy Hannafin the cobbler, and Dan O'Herlihy, as Don McGinnis, the unit commander. "The whole town is beside itself. Even the names of the shops have been changed to make it a northern town." Irish locations were also used to look like English cities from the past, as in the case of the filming of the notorious "'Sidney Street siege' in Dublin."[61] This 1960 British historical drama, which took place in London in 1911, was filmed in the back streets of Dublin because "there are no streets like this in London anymore". Sadly, this comment says a lot about the condition of inner city Dublin in 1962 that it could still pass for a street in London's East End fifty years earlier.

The most significant contribution to Irish film culture during this period was the production and release of George Morrison's two Gael Linn sponsored historical compilation films, which draw on the country's strength in terms of documentary rather than feature film production. In 1957 Gael Linn asked Morrison to make an historical film, for which he

---

60   "Co. Wicklow: Rathdrum sees stars" #11 21 August 1959.
61   "'Sidney Street siege' – in Dublin." #33: 22 January 1960.

obtained much of his footage from Continental film archives, since the Irish versions had been lost or destroyed. The first, *Mise Éire* (*I am Ireland*), was released in 1959 and told the story of the Irish revolutionary period through compiled documentary footage that Morrison collected. As a nationalist version of Irish historical events that told the story with much drama and set to the music of Seán O'Riada, it was received with great acclaim. Two years later, in 1961, Morrison produced another film, *Saoirse?* (*Freedom?*), this one an assessment the achievements of the independent state. The question mark in the title suggests Morrison's conclusion and *Saoirse?* was much less well received than the rather self-congratulatory *Mise Éire*.

None of the controversy is detectable in the *Amharc Éireann* films on the topic. The openings are recorded as momentous occasions, at which the luminaries of the revolution are all present. "Mise Éire: making Ireland's first historical film"[62] serves as the introduction to the topic, which begins at the National Library, where Morrison is pictured compiling old film tapes. "This film has been in the making for sixty years. George Morrison has been collecting and studying old films of Ireland." Clips of the IRA drilling are interspersed with shots of Kathleen Ní Bhrían, who locates historical documents and cuts the films, and her husband, Seán Ó Brían, who puts the images together in a series. Images follow of Countess Markiewicz at a rally just after she had been released from prison in England. Morrison is shown marking shots on the movieola and the commentator explains, "this is new technology used for focusing". Clips follow of Arthur Griffith, Count Plunkett and de Valera, described as "the one who won" at the election in Co. Clare. Peter Hunt recorded the sound for the film and Liam Butler and Padraig O'Rahellaigh from Radio Éireann did the narration. The film closes with a clip of O'Connell Street in 1916 and the commentator's reminder, "Mise Éire is made in Ireland by the Irish!"

"President and veterans at historic premiere,"[63] records the opening of *Mise Éire* at the theatre. "There was a battalion of Old IRA and Irish Citizen Army there at the first viewing of the film" and a week later

---

62   "Mise Éire: making Ireland's first historical film" #35: 5 February 1960.
63   "Presidents and veterans at historic premiere" #37: 19 February 1960.

"a crowd of Old IRA marched to the special showing." Their presence makes the opening very similar in stayle to the many other national commemorations covered in the series, in which the Old IRA is omnipresent with de Valera. All of the Dublin dignitaries were out for the occasion, including de Valera, the Lord Mayor, Sean T. O'Kelly, Donall Ó Morain and General Mulcahy. "It was a special occasion for de Valera, who also stars in the film," as was so much the case in other national celebrations. A number of men spoke on behalf of the Old IRA and after the film George Morrison was introduced to the public. The next film, "Premiere of historic film"[64] was on the opening of *Saoirse?* in 1961. Again, the Gael-Linn contingent was present with George Morrison, Donall Ó Morain and Sean O'Riada, and "lots of people who fought for Ireland" were present, again the Old IRA men and General Mulcahy. In closing, viewers were told that Gael Linn would be donating the proceeds from the opening to the veterans, while the *Mise Éire* opening was very much a stars-only event.

Self-promotion of this nature is inseparable from the *Amharc Éireann* series and Gael Linn's mandate, and it is particularly noticeable in the films focusing on Irish cultural life. Here, Gael Linn and many other Irish cultural organizations are shown contributing generously and energetically to the promotion of indigenous art and culture. But it must be noted that, despite the Irish Ireland message of the series, Ó Laoghaire cannot be accused of focusing on tradition to the exclusion of other, often much more light-hearted topics. There are a great many films on Irish popular culture, including fashion events,[65] competitions[66], beauty pageants[67] and fundraisers[68]; visits from internationally reknowned celebrities[69] and rock

64　"Premiere of historic film" #125: 27 October 1961.
65　"Fashion aids Cheshire Homes" #176: 6 October 1962.
66　"Lovely Legs contest" #116: 25 August 1961.
67　"Dublin 'Rose of Tralee' finalist #99: 28 April 1961.
68　"Variety Club's fancy dress ball" #183: 1 December 1962.
69　"Charlie Chaplin flies in" #150: 20 April 1962.

stars[70]; sporting events beyond the GAA[71]; and seemingly random and sometimes downright bizarre events like "Drinka pinta beer in 3 seconds,"[72] which were undoubtedly entertaining but defy classification beyond the category of popular entertainment.

This is not to say that such topics are undeserving of treatment – they clearly occupy a place in Irish society and popular culture in the early 1960s – but it is also clear that coverage of such topics served as the icing on the much weightier cake that features more consistently throughout the series. The real message, oft-repeated, is that Ireland is *Irish* – culturally rich, with its own language, dance, music and sport; with a vibrant artistic community that exists not only in the capital but also in the provinces, thanks to the work of dedicated individuals and their networks. Ireland is a country where tradition and modernity exist can hand-in-hand, where the success of one does not have to mean the exclusion of the other.

70   "Beatles pay unwelcome visit" #232: 9 November 1963.
71   "Dunboyne: Leinster Trophy car race" #268: 19 July 1964, ""Cold weather go karting" #238: 21 December 1963, ""Annual ice-breaking swim" #239: 28 December 1963.
72   "Drinka pinta beer in 3 seconds" #193: 9 February 1963, "Speedy midgets at Bray" #164: 27 July 1962.

Gael Linn Annual Debating Competition for Secondary Schools awards presented at the Shelbourne Hotel, Dublin. Donal Ó Morain and Dr. Patrick Hillery, Minister for Education, with members of the St. Louis Convent Monaghan team. 30 March 1963. *Reproduced with permission from the Irish Photo Archive.*

# Conclusion

The "Eyes of Ireland" short documentary films of the late 1950s overlapped with a period during which critical debates were taking place over the structure and control of television. A committee set up in 1952 submitted two reports to the Minister of Posts and Telegraphs, Michael Keyes, recommending a publicly owned and managed service. From 1953 onwards, BBC television was being received along Ireland's eastern seaboard from Wales, and from the new BBC transmitter in Belfast. Neil Blaney, Keyes's successor in 1957, continued in the same vein, stressing that an Irish television service, when it came, would be commercial in character, depending on its advertisers for revenue. Meanwhile, Leon Ó Broin, Secretary of the Department of Posts and Telegraphs, submitted a report in April 1956 calling attention to the moral danger posed to Irish audiences from British television. BBC television output was presented as an unwelcome and alien influence on Irish life and "wholly foreign to the ordinary Irish home."[1]

Seán Ormonde succeeded Blaney in December 1957 and set up the Television Commission, representing business, religious, Irish language and political institutions in March 1958. The Commission contained no journalists or broadcasters, except for one who retired six months after it began, saying it was useless. It met weekly for over thirteen months, submitted an Interim Report in December 1958 that was never published, and a Final Report on 8 May 1959. Its main recommendation was that a television service be set up as a profit-making enterprise, financed by revenue from advertisements and under a governing authority, the programming for which was the responsibility of a selected person. It also stated that the amount of Irish material should grow as the service expanded.

---

1   John Horgan, *Irish Media: A Critical History Since 1922* (London & New York: Routledge, 2001): 79.

In 1959, ITV began broadcasting from Britain and over 30% of Irish homes were receiving British television. Various proposals for an Irish television service followed, as did an open letter to the Commission in June 1959 proposing that no system of commercial television should receive the support of the government. In August 1959, Michael Hilliard, the new Fianna Fáil Minister for Posts and Telegraphs, announced the government's intention to set up a public authority for television and to transfer Radio Éireann's functions to it. The state thus proposed to enter into competition with private enterprise, British commercial networks, Irish and British newspapers and magazines, and display advertisers. Gael Linn submitted a proposal to establish and run a national Irish television station but it was rejected.

It was the competition from the North that finally prompted the Irish government to draft broadcasting legislation. It set up the new Authority first known as the Radio Éireann Authority and later the Radio Telefís Authority, which was required to "bear constantly in mind the national aims of restoring the Irish language and preserving and developing the national culture".[2] Initially then, RTÉ was charged with the duty of preserving the language, a policy very much in line with national broadcasting policy since the 1920s, which complemented the national goal of language preservation through compulsory Irish education in schools and economic development of the Gaeltacht. An advisory committee was set up to steer financial, technical and programming affairs until the Bill was drafted and the new Authority chosen, which met daily during the summer of 1960.

The Broadcasting Act of 1960 followed the public service model based of the BBC, which is financed under a mixed economy system. Responsibility for all broadcasting in the country was vested in the statutory, independent authority, Radio Éireann, renamed in 1966 the Radio Telefís Éireann Authority (RTÉ). Great emphasis was placed on its independence from both government and the civil service, which had controlled broadcasting since 1926.[3] The Bill was passed into law on 6 April 1960 and the

2   Horgan, p. 83
3   Martin McLoone, Introduction to *Television and Irish Society: 21 Years of Irish Television,* by Martin McLoone and John MacMahon, eds (Dublin: RTE-IFI, 1984): 6.

nine Authority members were nominated in May.[4] The members were each paid five hundred pounds per year and the Chairman one thousand. All nine remained in office for the five-year maximum term allowed under the Act, four of whom were replaced in 1965 when a new temporary Authority was set up for one year.

Plans previously prepared for the design of the studio building by Raymond McGrath were shelved in favour of Michael Scott's, who was engaged by the Authority to build the television studios at Montrose in Donnybrook. In November 1960 the first Director-General was appointed for a period of two years, an American named Edward Roth, a consultant with the National Broadcasting Corporation of America who had set up broadcasting stations in Mexico and Peru. Roth was paid seven thousand, five hundred pounds per year, making him the highest paid official in government service in Ireland. Work began on the Montrose site in Donnybrook in early 1961, while temporary offices were taken in Clarendon Street and Chatham Street, where the Authority made its headquarters. The new Authority hired a staff of roughly four hundred people employed in eleven sound studios.

The inauguration of Irish television on 31 December 1961, after almost five years of controversy and debate over its structure, financing, and potential role in what was still a conservative society,[5] was recorded in one of the *Amharc Éireann* newsreels.[6] In de Valera's opening address, he expressed his

4    The nine members were Eamonn Andrews, Chairman; Ernest Blythe, of the Abbey Theatre and the former Minister for Finance; Fintan Kennedy, General Secretary of the Irish Transport and General Workers' Union; Charles J. Brennan, who had been Chairman of the old Comhairle Radio Éireann; Dr. T.W. Moody, Senior Lecturer and Professor of Modern History at Trinity College Dublin, also from the old Comhairle; Áine Ní Cheannain, Gaelic teacher and writer; James Fanning, Editor of the *Midland Tribune* and founder of the Birr Little Theatre Group; E.B. Manus and Commander George Crosbie, who had both been members of the advisory committee.

5    See Martin McLoone and John MacMahon, eds, *Television and Irish Society: 21 Years of Irish Television* (Dublin: RTE-IFI, 1984), Robert J. Savage Jr. *Irish Television: a Political and Social History* (Cork: Cork University Press, 1996) and John Horgan, *Irish Media: A Critical History Since 1922* (London & New York: Routledge, 2001).

6    "Telifís rings in New Year" #135: 5 January 1962.

great hopes and fears for the new medium: "I must admit that sometimes when I think of television and radio and their immense power, I feel somewhat afraid. Like atomic energy it can be used for incalculable good but it can also do irreparable harm. Never before was there in the hands of men an instrument so powerful to influence the thoughts and actions of the multitude."[7] During its first year, the service transmitted home-produced material for eighteen hours a week. In January 1962 there were 35,766 licence-holders, which doubled by February and reached 150,000 by 1963. Early programming included Broadsheet, on public affairs; *Let's Draw*, a children's programme; *Beirt Eile*, on traditional music and dance; *Pick-of-the-Post*, covering domestic and international sports, as well as fashion, cookery and magazine programmes; and the famous weekly night-time programme hosted by Gay Byrne, *The Late Late Show*.

The coming of television signalled the end of an era for Irish Ireland. When Gael Linn lost the bid to run the new television station, Ireland missed out on an early opportunity to chance to have an Irish-language station.[8] It was rejected because the practical politicians of the Lemass era favoured competition and free trade over protectionism, even in language policy. The battle that took place between proponents of the commercial versus the public service model[9] over the form the national television service would take mirrored the political split between the traditional, Gaelic, protectionist view and the new generation's free market perspective on Ireland's proper path. The public service model won out technically but not for long, as viewer ratings shortly thereafter decided the content of RTÉ programming would be primarily American and British. So De Valera's apprehension regarding the power of the new medium was borne out, as

7    "Appendix 1: De Valera's Address on the opening of Telefís Éireann – 31 December
      1961," in *Television and Irish Society: 21 Years of Irish Television* (Dublin: RTE-IFI,
      1984): p. 149.
8    This was not rectified until 1996, when TG4 (originally known as Teilifís na Gaeilge)
      was established. Its headquarters are in the Connemara Gaeltacht. It was the third
      national station launched, following RTÉ One in 1961 as Teilifís Éireann, RTÉ Two
      in 1978, and TV3 in 1998.
9    This battle is outlined in detail in Doolan et al.

television was to prove a conduit for a predominantly urban and cosmopolitan set of images. Lemass, on the other hand, had no qualms about the service, offering the view that Irish people were citizens of the world as well as Ireland, and that certain values transcended national frontiers and were universal in their application.

From the very beginning, RTÉ was accused of not fulfilling its mandate to show Irish-language programming. The service itself was inevitably an agent of anglicization, staffed by foreigners in senior positions and urban, middle-class, university graduates unfriendly to Gaelic culture. Ernest Blythe, the only Irish person in a senior management position, resigned within six months of opening because he was unable to convince his superiors to give a distinctly Irish flavour to the station. However, since it survived on advertising revenue, Telifís Éireann could ill afford to ignore the desires of its viewers. In May 1962 the first Television Audience Measurement ratings were issued and, apart from the evening news, the most popular programmes were American. Television thus revealed the gap between the official image of the Irish people and the reality. The Gaeilgeoirí were forced to swallow a bitter pill and admit that the vast majority of the Irish public was simply not interested in Irish language programming.

The *Amharc Éireann* series ended in 1964, in part due to the influence of the newly established national television service and the decline in cinema audiences. The last newsreel issue was released on the week of 26 July, bringing the total number of issues to two hundred and seventy, including the trial issue of Gaelic News. The series ran for a total of eight years.

Gael Linn began a new Irish language documentary series, shot in colour, called *Fios Feasa* (*The Knowledge of Knowledge*), to be jointly produced by Ó Laoghaire and Mulkerns, but it only ran for four issues before being abandoned. Colm Ó Laoghaire and Jim Mulkerns both went on to other projects, while the rest of the production crew continued with their careers in journalism, academia and the arts. All of those involved in the *Amharc Éireann* series went on to become important names in the history of Irish film, broadcasting, literature, arts and culture.

*****

The period that began in the 1930s and 1940s with the growth of organizations and resurgence in Irish-language publishing, and grew throughout the 1950s through the efforts of Gael Linn and other cultural bodies, can now be seen as the beginning of Ireland's second cultural revival. While the first led to revolution and political independence, the second revival led to minority rights activism inspired by the examples of the French student movement and Martin Luther King's civil rights campaigns. The 1960s saw the birth and growth of the language rights movement in the Republic, with the Movement for Irish Language Rights and the Save the West campaign in the Republic and the Civil Rights Movement for Catholic rights in the North.

Well before then, the *Amharc Éireann* series was drawing Irish viewers' attention towards the various components of national cultural identity, and the need to save them for future generations. Undertaken when Ireland was urgently in need of an economic and psychological boost, Colm Ó Laoghaire's presentation of the country in the "Eyes of Ireland" short documentary films aimed to provide just that. By using the Irish language in film – a form of modern media associated with popular entertainment and success – to draw attention to the wealth of natural and human resources available for exploitation, Ó Laoghaire and Gael Linn initially attempted to eliminate the link between the Irish language and rural poverty in the public consciousness. The early collection of documentary films served as witness to the prelude to Ireland's material development from 1959 onward, and was visionary in its attempt to revive the Irish language by presenting a positive vision of Ireland and its native language before the Lemass years of prosperity. As Ireland's economic situation improved rapidly after 1959, the *Amharc Éireann* series also changed, from short documentary to the "Gaelic News" format. Moreover, the series' purposes changed from instilling confidence to reflecting on, and sometimes resisting, the changes that were taking place in Irish society.

Ó Laoghaire and Gael Linn looked at all facets of Irish life – past and future, traditional and modern – but always stressed the national element and affirmed Ireland's ability to thrive. The films on industrial and technological development embrace an economic nationalism, and assert Irish sufficiency when aided by state-sponsored bodies. The films on rural life are often critical of the lack of government action, because they value rural life equally, and see the opportunity and need for development in Ireland's traditional agricultural regions as well. The films admit to no conflict between being enthusiastic about development and progress, and defining Irishness as traditional and rural. Irish nationalists like Ó Laoghaire, like nationalists in other countries, were looking both backward and forward. The contradiction is key to understanding the series: along with the assertive use of the language, the conviction in Ireland's innate ability to succeed is what makes the film of *Amharc Éireann* a nationalist creation.

# Postscript

The politicians and civil servants of the Lemass era were more than willing to throw out the baby with the bathwater, so hard as Ó Laoghaire might have tried to unite Irish and modernization in the official mind, his plea fell on deaf ears – the language was cast aside and left to fend for itself, as an uncomfortable reminder of the failures of poor, backward Ireland. A corner was turned during this period in the definition of government priorities, away from the traditional policy of promoting and protecting the language as a marker of Irish national identity, and toward free market commercial and economic success.

The next thirty-odd years saw a decline in stature of the Irish language in the Republic, which was also reflected in the decline in Irish-language television, as RTÉ quickly decided that commercial needs overrode cultural and Irish programming continued to fall as a percentage of the total from the 1960s onwards.[1] The Language Freedom movement of 1964, which was really a freedom *from* Irish movement, was a prelude to the election campaign of Fine Gael in 1972, which promised to end the compulsory status of Irish in the school syllabus. In the early 1970s, this was partly a result of the fact that nationalism of any stripe, including linguistic, fell out of favour thanks to the violence in Northern Ireland. Thanks to this unwillingness on the part of the state to protect the language within the new context of political and economic interdependence, Irish language activists have had to fight from the rear ever since.

The only bright light in the late 1960s and early 1970s was the birth and growth of the language rights movement in the Republic, with the Movement for Irish Language Rights and the Save the West campaign in the Republic – the next chapters in Irish language activism. But even cultural independence was deemed incompatible with Ireland's new position

---

1    Watson 1996: 261.

in the international community, and the government proved unwilling to secure official language status for Irish as part of the country's negotiations to join the European Economic Community in 1973.

Unlike many other European regions, whose minority languages were recognized as official or working languages from the start, Ireland only recently secured a position of equality among the many lesser-used languages of the European Union.[2] This took place not because of a change in government opinion generated in Ireland, but rather as a reaction to external trends: Being an Irish speaker in the European Union is now about minority status and equal rights, whereas in the 1960s it was about national identity and state ideology. It is largely thanks to the work of the many political and cultural groups that work to raise awareness of the need to protect minority cultures that the profile and status of Irish has also risen. The fact that their arguments are now being heard is due to changes in international context and political ideology,[3] which are driving the ongoing integration process in the European Union, and giving an ear to organizations – and languages – that deserve to be heard.

2    Irish was given official and working language status in June 2005.
3    See Iarfhlaith Watson, "The Irish language and television: national identity, preservation, restoration and minority rights" in *British Journal of Sociology*, Vol. 4, Issue 2, June 1996: 255–74.

# Bibliography

Ainsworth, John "Kevin Barry, the Incident at Monk's Bakery and the Making of an Irish Republican Legend" *History* 87, no. 287 (2002): 372–87.

Aldgate, Anthony *Cinema and History: British Newsreels and the Spanish Civil War* London: Scholar Press, 1979.

Allen, Robert C., and Douglas Gomery *Film History: Theory and Practice* New York: Alfred A. Knopf, 1985.

Bale, John, and Mike Cronin, eds *Sport and Postcolonialism* Oxford and New York: Berg, 2003.

Baker, Susan "Nationalist Ideology and the Industrial Policy of Fianna Fáil: The Evidence of the *Irish Press* (1955–72)" *Irish Political Studies* 1 (1986): 67–77.

Beale, Jenny *Women in Ireland: Voice of Change* London: Macmillan Education, 1986.

Béaslaí, Piarás *Michael Collins and the Making of a New Ireland* Dublin: Phoenix Publishing Co., 1926.

Bell, Claudia, and John Lyall *The Accelerated Sublime: Landscape, Tourism and Identity* Westport, CT and London: Praeger, 2002.

Bolger, Pat, ed. *And See Her Beauty Shining There: The story of the Irish Countrywomen* Dublin: Irish Academic Press, 1986.

Brett, David *The Construction of Heritage* Cork: Cork University Press, 1996.

Brody, Hugh *Inishkillane: Change and Decline in the West of Ireland* London: The Penguin Press, 1973.

Brown, Terence *Ireland: A Social and Cultural History, 1922–79* Glasgow: Fontana Paperbacks, 1981.

Byrne, Evan "A Brief History of Soil Science at Johnstown Castle," *Irish Science Centres Awareness Network* Newsletter 8 (June 1999).

Carey, Tim *Hanged for Ireland: the 'forgotten ten' executed 1920–21: a Documentary History* Dublin: Blackwater Press, 2001.

Carroll, Clare, and Patricia King, eds *Ireland and Postcolonial Theory* Notre Dame, IN: University of Notre Dame Press, 2003.

Chubb, Basil, and Patrick Lynch, eds *Economic Development and Planning* Dublin: Institute of Public Administration, 1969.

Clerkin, Paul "Fifty years of Busarus" *History Ireland* 11, no. 2 (2003): 38–42.

Collins, Peter "The contest of memory: the continuing impact of 1798 commemoration" *Éire-Ireland* 34, no. 2 (1999): 28–50.

Commins, P. "Land policies and agricultural development." In *Irish Studies 2 Ireland: Land, Politics and People* Cambridge: Cambridge University Press, 1982: 217–40.

Connell, Carmel *Glasnevin Cemetery, Dublin, 1832–1900* Dublin: Four Courts Press, 2004.

Connolly, Tracey "The Commission on Emigration, 1948–54." In *The Lost Decade: Ireland in the 1950s* Cork: Mercier Press, 2004: 87–104.

Coogan, Tim Pat *Michael Collins: a biography* London: Hutchinson, 1990.

Coogan, Tim Pat, and George Morrison *The Irish Civil War* London: Seven Dials, 1999.

Cooke, Pat "Kilmainham Gaol: Interpreting Irish nationalism and Republicanism" <http://amol.org.au/omj/journal_index.asp> *Open Museum Journal* 2 (Aug 2002).

Corkery, Daniel *The Hidden Ireland: a Study of Gaelic Munster in the Eighteenth Century* Dublin: Gill and Son, 1924.

Corkery, Daniel *The Fortunes of the Irish Language* Cork: The Mercier Press, 1954.

Cormack, Michael J, and Niamh Hourigan *Minority Language Media: Concepts, Critiques, and Case Studies* Clevedon: Multilingual Matters, 2007.

Corner, John *The art of record: a critical introduction to documentary* Manchester: Manchester University Press, 1996.

Crist, Raymond E. "Migration and Population Change in the Irish Republic" *The American Journal of Economics and Sociology* 30, no. 3 (1971): 253–9.

Cronin, Michael *Translating Ireland: Translation, Languages, Cultures* Cork: Cork University Press, 1996.

Cronin, Mike *Sport and Nationalism in Ireland: Gaelic Games, Soccer and Irish Identity since 1884* Dublin: Four Courts Press, 1999.

Cronin, Mike "Projecting the Nation through Sport and Culture: Ireland, Aonach Tailteann and the Irish Free State, 1924–32" *Journal of Contemporary History* 38, no. 3 (2003): 395–411.

Cronin, Seán *Washington's Irish Policy 1916–86: Independence Partition Neutrality* Dublin: Anvil Books, 1987.

Crowley, Tony *The Politics of Language in Ireland, 1366–1922: A Sourcebook* London and New York: Routledge, 2000.

Cruise O'Brien, Conor *To Katanga and Back: a UN case history* London: Hutchinson & Co. Ltd., 1962.

Cruise O'Brien, Conor "The Congo (ONUC): the political perspective" *Irish Sword* 20, no. 79 (1996): 37–42.

Cullen, L.M. *An Economic History of Ireland since 1660* London: B.T. Batsford Ltd., 1972.

Daly, Mary *Industrial Development and Irish National Identity, 1922–39* New York: Syracuse University Press, 1992.

Daly, Mary "The Economic Ideals of Irish Nationalism: frugal comfort or lavish austerity?" *Éire-Ireland* 29, no. 4 (1994): 77–100.

Davis, John, ed. *Rural Change in Ireland* Belfast: The Queen's University of Belfast: The Institute of Irish Studies, 1999.

Davis, Troy *Dublin's American Policy: Irish-American Diplomatic Relations, 1945–52* Washington, DC: The Catholic University of America Press, 1998.

Dayal, Rajeshwar *Mission for Hammerskjold: the Congo Crisis* Princeton, NJ: Princeton University Press, 1976.

De Burca, Marcus *The GAA: A History (Second Edition)* Dublin: Gill and Macmillan, 2000.

De Fréine, Seán *The Great Silence: The study of a relationship between language and Nationality* Dublin and Cork: The Mercier Press, 1978.

De Witte, Ludo *The Assassination of Lumumba* London: Verso, 2001.

Delany, Enda "The Vanishing Irish? The Exodus from Ireland in the 1950s." In *The Lost Decade: Ireland in the 1950s* Cork: Mercier Press, 2004: 80–86.

Devereux, Eoin "Saving Rural Ireland – Muintir na Tire and its Anti-Urbanism, 1931–58" *Canadian Journal of Irish Studies* 17, no. 2 (1992): 23–30.

Dodd, Luke, ed. *Nationalisms: Visions and Revisions* Dublin: Film Institute of Ireland, 1999.

Dolan, Anne *Commemorating the Irish Civil War, 1923–2000* Cambridge: Cambridge University Press, 2003.

Dowling, William C. "John Ford's Festive Comedy: Ireland Imagined in *The Quiet Man*". *Éire-Ireland* 23, no. 1 (2002): 190–211.

Drudy, P.J., ed. *Irish Studies 2 Ireland: Land, Politics and People* Cambridge: Cambridge University Press, 1982.

Drudy, P.J. "Land, people and the regional problem in Ireland." In *Irish Studies 2 Ireland: Land, Politics and People* Cambridge: Cambridge University Press, 1982: 191–216.

Drudy, P.J., ed. *Irish Studies 4 The Irish in America: Emigration, Assimilation and Impact* Cambridge: Cambridge University Press, 1985.

Ellis, Jack C. *The Documentary Idea* Englewood Cliffs, NJ: Prentice Hall, 1989.

Fallon, Brian *An Age of Innocence: Irish Culture 1930–60* New York: St. Martin's Press, 1998.

Fanning, Ronan *Independent Ireland* Dublin: Helicon Ltd., 1983.

Farrell, Brian *Seán Lemass* Dublin: Gill and Macmillan, 1983.

Fielding, Raymond *The American Newsreel, 1911–67* Norman: University of Oklahoma Press, 1972.

Findlay, Trevor *The Blue Helmets' First War? Use of Force by the UN in the Congo, 1960–64* Clementsport: The Canadian Peacekeeping Press, 1999.

FitzGerald, Garret *Planning in Ireland: a P.E.P. Study* Dublin: Institute of Public Administration & London: Political and Economic Planning, 1968.

Fitz-simon, Christopher *The Irish Theatre* London: Thames and Hudson Ltd., 1983.

Foster, R.F. *Modern Ireland, 1600–1972* London: Penguin Books, 1989.

Gael-Linn web site: <http://www.gael-linn.ie>.

Gaelachas Teo web site: <http://www.gaelachas.com/gaelachas.htm>.

Garvin, Tom *Evolution of Irish nationalist politics* New York: Holmes and Meier, 1981.

Garvin, Tom *Nationalist revolutionaries in Ireland, 1858–1928* Toronto: Oxford University Press, 1987.

Garvin, Tom *1922, The birth of Irish democracy* New York: St. Martin's Press, 1996.

Gibbons, Luke "Topographies of Terror: Killarney and the Politics of the Sublime" *South Atlantic Quarterly* 95, no. 1 (1996): 23–44.

Gibbons, Luke *Transformations in Irish Culture* (Critical Conditions: Field Day Essays) Notre Dame, IN: University of Notre Dame Press, 1996.

Gibbs, David N. *The Political Economy of Third World Intervention: Mines, Money, and U.S. Policy in the Congo Crisis* Chicago: University of Chicago Press, 1991.

Gibbs, David N. "Dag Hammarskjold, the United Nations, and the Congo Crisis of 1960–1: a Reinterpretation" *The Journal of Modern African Studies* 31, no. 1 (1993): 163–74.

Gillmor, Desmond A. "Irish Mineral Development and Canadian participation" *Canadian Geographic Journal* 82, no. 2 (1971): 172–81.

Gillmor, Desmond A. *Economic Activities in the Republic of Ireland: A Geographical Perspective* Dublin: Gill and Macmillan, 1985.

Gillmor, Desmond A. "The Irish Sea Fisheries: Development and Curtailment of a Renewable Resource Industry" *American Journal of Economics and Sociology* 46, no. 2 (April 1987): 165–78.

Gillmor, Desmond A., ed. *The Irish Countryside: Landscape, Wildlife, History, People* Dublin: Wolfhound Press, 1989.

Girvin, Brian *Between Two Worlds: Politics and Economy in Independent Ireland* Savage, MD: Barnes and Noble Books, 1989.

Goggin, Carolan "The Boats: The New Ross Galley" *Newsletter of the Inland Waterways Association of Ireland* 29, no. 1 (2002): 1–4.

Goldthorpe, J.H., and C.T. Whelan, eds *The Development of Industrial Society* Proceedings of the British Academy, The Third Joint Meeting of the Royal Irish Academy and the British Academy, Oxford: Oxford University Press, 1990.

Guinness, Desmond "The E.S.B. Buildings: will they survive?" *Quarterly Bulletin of the Irish Georgian Society* 4 (1961): 29–34.

Harbison, Peter *Guide to the National Monuments of Ireland* Dublin: Gill and Macmillan, 1970.

Hart, Peter *The I.R.A. at War 1916–23* Oxford: Oxford University Press, 2003.

Heathcote, Nina "Ireland and the United Nations operation in the Congo" *International Relations* 3, no. 11 (1971): 880–902.

Hederman, Mark Patrick, and Richard Kearney, eds *The Crane Bag Book of Irish Studies (1977–81)* Dublin: Blackwater Press, 1982.

Helleiner, Jane "'Women of the Itinerant Class': gender and anti-traveller racism in Ireland" *Women's Studies International Forum* 20, no. 2 (1997): 275–87.

Heverin, Aileen *The Irish Countrywomen's Association: A History, 1910–2000* Dublin: The Irish Countrywomen's Association and Wolfhound Press, 2000.

Hobsbawm, Eric J., and Terence Ranger, eds *The Invention of Tradition* Cambridge: Cambridge University Press, 1983.

Horgan, John *Irish Media: A Critical History Since 1922* London & New York: Routledge, 2001.

Howe, Stephen *Ireland and Empire: colonial legacies in Irish history and culture* New York: Oxford University Press, 2000.

Hutchinson, John *The Dynamics of Cultural Nationalism: The Gaelic Revival and the Creation of the Irish Nation State* London: Allen & Unwin, 1987.

Igoe, Vivien *Dublin Burial Grounds & Graveyards* Dublin: Wolfhound Press, 2001.

Inland Waterways Association of Ireland website: <http://www.iwai.ie>.

Irish Film Archive: "Information about Amharc Éireann magazine and newsreel series taken from discussion with Colm Ó Laoghaire, 28 September 1993".

Jacobsen, John Kurt *Chasing Progress in the Irish Republic: Ideology, democracy and dependent development* Cambridge: Cambridge University Press, 1994.

James, Alan *Keeping the Peace in the Cyprus Crisis of 1963–64* New York: Palgrave, 2002.

Johnson, Nuala "Building a nation: an examination of the Irish Gaeltacht Commission Report of 1926" *Journal of Historical Geography* 19, no. 2 (1993): 157–68.

Keaney, Marion *Athlone bridging the centuries* Mullingar: Westmeath county council, 1991.

Kearns, Kevin C. "Resuscitation of the Irish Gaeltacht" *Geographical Review* 64, no. 1 (1974): 82–110.

Kearns, Kevin C. "Ireland's Mining Boom: Development and Impact" *The American Journal of Economics and Sociology* 35, no. 3 (1976): 251–70.

Kearns, Kevin C. "Development of the Irish Peat Fuel Industry" *The American Journal of Economics and Sociology* 37, no. 2 (1978): 179–93.

Kearns, Kevin C. "Population ship and settlement patterns of Irish Travellers" *Irish Geography* 11 (1978): 23–34.

Kearns, Kevin C. *Dublin Tenement Life: An Oral History* Dublin: Gill and Macmillan, 1994.

Kearns, Kevin C. "Irish Tinkers: an itinerant population in transition" *Annals of the Association of American Geographers* December 67, no. 4 (1997): 538–54.

Kelly, Mary J., and Barbara O'Connor, eds *Media Audiences in Ireland: Power and Cultural Identity* Dublin: University College Dublin Press, 1997.

Kennedy, Michael, and Joseph Morrison Skelly, eds *Irish Foreign Policy, 1919–66: From Independence to Internationalism* Dublin: Four Courts Press, 2000.

Keogh, Dermot *Twentieth-Century Ireland: Nation and State* New York: St. Martin's Press, 1995.

Keogh, Dermot, Finbar O'Shea, and Carmel Quinlan, eds *The Lost Decade: Ireland in The 1950* Dublin: Mercier Press, 2004.

Kilmainham Jail Restoration Society *Kilmainham: The Bastille of Ireland* Dublin: The Kilmainham Jail Restoration Society, 1961.

King, Carla "Co-operation and Rural Development: Plunkett's Approach." In *Rural Change in Ireland* Belfast: The Queen's University of Belfast – The Institute of Irish Studies, 1999: 45–57.

Kirk, John M., and Dónall P. Ó Baoill, eds *Travellers and their Language* Queen's University Belfast: Cló Ollscoil na Banríona, 2002.

Kockel, Ullrich, ed. *Culture, Tourism and Development: The Case of Ireland* Liverpool: Liverpool University Press, 1994.

Lee, J.J., ed. *Ireland 1945–70* Dublin: Gill and Macmillan & New York: Barnes and Noble Books, 1979.

Lee, J.J. *Ireland 1912–85: Politics and Society* Cambridge: Cambridge University Press, 1989.

Lefever, Ernest W. *Crisis in the Congo: A United Nations Force in Action* Washington, DC: The Brookings Institution, 1965.

Lemass, Sean "The Role of State-sponsored Bodies." In *Economic Development and Planning* Dublin: Institute of Public Administration, 1969: 177–93.

Lloyd, David *Ireland after History* Notre Dame, Indiana: University of Notre Dame Press in association with Field Day, 1999.

Lowenthal, David "European and English Landscapes as National Symbols." In *Geography and National Identity* Oxford: Blackwell, 1994.

Lyons, F.S.L *Ireland Since the Famine* London: Fontana Paperbacks, 1973.

McAleese, Dermot "American investment in Ireland." In *Irish Studies 4: The Irish in America: Emigration, Assimilation and Impact* Cambridge: Cambridge University Press, 1985: 329–51.

McCabe, Ian "JFK in Ireland" *History Ireland* 1, no. 4 (1993): 38–42.

McCaughren, Tom *The Peacemakers of Niemba* Dublin: Browne and Nolan Ltd., 1966.

MacCuaig, Padraig *A History of Kilmainham Gaol, 1796–1924* Dublin: The Stationery Office, 1995.

MacDonald, Frank *The Construction of Dublin* Dublin: Gandon Editions, 2000.

MacGóráin, Riobard "Scannáin, Amhráin agus Dramaí." In unknown collection
(obtained copy from Gael-Linn archives): 67–76.

McIlroy, Brian *World Cinema 4: Ireland* Trowbridge: Flicks Books, 1989.

McKeown, Sean "The Congo (ONUC): the military perspective" *Irish Sword* 20,
no. 79 (1996): 43–7.

McKernan, Luke *Topical Budget: The Great British News Film* London: British Film
Institute, 1992.

McLoone, Martin and John MacMahon, eds *Television and Irish Society: 21 Years of
Irish Television* Dublin: An RTÉ-IFI publication, 1984.

MacQueen, Norman "Ireland and the United Nations Peacekeeping Force in Cyprus"
*Review of International Studies* 3 (1983): 95–108.

Mandle, W.F. "The I.R.B. and the beginnings of the Gaelic Athletic Association" *Irish
Historical Studies* 20, no. 80 (1977): 418–38.

Manning, Maurice "The Farmers." In *Ireland 1945–70* Dublin: Gill and Macmillan &
New York: Barnes and Noble Books, 1979: 48–60.

Mathews, Alan "The State and Irish agriculture." In *Irish Studies 2 Ireland: Land,
Politics and People* Cambridge: Cambridge University Press, 1982: 241–70.

Mathews, P.J. *Revival: The Abbey Theatre, Sinn Féin, The Gaelic League and the Co-
operative Movement* Notre Dame, IN: University of Notre Dame Press in association with Field Day, 2003.

Maume, Patrick "Young Ireland, Arthur Griffith, and Republican ideology: the question of continuity" *Éire-Ireland* 34, no. 2 (1999): 155–74.

Miller, David *On Nationality* Oxford: Clarendon Press, 1995.

Murphy, Gary "The Irish Government, the National Farmers Association, and the
European Economic Community, 1955–64" *New Hibernia Review* 6, no. 4
(Winter 2002): 68–84.

Nairn, Tom *Faces of Nationalism: Janus revisited* London & New York: Verso, 1997.

O'Brien, Harvey "Projecting the Past: historical documentary in Ireland" *Historical
Journal of Film, Radio and Television* 20, no. 3 (2000): 335–50.

O'Brien, Harvey *The Real Ireland: the evolution of Ireland in documentary film* Manchester: Manchester University Press, 2004.

O'Connor, Barbara and Michael Cronin, eds *Tourism in Ireland: a critical analysis*
Cork: Cork University Press, 1993.

O'Connor, John E., ed. *Image as Artifact: The Historical Analysis of Film and Television*
Malabar, FL: Robert E. Krieger Publishing Company, 1990.

Ó Cuív, Brian, ed. *A View of the Irish Language* Dublin: Government Publications Office, 1969.

O'Donnell, Peadar *The Gates Flew Open* Cork: The Mercier Press, 1966.

O'Donoghue, Thomas A. "Sport, Recreation and Physical Education: The Evolution of a National Policy of Regeneration in Eire, 1926–48" *British Journal of Sports History* 3, no. 2 (1986): 216–33.

O'Donovan, Donal *Kevin Barry and his time* Dublin: Glendale, 1989.

O'Farrell, Padraic *Who's Who in the Irish War of Independence and the Civil War, 1916–23* Dublin: Lilliput Press, 1997.

O'Grady, Joseph P. "Stopover at Shannon" *Air Power History* 1996 43, no. 3 (1996): 34–47.

Ó hAllmhuráin, Gearóid *A Pocket History of Irish Traditional Music* Dublin: The O'Brien Press, 1998.

Ó Laoghaire, Colm "Gael-Linn 'Vest Pocket' Documentaries" *Irish Film Quarterly* 1, no. 1 (March 1957): 9–11.

Ó Laoghaire, Nora. Author's interview. Dublin, 19 November 2003.

O'Neill, Kevin "A Demographer looks at *Cúirt an Mheán Oiche*" *Éire-Ireland* 19, no. 2 (1984): 135–42.

Ó Riagáin, Pádraig *Language Policy and Social Reproduction, Ireland 1893–1993* Oxford: Clarendon Press, 1997.

O Riain, Michael *Aer Lingus, 1936–86: A Business Monograph* Dublin: Gill and Macmillan, 1986.

Ó Tuathaigh, M.A.G. "The land question, politics and Irish society, 1922–60." In *Irish Studies 2 Ireland: Land, Politics and People* Cambridge: Cambridge University Press, 1982: 167–90.

Patterson, Henry "Seán Lemass and the Ulster Question" *Journal of Contemporary History* 34, no. 1 (1999): 145–59.

Patterson, Henry *Ireland since 1939* Oxford: Oxford University Press, 2002.

Pettitt, Lance *Screening Ireland: Film and television representation* Manchester: Manchester University Press, 2000.

Piper, Leonard *Dangerous Waters: the life and death of Erskine Childers* London and New York: Hambledon and London, 2003.

Moore Quinn, E. "Portrait of a Mythographer: Discourses of Identity in the work of Father James McDyer" *Éire-Ireland* 38, nos. 1–2 (2003): 123–40.

Rockett, Kevin, Luke Gibbons and John Hill *Cinema and Ireland* London and Sydney: Croom Helm, 1987.

Rouse, Paul "The Politics of Culture and Sport in Ireland: A History of the GAA Ban on Foreign Games, 1884–1971. Part One: 1884–1921" *International Journal of the History of Sport* 10, no. 3 (1993): 330–60.

Ryan, Ray, ed. *Writing in the Irish Republic: Literature, Culture, Politics 1949–99* London: Macmillan Press Ltd., 2000.

Ryder, Sean "Speaking of '98: Young Ireland and Republican memory" *Éire-Ireland* 34, no. 2 (1999): 51–69.

Savage Jr., Robert J. *Irish Television: A Political and Social History* Cork: Cork University Press, 1996.

Savage Jr., Robert J. *Seán Lemass* Dublin: Dundalgan Press Ltd., 1999.

Savage Jr., Robert J., ed. *Ireland in the New Century: Politics, Identity and Culture* Dublin: Four Courts Press, 2003.

Savage Jr., Robert J. *A Loss of Innocence? Television and Irish Society 1960–72* (Manchester: Manchester University Press/Palgrave Macmillan, 2010).

Sawyers, June Skinner *Celtic Music: A Complete Guide* De Capo Press, 2001.

Sayers, Peig *An Old Woman's Reflections* London: Oxford University Press, 1962.

Scherer, John L. *Blocking the Sun: The Cyprus Conflict* Minneapolis, Minnesota: University of Minnesota, 1997.

Shaw-Smith, David *Ireland's Traditional Crafts* London: Thames and Hudson Ltd., 1984.

Shiel, Michael J. *The Quiet Revolution: The Electrification of Rural Ireland, 1946–76* Dublin: The O'Brien Press, 1984.

Skelly, Joseph Morrison *Irish Diplomacy at the United Nations, 1945–65: National Interests and the International Order* Dublin: Irish Academic Press, 1997.

Slide, Anthony *The Cinema and Ireland* Jefferson, North Carolina and London: MacFarland & Co., Inc. Publishers, 1988.

Tierney, Fr. Mark *The Story of Muintir na Tíre, 1931–2000: the first seventy years.* Tipperary: Muintir na Tíre, 2004.

Tobin, Fergal *The Best of Decades: Ireland in the 1960s* Dublin: Gill and Macmillan, 1984.

Tucker, Vincent "Images of Development and Underdevelopment in Glencolumbcille, County Donegal, 1830–1970." In *Rural Change in Ireland* Belfast: The Queen's. University of Belfast: The Institute of Irish Studies, 1999: 84–115.

Wallace, Patrick F. *A Guide to the National Museum of Ireland* Dublin: Town House Dublin in association with the National Museum of Ireland, 2000.

Walsh, Brendan "Economic Growth and Development, 1945–70." In *Ireland 1945–70* Dublin: Gill and Macmillan & New York: Barnes and Noble Books, 1979: 27–37.

Watson, Iarfhlaith "The Irish language and television: national identity, preservation, restoration and minority rights" *British Journal of Sociology*, Vol. 4, Issue 2, June 1996: 255–74.

Watson, Iarfhlaith "A History of Irish Language Broadcasting: National Ideology, Commercial Interest and Minority Rights." In *Media Audiences in Ireland: Power and Cultural Identity* Dublin: University College Dublin Press, 1997: 212–30.

Whelan, Kevin *Fellowship of Freedom: The United Irishmen and 1798* Cork: Cork University Press, 1998.

White, Jerry "Translating Ireland back into Éire: Gael Linn and film making in Irish" *Éire-Ireland* 38, nos. 1/2 (2003): 106–22

# Filmography

## A. Single-item "Eyes of Ireland" short documentary films

1. Iascairí ar Scoil – Howth Fishing School, June 1956
2. Aerphort na Sionainne – Shannon Airport, July 1956
3. Mianaigh Thrá Dhá Abhann – Avoca Mines, August 1956
4. Bantracht na Tuaithe – Irish Countrywomen's Association, September 1956
5. Bréidín Thír Chonaill – Donegal Tweeds, October 1956
6. Gáirdín na nAinmhithe – Dublin Zoo, November 1956
7. Oiliúint Bainicín – Mannequin Schools, December 1956
8. Ospidéal na N-Ainmhithe – Animal Dispensary, January 1957
9. Cúrsaí Óstán – Hotel Training Courses, February 1957
10. Báid Solais – Lightboats, March 1957
11. Glaoch na Spéire – The Call of the Sky, April 1957
12. Mná Spéire – Air Hostess Training, May 1957
13. Bua na Móna – Milled Peat Production, June 1957
14. Fleadh Cheoil – Music Festival, July 1957
15. Leictriú Chonamara – Rural Electrification in Connemara, August 1957
16. Saoire ar Sionainn – Shannon Cruises, September 1957
17. Aer Spóirt – Dublin Gliding Club, October 1957
18. Pictiúirí le Páistí – Child Art Contest, November 1957
19. Obair Miotal na hÉireann – Irish Metalwork, December 1957
20. Gloine Phortláirge – Waterford Glass, January 1958
21. Dún Mór na Scadán – Dunmore Herring Catch, February 1958
22. Foilsiú Nuachtán – How a Newspaper is Published, March 1958
23. Marcaigh an Airm – Army Equitation School, April 1958
24. Réadlann Fathfearnáin – Rathfarnham Observatory, May 1958

25.    Gáirdíní na Lus – Botanic Gardens, June 1958
26.    Caiseal na Rí – Rock of Cashel, July 1958
27.    Fír Tine (cut off) – Dublin Fire Brigade, August 1958
28.    Snámh Sábhála – Life Saving Course, September 1958
29.    Féiríní Cuimhne – Irish Souvenirs, October 1958
30.    Madraí ar Saoire – Dogs' Hotel, November 1958
31.    Margadh na nÉan – Bird Market, December 1958
32.    Peil Chise – Basketball, January 1959
33.    Cuairt ar Chill Áirne – Visit to Killarney, February 1959
34.    Calafort Átha Cliath – Port of Dublin, March 1959
35.    Téarnamh as Polio – Polio Clinic, April 1959
36.    Tórramh an Bhairrile – Coopering in Guinness, April 1959

36 magazine-style films were made (38 were shot but 2 were never made)
from June 1956 to April 1959, when the news films began.

## B.  "Gaelic News" films

Trial issue: 5 June 1959

1.    First tanker at Cork refinery
2.    Final of National League between Offaly and Kerry

1: 12 June 1959

1.    The Balmoral Show
2.    Dublin Bay dinghies
3.    Ulster senior football championship at Lurgan: Armagh v. Derry
4.    The last Howth tram

2: 19 June 1959

1.    New Hogan stand and Railway Cup final
2.    Luxury liner docks at Dublin
3.    Pet's corner at the Zoo

3: 26 June 1959

1. Historic election campaign
2. NFA seminar: foreign delegates visit Kildare farms
3. Motorcycling: Leinster 200

4: 3 July 1959

1. Inauguration of the President
2. National Currach Championships
3. Disney in Dublin
4. International clay pigeon shoot

5: 10 July 1959

1. President's first public function
2. Leinster senior football final
3. Archbishop of Liverpool visits Dublin
4. Veterans on the road

6: 17 July 1959

1. An Uaimh: Leinster senior football semi-final
2. Westport: international angling
3. US visitors see Irish buildings

7: 24 July 1959

1. Leinster senior hurling final
2. Bi-centenary of Irish firm
3. Woodbrook: Max Faulkner's triumph
4. Belfast: the Twelfth

8: 31 July 1959

1. Dublin: Mr. Aiken attends economic conference
2. Weekend leisure: golf-climbing-rowing
3. Cork: President opens Trabolgan Irish College

9: 7 August 1959

1. Thurles: Munster hurling final
2. Autumn fashions
3. Crosshaven: Yachting Champtionship final

10: 14 August 1959

    1.      Tullamore: Leinster senior football final
    2.      Ras Tailteann cross-country bicycle race
    3.      Galway races

11: 21 August 1959

    1.      President presents Aga Khan trophy
    2.      Rathdrum sees stars
    3.      Ulster Grand Prix
    4.      Irish boxers train for South Africa

12: 28 August 1959

    1.      Croke Park: All-Ireland semi-final
    2.      Portlaoise: training gun dogs
    3.      Galway Bay: demonstration of Seine net fishing
    4.      Dublin Zoo: tiger cubs growing up

13: 4 September 1959

    1.      Co. Dublin: water polo at Blackrock
    2.      Croke Park: All-Ireland semi-final
    3.      Mosney: stars entertain orphans
    4.      Donegal: Moville Angling Festival

14: 11 September 1959

    1.      "Rose of Tralee" final
    2.      Red Cross water safety championships
    3.      Clonakilty: road bowling
    4.      Co. Cork: aerial crop spraying demonstration

15: 18 September 1959

    1.      All-Ireland hurling final: Waterford and Kilkenny draw

16: 25 September 1959

    1.      Carlow: interprovincial rowing finals
    2.      All-Ireland camogie final: Dublin outplay Mayo
    3.      Canoe camping holidays
    4.      Irish-American enterprise: Minister opens a bubble-gum factory at Kilcock

17: 2 October 1959

1.    Co. Cork: An Taoiseach opens Whitegate refinery

2.    Congress of Trade Unions first meeting since amalgamation

3.    New showrooms for Gaeltarra Eireann

4.    Killaloe: first national waterski championships

18: 9 October 1959

1.    All-Ireland football final: Kerry beats Galway

19: 16 October 1959

1.    All-Ireland hurling replay final: Waterford victory

20: 23 October 1959

1.    Kerry goes to Listowel races

2.    New trade mark for tweed

3.    Irish windows for Johannesburg Cathedral

4.    Roscrea: farming with a difference

21: 30 October 1959

1.    Oireachtas Week gatherings

2.    Kitchen and Cellar Week: wagon wheels in Phoenix Park

3.    Dublin Airport: helicopter shows its paces

22: 6 November 1959

1.    Kilkenny: Waterford and Kilkenny draw in National League

2.    Dublin: Lord Mayor Brady lights up new cinema canopy

3.    Shelbourne Park: The Flogging Reel wins McAlinden Gold Cup

4.    Thrills for Dubliners: speedboats on Liffey

23: 13 November 1959

1.    Belfast: Gael Linn camogie cup – Leinster beat Ulster

2.    President at meeting of Irish speaking priests

3.    Dublin: new B+I ship launched

4.    French fashion show in Dublin

24: 20 November 1959

1.    Maynooth: An Taoiseach opens new cattle mart

2.      Fashion jewelry revives Celtic tradition
3.      Tipperary: beagles at Holycross inter-hunt meeting
4.      Dublin: Malayans celebrate independence anniversary

25: 27 November 1959

1.      Croke Park: Dublin best Roscommon in National League
2.      Film unit at Dalkey but where's the monster?
3.      RDS Ballsbridge: November bloodstock sales

26: 4 December 1959

1.      It might have been worse
2.      Co. Dublin: indoor athletics at Stillorgan
3.      At Ringsend Tech: "do-it-yourself" boat-builders
4.      Dublin Zoo: Maeve visits the baby camels

27: 11 December 1959

1.      Drogheda: Dublin beat Louth in National League
2.      Malahide: Mr. Dillon at Fine Gael study session
3.      One way to keep warm: table tennis
4.      Dublin Bay yachtsmen hold a Georgian ball

28: 18 December 1959

1.      Ban-Ghardai passing-out parade
2.      Dublin shops highlight Christmas

29: 25 December 1959

1.      Wicklow storm damage – who pays?
2.      Dun Laoghaire: new life raft demonstration
3.      Fashion show to aid world refugee year

30: 1 January 1960

1.      Old Nordic feast visits Ireland: "Santa Lucia" visits Ireland
2.      Indoor sports 1: strong men in training
3.      Indoor sports 2: don't fence me in
4.      The new Abbey: building starts soon

31: 8 January 1960

1.      Shannon flood disrupts transport
2.      Dublin dog show society holds championship show

3.     Clontarf Baths: Christmas Day swim
4.     "Panto" time: Cinderella comes to Crumlin

32: 15 January 1960

1.     Branch lines close: Kenmare's last train
2.     Co. Dublin: motorcyclists "splash" in Stapleton Cup trial
3.     Co. Tipperary: New Year's coursing at Nenagh

33: 22 January 1960

1.     Co. Armagh: 2nd Ulster Cross-Country Classic
2.     Spring fashions here already
3.     Tuam, Co. Galway: "Young Farmer of the Year" at home
4.     "Sidney Street siege" – in Dublin

34: 29 January 1960

1.     Johnstown Castle passed to Foras Taluntais
2.     National Stadium: junior boxing championships
3.     Co. Dublin: Irish motor racing winter trial
4.     Export of horses: protests continue

35: 5 February 1960

1.     Belfast shipyard builds novel liner
2.     "Breaking the ice" at Howth
3.     Dublin: Indian League celebrations
4.     Belfast: Freddie Gilroy in training
5.     Mise Eire: Ireland's first historical film

36: 12 February 1960

1.     Dublin actors' show aids World Refugee Year
2.     Judo Club – an oriental sport in Ireland
3.     Co. Dublin: South Dublin Harriers meet at Blessington
4.     Irish-German society annual dance

37: 19 February 1960

1.     Croke Park: Dublin beat Galway in National League
2.     Students stage boycott march
3.     "Sportmen of the Year" awards
4.     President and veterans at historic premiere

38: 26 February 1960

1.  Belfast: Balmoral Show
2.  Dublin Zoo: Variety Club treat for disabled children
3.  Greyhounds under the hammer
4.  Irish team stages "rally" for charity

39: 4 March 1960

1.  Shannon air disaster
2.  Croke Park: Ulster beat Leinster in Railway Cup semi-final
3.  Fine Gael Ard-Fheis: General Mulcahy retires
4.  Dublin: Gilroy-Jordan exhibition match

40: 11 March 1960

1.  Belfast: exhibition of Gaelic books
2.  Dundalk cinema gutted by fire
3.  Flour Millers' Association launch cookery drive
4.  Gort: Galway Blazers point-to-point

41: 18 March 1960

1.  Dun Laoghaire: Amateur Ballroom Challenge trophy
2.  Athlone: All-Army Cross-Country Championships
3.  Dublin: technical students show hairstyles
4.  Roundwood, Co. Wicklow: ploughing championships

42: 25 March 1960

1.  Variety Club of Ireland elects "Lady of the Year"
2.  St. Patrick's Day: industrial parade in Dublin
3.  Ulster beat Munster in Railway Cup final
4.  Irish Kennel Club Championship show

43: 1 April 1960

1.  Dublin stars attend charity premiere
2.  Celbridge, Co. Kildare: foster mother for a foal
3.  Co. Louth: ICA members at novel cookery course
4.  North Kilkenny hunt: point-to-point

44: 8 April 1960

1. Co. Cork: drag hunting at Clogheen
2. Young artists show their mettle
3. Curragh camp, Kildare: All-Army physical training championship
4. Cork amateurs stage "Merry Widow"

45: 15 April 1960

1. Dublin: National Wrestling Tourament
2. Lifeboats away – in seven minutes!
3. Celbridge, Co, Kildare: Olympic hunter trials

46: 22 April 1960

1. National senior boxing: Perry outpoints Gallagher
2. Co. Meath: racing at An Uaimh
3. Clonmel, Co. Tipperary: 50 mile senior cycling championship
4. Dublin: fashion show aids Unicef – with dachshunds!

47: 29 April 1960

1. Ballina, Co. Mayo: An Taoiseach opens 3 million pound drainage scheme
2. Gormanstown College: swimming association holds coaching course
3. Dublin: first Irish boatshow
4. "Careless Love": highlight of National Ballet season

48: 6 May 1960

1. President receives Freedom of Clonmel
2. Taghmon, Co. Wexford: national handball final
3. Punchestown: first ever brush fences
4. Dublin Airport: to Ireland – the easy way!

49: 13 May 1960

1. Arbour Hill, Easter Week commemoration
2. French ambassador opens Roualt exhibition
3. Cork: Tipperary beats Cork in National League final

50: 20 May 1960

    1.      Trinity College honours President
    2.      Croke Park: Down beats Cavan in National League final
    3.      "Italian fortnight" in Dublin: summer styles from Rome
    4.      Bastketball Championships: Dublin Celtic outplay St. Colmcille

51: 27 May 1960

    1.      Dr. Nkrumah in Dublin
    2.      Belfield athletics, Universities v. N.A. & C.A.I team
    3.      How to run a farm indoors
    4.      Portstewart: 100 mph win in North West "200"

52: 3 June 1960

    1.      Belfast: Balmoral show
    2.      International fencing
    3.      Clonmel: ladies walking race
    4.      Moto-ball in Co. Wicklow

53: 10 June 1960

    1.      Galway: Donegal win National Curragh Championship
    2.      Final of schools Irish debating contest
    3.      Athy: sorting peas – by "Electric Eye"
    4.      U.C.D. beat Trinity in Liffey race

54: 17 June 1960

    1.      First jet service via Shannon to Europe
    2.      ITGWU Congress in Buncrana
    3.      Teelin, Co. Donegal: vocational officers see Gael-Linn project
    4.      Boyle, Co. Roscommon: Fleadh Ceoil na hEireann

55: 24 June 1960

    1.      Ballinasloe sports and national relay
    2.      Dublin: All-Ireland Old-Time Dance Championships
    3.      Grasstrack meet in Wicklow
    4.      Trinity Week: regatta at Dun Laoghaire

56: 1 July 1960

    1.      Ballinglen, Co. Wicklow: Taoiseach unveils plaque to '98 men

2. Co. Meath: agricultural delegates see animal research station
3. Laytown races
4. Dublin: independent arts show their work

57: 8 July 1960

1. Portmarnock: The Canada Cup
2. Blackrock: Varsities International spring-board diving
3. Dublin to Wicklow: 13th annual veteran car run

58: 15 July 1960

1. US postman on goodwill visit
2. Westport anglers enjoy "free-and-easy" festival
3. The Curragh: Army Week shooting contest
4. Close finish in Skerries "100"

59: 22 July 1960

1. Fitzwilliam Ladies' Singles Final
2. Athy Dog Show
3. All-Ireland Pipe-Band Championship
4. The "Twelfth" at Finaghy

60: 29 July 1960

1. International boxing – Maxie Earle rallies to defeat Paddy Stapleton
2. Oldcastle, Co. Meath: first Fleadh Rinnce
3. Dalkey: wet time at Watersports!
4. Weston airfield: the gentle art of sky-diving

61: 5 August 1960

1. "Operation Sarsfield" gets under way
2. Phoenix Park: cars race for Gold Flake trophy
3. Leinster Senior Final: Wexford's narrow margin over Kilkenny

62: 12 August 1960

1. Thurles: Munster senior hurling final: Tipperary beats Cork
2. Horse Show Week: fifteenth annual Cavalry Ball
3. Horse Show Week: international jumping opens
4. St. Stephen's Green: art in the open air

63: 19 August 1960

1.    Kerry beat Galway to qualify for final
2.    Dublin Airport: Red Cross doctor leaves for Congo
3.    Arklow: inter-provincial water polo: Ulster 8, Leinster 3
4.    Co. Cork: US students enjoying Irish holiday

64: 26 August 1960

1.    Rockwell College: President attends Muintir na Tire rural week
2.    Thurles Show
3.    Congo airlift: An Taoiseach inspects 33rd battalion
4.    College Park: Gormley breaks 1500 metres record

65: 2 September 1960

1.    Croke Park: Down & Offaly in epic draw
2.    Paintings by Maeve de Markievicz
3.    National Stadium: Olympic boxers in training
4.    Naval cadets to train with Irish Shipping

66: 9 September 1960

1.    Co. Cavan: new airstrip for midlands
2.    Santry Stadium: international tennis stars
3.    New look in autumn fashions
4.    Blackrock: Red Cross Water Safety Championships

67: 16 September 1960

1.    Hurling final: Wexford surprise Tipperary

68: 23 September 1960

1.    Croke Park: Down qualify for final
2.    Gael-Linn scholarships: Dublin children off to Gaeltacht
3.    Drogheda: Leinster win inter-provincial rowing
4.    Clarenbridge: Galway Oyster Festival

69: 30 September 1960

1.    Cork Road Safety Week
2.    Irish forces in the Congo

70: 7 October 1960

1.    Football final: first ever victory for North

71: 14 October 1960

1. Balbriggan: enjoying themselves at "Sunshine House"
2. Castleblaney Agricultural Show
3. Weston airfield: 1st international parachute rally
4. Nowadays – "say it with plastics"

72: 21 October 1960

1. Croke Park: Down beat New York
2. Belfast: Porkers' Day at Balmoral Autumn Show
3. Dublin: fashion show aids polio clinic
4. Baldonnel: last of the famous aircraft: Spitfire retire

73: 28 October 1960

1. New Cork dockyard: Taoiseach lays keels on first ship
2. Dublin Nigerian independence ball
3. Dundalk races: "Settlement" wins Carrickmacross Handicap
4. Garda depot auction: "Who wants a squad-car?"

74: 4 November 1960

1. Termonfeckin, Co. Louth: ICA Congress discusses rural water supplies
2. Malahide: youngsters star in speedboat race
3. Co. Leix: open-cast mining with world's largest excavator
4. Ruskey, Roscommon: Kerry girl wins national beauty contest

75: 11 November 1960

1. Croke Park: Offaly beat Dublin in National League
2. National Stadium boxing: two-round win for Belfast hard-hitter
3. Naas races: Blessington handicap chase
4. Coolkeeragh: Derry's first oil-fired power station

76: 18 November 1960

1. Mansion House: Fianna Fail Ard-Fheis
2. New Ross: National Ploughing Championships
3. Newtownards: Ulster Table Tennis Championships
4. Malayan Students celebrate "Mardeka"

77: 25 November 1960

 1.  Our Congo Dead: the last journey

78: 2 December 1960

 1.  UCD students honour Kevin Barry
 2.  Croke Park: All-Ireland camogie final: Dublin beat Galway
 3.  Bagenalstown, Carlow: "new look" in pig production methods
 4.  Variety Club film ball aids disabled children

79: 9 December 1960

 1.  Taoiseach at opening of Grand Opera season
 2.  Co. Waterford: winter beagling at Tallow
 3.  "Irishmen in Papal Army" exhibition
 4.  Dublin Bay yachtsmen hold "Bavarian Ball"

80: 16 December 1960

 1.  Dublin Creation Ball to help remedial clinic
 2.  Badminton championships: men's doubles
 3.  "Furs of the future" at chinchilla show
 4.  Taking census of the travelling people

81: 23 December 1960

 1.  Removal of the remains of late Col. McCarthy
 2.  Scholarship children home from Gaeltacht
 3.  Dublin-New York: Irish jet liner: inaugural flight

82: 30 December 1960

 1.  Irish airline office opened on 5th Avenue
 2.  Raheny clay pigeon Christmas shoot
 3.  Racing at Shelbourne Park
 4.  Christmas in Dublin streets

83: 6 January 1961

 1.  Christmas Day swim
 2.  "Puss in Boots" comes to Drimnagh
 3.  A "wet" Christmas at Howth too!
 4.  Saggart, Co. Dublin: St. Stephen's Day motor cycle trials

84: 13 January 1961

1. Kiltegan, Co. Wicklow: "Young Farmer of the Year" at home
2. Shannon Free Airport industrial boom
3. Co. Limerick: Kilfeacle beagle hunt ball
4. Best of children's art on show

85: 20 January 1961

1. 3rd Congo airlift: 34th battalion leaves
2. Dublin: schoolboy shows unique collection of newspapers
3. Naas racecourse: Leinster Junior Cross-Country Championship

86: 27 January 1961

1. Return of Galway mace and sword
2. Brittas, Co. Dublin: Manders Cup trial
3. Spring fashions here already
4. Olympic games: "Inkblots and Crackpots" version!

87: 3 February 1961

1. Junior boxing championships: lightweight final
2. Lisburn: international exhibition of children's art
3. Dublin: East Ireland fencing championship: men's foils section
4. Topical notes at Belfast Arts Ball

88: 10 February 1961

1. Ennis, Co. Clare: novel road safety campaign
2. Senior cross-country championships
3. Seashore motif in Spring clothes
4. West Clare railway: the last run

89: 17 February 1961

1. Mansion House, Dublin: Fine Gael Ard-Fheis
2. Wexford: Killinick and Bree hold joint meet
3. Basketball: Leinster blitz tournament
4. Sportstars of 1960

90: 24 February 1961

1. Inishturk relieved: supplies by helicopter
2. State aid for "children to Gaeltacht" scheme

3.     Rotary Club Week: opening of poster contest
4.     Dublin Zoo: Variety Club children's treat

91: 3 March 1961

1.     Co. Wicklow: All-Ireland Junior Cross-Country Championship
2.     Dublin: the last of the old Abbey
3.     RDS bull show and sales
4.     Tubbercurry, Sligo: Western Drama Festival

92: 10 March 1961

1.     Students' "Ban the Bomb" march ends in explosion
2.     Archbishop of Dublin receives new Irish hymnal
3.     Prime Minister of Canada arrives in Dublin
4.     Belfast: commissioning of Indian aircraft carrier "Vikrant"

93: 17 March 1961

1.     "Free-style" wrestling at the Mansion House
2.     Dublin's first drive-in bank
3.     Arbor Day at Palmerstown school
4.     Variety Club of Ireland: children's fancy dress parade

94: 24 March 1961

1.     Cork: St. Patrick's Eve torchlight parade
2.     Cary Grant visits Dublin
3.     Patrician Year: impressive scenes at Armagh
4.     Downpatrick: Church of Ireland honours St. Patrick

95: 31 March 1961

1.     English stars attend charity premiere
2.     Naas races: Tuna Gail wins Paddy's Sister stakes
3.     Wrestling: new craze sweeps country
4.     Galway to Dublin by barrel

96: 7 April 1961

1.     New look for old cars: latest edition
2.     Shannon Airport: six cheat death
3.     Dundalk: moving scenes in passion play

97: 14 April 1961

1.     Congo troops get UN medals
2.     Kildare: national hunter trials
3.     Lovely legs contest
4.     National Stadium boxing: McLoughlin beats McCarthy

98: 21 April 1961

1.     Dublin children leave for Gaeltacht
2.     President opens Thurles Drama Festival
3.     The "Caravelle" jet at Dublin airport
4.     Falcon Gun Club annual shoot

99: 28 April 1961

1.     Dublin "Rose of Tralee" finalist
2.     Fashions for summer (when it comes)
3.     Fitzwilliam, Dublin: Hard Court Championship, semi-finals
4.     Mysterious happenings at Howth

100: 5 May 1961

1.     Honorary degrees for visiting churchmen
2.     Newport, Co. Mayo: Gael-Linn handball final
3.     Controversial play in rehearsal
4.     Belfast 15 million pound Canberra completed

101: 12 May 1961

102: 19 May 1961

1.     Cobh: new American ambassador arrives
2.     Croke Park: National League final, Kerry beats Derry

103: 26 May 1961

104: 2 June 1961

1.     Lambretta Club of Ireland annual rally
2.     Prime Minister of Indonesia arrives in Dublin
3.     Belfast: Balmoral agricultural show

105: 9 June 1961

3. Tralee Kingdom County Fair
4. Bray Regatta
5. Cotton for glamour fashion show
6. Dublin University hill climb

106: 16 June 1961

1. Prince Rainier and Princess Grace in Ireland

107: 23 June 1961

108: 30 June 1961

1. Co. Louth: container ferry service for Greenore
2. Cardinal Agagianan in Dublin
3. 35th battalion leaves for Congo

109: 7 July 1961

1. Israeli language scholar visits Mayor Briscoe
2. Congo: 34th battalion return

110: 14 July 1961

111: 21 July 1961

1. Dogs on show at Bray
2. Mansion House: Road Safety Week exhibition
3. Fitzwilliam: Irish Open Tennis Championships
4. Belfast: "the Twalfth"

112: 28 July 1961

1. International golf
2. Car races
3. Miss Dublin contest

113: 4 August 1961

1. Howth harbour: the Asgard comes home

114: 11 August 1961

1. Summer school for athletes
2. Senators & TDs tour Bord na Mona works
3. The circus comes to town

115: 18 August 1961

1.    Climax of the horse show Aga Khan Cup
2.    National Stadium international boxing: Germany v. Ireland
3.    Croke Park: All-Ireland semi-final: Down beats Kerry

116: 25 August 1961

1.    Thurles: Munster hurling final
2.    Autumn fashions
3.    Lovely Legs contest

117: 1 September 1961

1.    Gormanstown Castle: international scout leaders' conference
2.    Athlone: FCA officers commissioned
3.    Blackrock: Red Cross water safety contests

118: 8 September 1961

119: 15 September 1961

1.    Shannon air disaster: 83 dead – no survivors
2.    Medical congress delegates visit brewery
3.    Co. Wicklow: hill climb at Kilpeddar
4.    Autumn fashions preview

120: 22 September 1961

121: 29 September 1961

122: 6 October 1961

1.    75 escape in pilgrim plane crash
2.    Lively banter at theatre symposium
3.    Mansion House: television and radio show

123: 13 October 1961

1.    Dublin mill destroyed by fire
2.    Exhibition of Epstein bronzes
3.    FCA manoeuvres in the midlands

124: 20 October 1961

1.    Mountjoy Prison unveils memorial to patriots

2.      Irish fortnight at Dublin department store

3.      Old Bawn Moran Cup motorcycle trial

125: 27 October 1961

1.      Cork airport: inaugural flight

2.      Georgian Society protest to ESB

3.      Premiere of historic film

126: 3 November 1961

1.      Dublin students Ban the Bomb protest

2.      Co. Offaly: Bord na Mona briquette factory opened

3.      Japanese goods on display

4.      Drogheda: Miss Dublin wins beauty contest

127: 10 November 1961

1.      Bob Hope visits Ireland

2.      Weston airfield: Leinster Aero Club's new training plane

3.      Dublin University: distinguished speakers at Historic Society
        meeting

4.      AA Battery prepare for Congo service

128: 17 November 1961

1.      Tribute paid to Congo dead

2.      "Wintersports" in Dublin mountains

3.      National Stadium: international boxing, Ireland v. USA

4.      Malayan independence ball

129: 24 November 1961

1.      Dublin Castle: Dublin Brigade veterans honour executed
        comrades

2.      Liverpool ship aground at Drogheda

3.      Cork: Irish Christian Brothers 150th anniversary

4.      Glencree: Dublin University motorcycle trials

130: 1 December 1961

1.      Mansion House: chinchillas on show

2.      Trinity College: Christmas cards help world's refugees

3.      Stars attend charity premiere

4.      International awards for Radio Eireann actors

131: 8 December 1961
1. Bord Iascaigh Mhara: presentation to Galway skipper
2. Kilmainham prison shooting the "Quare Fella"
3. Variety Club fancy dress ball

132: 15 December 1961
1. Dr. Cruise O'Brien arrives from New York
2. Taoiseach reviews 36th battalion
3. National Stadium boxing: Taylor (England) defeats McGrane (Ireland)
4. Cork dockyard: new Irish fishing vessel launched

133: 22 December 1961

134: 27 December 1961
1. Clay pigeon association annual shoot
2. "Search for a Ballad Singer" area finals
3. Co. Wicklow: muddy going at car trials

135: 5 January 1962
1. Cappagh hospital outdoor party for handicapped children
2. Fancy dress on wheels
3. Telifís rings in the New Year

136: 12 January 1962

137: 19 January 1962

138: 26 January 1962

139: 2 February 1962

140: 9 February 1962

141: 16 February 1962
1. Dancing competition
2. Basketball
3. Halla Damer: Taoiseach attends new Irish drama
4. Fancy dress ball

142: 23 February 1962

143: 2 March 1962

144: 9 March 1962

    1.     Stars attend charity premiere
    2.     Awards ceremony held by Spanish firm to honour Irish personalities
    3.     Mansion House: international wrestling
    4.     Mr. de Valera revisits Kilmainham Gaol

145: 16 March 1962

    1.     Gay time at Arts Ball
    2.     Dogs at School
    3.     Lord Mayor of London visits Dublin

146: 23 March 1962

    1.     Irish entertainers leave for Congo

147: 30 March 1962

    1.     President back from Rome
    2.     National fencing championships
    3.     Parade of summer fashion
    4.     Cork boat show

148: 6 April 1962

    1.     General McKeown: his homecoming

149: 13 April 1962

150: 20 April 1962

    1.     Charlie Chaplin flies in
    2.     Irish Theatre Ballet, Cork visits Dublin
    3.     "Irish Cedar" launched in Holland

151: 27 April 1962

    1.     Dutch ship "visits" Arklow

152: 4 May 1962

    1.     Belfast greets Satchmo

2.      French fortnight in Dublin

3.      Castledermot karting season starts

153: 11 May 1962

154: 18 May 1962

155: 25 May 1962

156: 1 June 1962

1.      Dublin: Berlin Wall exhibition

157: 8 June 1962

1.      Bord Iascaigh Mhara Minister sees boatbuilding at Killibegs

2.      Dublin airport: Aer Lingus fleet annual blessing

3.      Quiet poll at Stormont elections

4.      Mount Venus TCD car club hill climb

158: 15 June 1962

159: 22 June 1962

1.      Gorey: "strange contrasts" at Fleadh Ceoil

160: 29 June 1962

1.      Skyscraper to replace Dublin theatre

2.      Co. Wicklow: have you any wool?

3.      Balbriggan: new plastics factory opened

4.      16th annual veteran car run

161: 6 July 1962

162: 13 July 1962

1.      End of an era: Theatre Royal closes

163: 20 July 1962

1.      Car-racing 91mph win for Templeton at Phoenix Park

2.      Lisburn-Belfast: Ireland's first motorway

3.      Belfast: the Twelfth

164: 27 July 1962

1.      Speedy midgets at Bray

2.      Welcome for Cardinal Brown
3.      Dublin: Canadian fleet in

165: 3 August 1962

166: 10 August 1962

1.      Living Art Exhibition
2.      Shannon boat rally
3.      James Stewart to start oil strike?
4.      Polo in the park

167: 17 August 1962

1.      Ras Tailteann Fabulous Shay winner
2.      Ennis Fleadh Ceoil
3.      Aga Khan Cup for Italy

168: 24 August 1962

1.      Water sports at Dalkey
2.      Belfast: unemployment increases workers protest
3.      Blackrock baths: Ronnie Jones wins 800 metres
4.      Co. Meath: oil drilling commences

169: 31 August 1962

1.      Dublin Zoo: baby camels on view
2.      "Ike" in Wexford
3.      Kells flying display at Headford Estate
4.      Co. Tipperary: farming for fish

170: 1 September 1962

1.      Hurling final: close win for Tipp

171: 8 September 1962

1.      Autumn fashions on parade
2.      Leinster Championships Rifle Shoot
3.      Mansion House: Ideal Homes exhibition
4.      Rose of Tralee final 1962

172:15 September 1962

1.      Bellingham Castle: sportsmen shoot for charity

2.     National Ballet Company in rehearsal
3.     Mr. Acker Bilk at Bray
4.     Santry: contrasts in horse power

173: 22 September 1962

1.     The Final: Kerry are Champions

174: 29 September 1962

1.     President at Augustinian Centenary mass
2.     Kinsealy agricultural research station
3.     Leixlip: Jackson Trophy car trial
4.     Theatre Royal final scene

175: 6 October 1962

1.     President attends Irish play
2.     Dublin: 13th century dwellings found at High Street

176:13 October 1962

1.     Fashion aids Cheshire Homes
2.     Models with a difference
3.     Chambers of Horrors for medical students
4.     Newry: unemployment in the North – protests continue

177: 20 October 1962

1.     Football: Oireachtas Cup – Waterford outplay Tipp
2.     Hair styles by Simon of London
3.     Miss Ireland 1962

178: 27 October 1962

1.     Shelbourne Park: "Annaglaive Star" wins McAlinden Cup
2.     Fencing: Irish Foil Championships
3.     Oireachtas Art Exhibition
4.     Canoe enthusiasts meet at Dalkey

179: 3 November 1962

1.     International badminton circus
2.     Beagling in Co. Wicklow
3.     Motorracing: muddy going at Nicholson Trophy
4.     Kevin Barry remembered

180: 10 November 1962

  1.      Helen Shapiro
  2.      International wrestling
  3.      Thurles National Ploughing Championships
  4.      Congo 38th fly out

181: 17 November 1962

  1.      Theatre closes, but variety fights back
  2.      Naas: Army's school for apprentices
  3.      Congo dead laid to rest

182: 24 November 1962

  1.      Fianna Fail Ard-Fheis
  2.      Detroit diesels for CIE
  3.      RDS bloodstock sales
  4.      Doing the Madison

183: 1 December 1962

  1.      Irish Open Snooker Championship
  2.      Fire damages CIE premises
  3.      National Stadium boxing: Terenure v. Transport
  4.      Variety Club's fancy dress ball

184: 8 December 1962

  1.      Cardinal and bishops home from Rome
  2.      Four Courts garrison, 42nd anniversary
  3.      Dublin University: honoris causa Michael MacLiammoir

185: 15 December 1962

  1.      US Secretary of State pays visit
  2.      Christmas lights

186: 22 December 1962

  1.      New look for air hostesses
  2.      Innovation in schoolrooms prefabrication
  3.      Do-it-yourself fur coats/ Muscles for everyone

187: 29 December 1962

1. Swimmers "break the ice"
2. Moving crib tells Christmas story
3. Speedboat skills

188: 5 January 1963

1. 200 escape death: Belfast-Dublin rail crash
2. Baldoyle races despite snow and ice
3. New 1,000 HP diesel engines for CIE
4. Storm damage to Dublin-Wexford line

189: 12 January 1963

1. Corvette "Maeve" arrests Russian ship
2. Radar to enforce speed limit
3. National Stadium: bantam weight fights – Hamrock beats No-one
4. Keeping warm in the big freeze

190: 19 January 1963

1. Hotel and Catering exhibition
2. Irish Hawthorn, Ireland's largest tanker
3. The homeless ones
4. Stars and slapstick

191: 26 January 1963

1. Airlift to Kippure
2. Heavyweight: unpopular win for Chadwick
3. The ancient dancers of India

192: 2 February 1963

1. Judo black belts awarded
2. Fashions for Spring, if it comes!
3. Art students get twisted
4. Caltex sports awards

193: 9 February 1963

1. Drinka pinta beer in 3 seconds
2. Rough riding at Ticknock trials

3.  National Stadium: Perry's farewell appearance, Gilroy v. Perry
4.  President and stars at charity premiere

194: 16 February 1963

1.  Belfast: Balmoral livestock show
2.  Ladies fencing tournament
3.  Rudden wins cross country championship
4.  Blind boy plays chess

195: 23 February 1963

1.  Cork Food Fair
2.  Pere Pire friend of the homeless on visit
3.  Garden of Remembrance near completion
4.  Point-to-point races in Fermoy

196: 2 March 1963

197: 9 March 1963

1.  Colourful beachwear from synthetics
2.  Abbeyfeale: Most Irish Town award
3.  Amateur Ballroom finals

198: 16 March 1963

1.  3,500 in the Long Walk
2.  Preserve Georgian Dublin
3.  Croke Park: Ulster regain football title

199: 23 March 1963

1.  Stars of the Year, Gaelic Sports Writer awards
2.  Kennel Club Annual Show
3.  Speedboats in 50 mph contest
4.  Barmen visit Belfast brewery

200: 30 March 1963

1.  Shelbourne Park: Arhur's Ship wins March sweepstake
2.  All-Ireland Schools Debating Contest
3.  Naas Senior Cross-Country Championship
4.  New car air ferry service

201: 6 April 1963
1.    Toys, buy now for Christmas
2.    Inter-county badminton
3.    Moving production of passion play

202: 13 April 1963
1.    Celbridge: Olympic hunter trials
2.    National Stadium: Irish Judo Association's big show
3.    Irish Theatre Ballet features "Charlestown"

203: 20 April 1963

204: 27 April 1963
1.    Dublin Rose of Tralee chosen
2.    Minister reviews new Garda recruits
3.    Dublin: Bus strike

205: 4 May 1963

206: 11 May 1963
1.    Shelbourne Park: Easter Cup final
2.    RDS Spring Show
3.    Royal Hibernian Academy exhibition
4.    Leopardstown: Gay Challenger wins Gold Flake stakes

207: 18 May 1963

208: 25 May 1963

209: 1 June 1963
1.    Fleadh Ceoil at Mullingar

210: 8 June 1963
1.    Dev at Cathedral
2.    M.E.C. trials at Dun Laoghaire
3.    Miss Cinema 1963
4.    Annual blessing of Aer Lingus fleet

211: 15 June 1963
1.    Annual veteran car run

2.      Sheepdogs show their pace
3.      Dublin tenements growing alarm

212: 22 June 1963

1.      Bodenstown: Wolfe Tone remembered
2.      Kells: second annual airshow
3.      International clay pigeon shoot
4.      Belfast shipyards busy again

213: 29 June 1963

214: 6 July 1963

1.      Ireland-France: student exchange scheme by Caravelle jet
2.      Variety Club of Ireland: polio children's new "Sunshine Coach"
3.      First aid for youngsters
4.      Motorcycling: Skerries "100"

215: 13 July 1963

1.      Finaghy: the Twalfth
2.      Blessington Metropolitan Regatta
3.      International trade apprentice competition
4.      Polish riders win Ras Tailteann

216: 20 July 1963

1.      Foreign trade body visit Dundalk brewery

217: 27 July 1963

1.      Congolese premier visits Ireland
2.      Annual pilgrimage to Croagh Patrick

218: 3 August 1963

1.      Luxury liner at Dun Laoghaire
2.      Danish frigates visit Dublin

219: 10 August 1963

1.      Dollars aid Kilmainham restoration
2.      International water skiing
3.      Ireland wins Aga Khan trophy

220: 17 August 1963

1. Exhibition of Living Art
2. Farmers demonstrate at Athlone
3. Harlem Globetrotters in Dublin
4. Artillery shoot at Glen of Imaal

221: 24 August 1963

1. Dunboyne Crossett wins Leinster "200"
2. Collins and Griffith remembered
3. Co. Wicklow: horse show at Blessington
4. Be prepared – Annual Scouts Contest

222: 31 August 1963

1. Croke Park: hurling final, Kilkenny are champions

223: 7 September 1963

1. Abbey Theatre: foundation stone laid
2. Elvis sends them in NY Fair
3. Trinity College: Garda sports at College Park
4. Miss Ireland 1963

224: 14 September 1963

1. Ragusa home from St. Ledger
2. Carrickmacross: Ulster v. Leinster in camogie semi-final
3. Dublin docks: ships idle – strikers march

225: 21 September 1963

1. Football final September 1963, Dublin v. Galway

226: 28 September 1963

1. Liberty Hall: Dublin's highest building goes up and up
2. Croke Park: Junior Tailteann Games
3. Long distance walk for world charity
4. Mighty Midgets: last race of karting season

227: 5 October 1963

1. Liam Martin's exhibition captures disappearing Dublin
2. Curragh Camp memorial to Congo dead
3. Big circus laughs for young and old

228: 12 October 1963

1.    Shelbourne Park: October stakes semi-final
2.    Irish barmen get the shakes
3.    Furs for winter
4.    Motor-cycling, muddy going at Kilbride

229: 19 October 1963

1.    FCA officers commissioned
2.    Racing at Naas
3.    New measures to curb rising road toll

230: 26 October 1963

1.    Toy time again
2.    Maynooth: Fr. Eoghan O'Gramhna centenary remembrance
3.    Limerick: 30,000 farmers in protest march

231: 2 November 1963

1.    Kevin Barry remembered
2.    Belfast: new airport at Aldergrove
3.    Cork Science and Technology exhibition
4.    Mr. Donal Ua Buachalla laid to rest

232: 9 November 1963

1.    Beatles pay unwelcome visit
2.    McKee Barracks: Taoiseach reviews 2nd infantry troops
3.    Dublin-Malaga: Aer Lingus winter sunshine flight
4.    Miss Cinema 1963

233: 16 November 1963

1.    Housewives protest march over turnover tax
2.    Miss Cinema 1963
3.    Co. Galway: Ploughing Championships at Athenry

234: 23 November 1963

1.    John F. Kennedy, 1917–63: a remembrance

235: 30 November 1963

1.    Belfast shipyard closedown averted

2. New copy anything machine displayed
3. Memorial plaque to 1913 Volunteers

236: 7 December 1963

1. First aid for youngsters
2. Cork collector's art treasures
3. Rasslin' Rogues

237: 14 December 1963

1. Christmas in the city

238: 21 December 1963

1. Swedish ceremony of light
2. Cold weather go karting
3. Blind children's party
4. High speed midgets at Bray

239: 28 December 1963

1. Annual ice-breaking swim
2. Irish Kennel Club dog show
3. Factory gutted by fire

240: 4 January 1964

1. New Year sale fever
2. John Huston becomes Irish citizen
3. "The Thing" removed from O'Connell Bridge
4. Brittas Bay: further attempts to float beached coaster

241: 11 January 1964

1. Royal College of Surgeons: honorary fellowship for President de Valera
2. National Stadium: pantomania!
3. Tackling Ireland's apartheid problems

242: 18 January 1964

1. Book commemorates Kennedy's visit
2. Co. Meath: Trim Housing scheme opened
3. Co. Waterford: bad herring season at Dunmore East

243: 25 January 1964

　　1.　　Sportstars '63
　　2.　　Basketball: Dublin beat Mullingar
　　3.　　On patrol with Corvette "Maeve"

244: 1 February 1964

　　1.　　New look in army uniforms
　　2.　　Mink farm at Swords
　　3.　　Fashions for bedtime
　　4.　　James Larkin remembrance ceremony

245: 8 February 1964

　　1.　　Dublin Airport: British and Japanese ambassadors fly in
　　2.　　Sutton: power boat thrills
　　3.　　Dublin city: dangerous buildings demolition continues

246: 15 February 1964

　　1.　　Trams, where are they now?
　　2.　　Slua Mhuiri officers commissioned
　　3.　　Garda depot moves to Templemore
　　4.　　Variety Club Week helps blind children

247: 22 February 1964

　　1.　　Do-it-yourself exhibition
　　2.　　Motor cycling trials at Brittas
　　3.　　Art exhibition in pub!

248: 1 March 1964

249: 8 March 1964

　　1.　　Actors' Equity Variety Show
　　2.　　Co. Meath ploughing contest
　　3.　　Dublin Bay: "Boat Week" water events
　　4.　　Tank exercises at Curragh

250: 15 March 1964

　　1.　　Galway: Atlantic fishermen join strike – temporary truce
　　　　　announced

2.     Gael Linn development scheme in Carna

251: 22 March 1964

1.     Leopardstown: international cross-country protest
2.     Karting at Athy
3.     Moving production of passion play

252: 29 March 1964

1.     Stillorgan: first horse show of the season
2.     Irene Gilbert summer fashions
3.     Baldonnel: new helicopter crews in training

253: 5 April 1964

254: 12 April 1964

1.     Curragh camp: 40th battalion in training for Cyprus

255: 19 April 1964

1.     40th battalion away
2.     Abbey players leave for Shakespeare festival

256: 26 April 1964

1.     Boxing: National Senior Championships, McCourt beats McGrane
2.     Anti-apartheid movement strengthens
3.     Dublin's changing skyline

257: 3 May 1964

258: 10 May 1964

259: 17 May 1964

1.     Clones: Fleadh Ceoil

260: 24 May 1964

1.     New American embassy opened
2.     What's new in hair fashion
3.     Malahide: new indoor jumping arena
4.     International wrestling: Feeney (Ireland) beats Weston (Scotland)

261: 31 May 1964

    1.      Dublin University: Trinity Week sports
    2.      Miss Cinema semi-finals
    3.      CIE driving school skids for safety

262: 7 June 1964

    1.      Let the Language Live
    2.      Dublin stores Irish Week
    3.      Steam locomotives back at work

263: 14 June 1964

    1.      Continued expansion at Shannon industrial zone
    2.      Keeping the waterways clear
    3.      International railway conference delegates see Killarney
    4.      New 3 million pound jet for Aer Lingus

264: 21 June 1964

    1.      US coastguards visit Dublin
    2.      Curragh Camp: army motor cycle trials
    3.      Castletown House: field sports fair
    4.      Bodenstown: Wolfe Tone commemoration

265: 28 June 1964

266: 5 July 1964

    1.      Glenageary Horse Show
    2.      Taoiseach opens new Guinness laboratory
    3.      The Royal Showband buys a horse
    4.      Atom-powered "Savannah" at Dublin port

267: 12 July 1964

    1.      Arbour Hill: ex-servicemen lay wreath
    2.      Drogheda: international karting
    3.      Floating 4,000 tons of concrete – Dun Laoghaire harbour

268: 19 July 1964

    1.      President of Pakistan in Dublin
    2.      Kilmainham prison: restoration work continues
    3.      Dunboyne: Leinster Trophy car race

269: 26 July 1964

# Index

# Reimagining Ireland

Series Editor: Dr Eamon Maher, Institute of Technology, Tallaght

The concepts of Ireland and 'Irishness' are in constant flux in the wake of an ever-increasing reappraisal of the notion of cultural and national specificity in a world assailed from all angles by the forces of globalisation and uniformity. Reimagining Ireland interrogates Ireland's past and present and suggests possibilities for the future by looking at Ireland's literature, culture and history and subjecting them to the most up-to-date critical appraisals associated with sociology, literary theory, historiography, political science and theology.

Some of the pertinent issues include, but are not confined to, Irish writing in English and Irish, Nationalism, Unionism, the Northern 'Troubles', the Peace Process, economic development in Ireland, the impact and decline of the Celtic Tiger, Irish spirituality, the rise and fall of organised religion, the visual arts, popular cultures, sport, Irish music and dance, emigration and the Irish diaspora, immigration and multiculturalism, marginalisation, globalisation, modernity/postmodernity and postcolonialism. The series publishes monographs, comparative studies, interdisciplinary projects, conference proceedings and edited books.

Proposals should be sent either to Dr Eamon Maher at eamon.maher@ittdublin.ie or to ireland@peterlang.com.

Vol. 1    Eugene O'Brien: 'Kicking Bishop Brennan up the Arse':
          Negotiating Texts and Contexts in Contemporary Irish Studies
          ISBN 978-3-03911-539-6. 219 pages. 2009.

Vol. 2    James P. Byrne, Padraig Kirwan and Michael O'Sullivan (eds):
          Affecting Irishness: Negotiating Cultural Identity Within and
          Beyond the Nation
          ISBN 978-3-03911-830-4. 334 pages. 2009.

Vol. 3    Irene Lucchitti: The Islandman: The Hidden Life of Tomás
          O'Crohan
          ISBN 978-3-03911-837-3. 232 pages. 2009.